PREVAILING *Winds*

WHEN THE STORMS OF LIFE TAKE CONTROL

BY

STANLEY P. JORDAN

Tate Publishing, LLC.

Published in the United States of America
by Tate Publishing, LLC
127 East Trade Center Terrace
Mustang, OK 73064
(888) 361–9473

ISBN: 1-59886-13-1-X

This book is dedicated to:
Reverend Clive and Anna Meidahl

*whose unfailing love has been
my constant ballast,
whose selfless, godly advice
has been the parallel rule
that has kept my ship upon her true course
and whose confidence in my
destiny has frapped my ship
during many of the most difficult
moments in my life.*

TABLE OF CONTENTS

Acknowledgements

In writing this, my first book, I am so grateful for all of the people who have helped this dream become a reality. There are not enough words to express my heartfelt gratitude or my enduring debt in part to each person listed here.

I would like thank God for giving me the insight into His Holy Word, and then giving me the idea and desire to pen this work. Without Him, I can do nothing and would be nothing.

I would like to thank my wonderful, loving wife, Marsha, without whose support this book would not be a reality. Thank you for all of the support you have given me when I got down on myself and was fed up with the daily grind of writing. I could not have done this without you. You kept me going when I wanted to quit and burn every page that I had written. I would also like to thank my beautiful children for their support: Wesley, Aleesha and Ethan. Thank you for not making too much noise upstairs and for bringing me chocolate-chip cookies when you thought that I needed a snack.

I would like to thank Tate Publishing for believing in this book and me enough to bring it to life and publish it. When so many writers never get the opportunity to see their baby put into print, I am honored by your commitment to me and to this book. Thank you for giving the feet of my dreams a road upon which to walk.

I would like to thank Miss Fran Barter, who so graciously helped in the first edit before the manuscript was even sent off to the publisher. Your keen insight into the flow and rhythm of the book has helped me to fashion a work of which I can be proud. Thank you for all of your help and for all of the kind words, which I am not sure that I deserve or resemble.

Lastly, I would like to thank all of the other people who have helped or contributed to the book, whether it was in words of encouragement, in the editorial process itself, or in the marketing of the final product. Mom and Dad—thanks for encouraging me to write. Rev. Clive and Mrs. Anna Meidahl—thanks for being my continual mentors. Reverend Steve and Darla Edlin—thanks for your honest encouragement over many meals at Zebb's and The Roadhouse Grille. I owe you several meals! Rev. Mary Edlin—thanks for believing in me and the gift that God has given. The Reverends Andy DeRier and Chris Gray—thanks for giving me the opportunity both to share the ideas in this book with your congregations and to fail miserably in your pulpits in my attempts at communicating these thoughts. Jann McMurry—thanks for loving the way I write and for sharing some of my more memorable treatises with those who needed to hear them. The staff at the Palmyra King's Daughters Library—thanks for getting me most of the research books I utilized on this project.

FORWARD

I am persuaded that this book will be a blessing to all serious Christians throughout the world. Stanley Jordan has gone through storms that many would find similar to their own, but, like he found out, until you discover their purpose you just keep wandering around and repeating them. The purpose of this book is to prevent you from having to repeatedly endure the same storms in your life. The teaching in this book is not just theory, but comes from years of experience and the personal dealings of the Lord.

This book is a study book for your personal library as well as a practical guide to living which includes some vibrant revelations and life challenges. You are bound to receive from the Lord in these pages as you open your heart to some divine answers to your own storms. You will never think of your storms in the same way after reading this book.

Some thoughts from this book that are particularly relevant include, "The key to surviving any of the storms of life is discernment," and "dealing with the storms of life is like opening a safety deposit box. It requires two keys." These concepts are intertwined through the pages as common, powerful threads to successfully dealing with the situations life throws at you. As for you, dear reader, do you know what to do in the midst of your own storm? Do you know where it came from? Do you know how to prepare for or prevent the next one from desolating you land? You can and you should. This book will answer those questions and many more.

I thank the Lord for someone like Stan who can put his experiences into print. Let the Lord speak to you and encourage your heart as you consider the storms in your own life.

In Christ,

Rev. Mary L. Edlin

Reverend Mary L. Edlin
Apostolic Overseer of Faith Temple
Rochester, New York

Preface

As I sit to pen this preface, I am faced with the weight of writing this book. With so many natural disasters taking place all around us, it is incredible to see the thousands of people who have recently been thrust headlong into storms they never wished to face and were ill prepared to handle. In the wake of the destruction, many have endeavored to shift the blame for these disasters onto others, but to what avail is that? Does that ever help anyone? Does a scapegoat somehow wipe away the pain and magically restore our shattered kingdoms? The tough truth is, no. Storms come in all levels of destruction and descend unbiased upon all colors of flesh. The storms do not care about our social status or race and religion, and so we, too, must refrain from playing these childish games. In the aftermath of destruction, what we need most is the ability to survive with our pride intact and our honor unblemished. We do not need to finger point at who didn't do what fast enough or more effectively. Picking up the pieces and rebuilding is not an easy task, and wasting time throwing dirt at others will only help dirty us more. What it all boils down to is that we must all take the individual initiative in preparing for the worst that life may hurl at us. We must not blame our family or government for not being prepared. It is solely our responsibility to be prepared. And even though that "once in 200 years storm" may never arrive during our lifetime, the uneasy truth is that it may even if we wish it would not. So what is a person to do? Prepare, pure and simple. That is what this book is all about.

What I have endeavored to give you, my dear reader, is as comprehensive a manual on the storms of life as there is out there. My purpose in writing this book is to help every person who reads it to better understand, prepare for and survive the storms of life. I will not, however, give the reader a detailed description of exactly what to do when your particular storm pounds down upon you. There are too many variables for anyone to give you a three-step technique in how to conquer and survive. One of the keys in making it through your rough weather is found in understanding the psychology of survival. Although I will stress preparedness throughout this book, it takes more than knowledge or skills to survive the storms of life. "A key ingredient in any survival situation is the mental attitude of the individual(s) involved. Having survival skills is important; having the will to survive is essential. Without a desire to survive, acquired skills serve little purpose and invaluable knowledge goes to waste."[1]

What I have given you is a guidebook and a starting-off point from which you can become better navigators of life. It is not up to me, your pastor, your parents, or your president and chief executive officer to tell you specifically how to deal with the maelstroms that slam into your life. I can give you my insights and personal beliefs based upon the Word of God, the ultimate authority on truth in the universe, but I cannot tell you exactly what you should do. No man can, and no man should try. That is why I stress the importance of discernment in this book. You must choose your own path with the help of God. The Bible says that God orders the steps of a good man; a spiritual leader or a dynamic cult founder does not order them. It is up to every one of you to find out from God Himself what your particular path should be. The matter is solidly between you and God. I can help point out some productive and unproductive behaviors, and I can give you my insights, but I cannot and will not tell you what to do.

You will do well to remember to, "Lean on, trust in, and be confident in the Lord with all of your heart and mind and do not rely on your own insight or understanding. In all your ways know, recognize, and acknowledge Him, and He will direct and make straight and plain your paths. Be not wise in your own eyes; reverently fear and worship the Lord and turn [entirely] away from evil. It shall be health to your nerves and sinews, and marrow and moistening to your bones" (Proverbs 3:5–8 AMP). When you realize how much God has invested in you and how much He loves you, then you will realize that He wants you to make it. God wants you to prosper and to have good success. The Creator of the universe has plans for you to give you a hope and a future. He is the most gracious, loving, ever-present help and comforter around, and He wishes you good success. You have an important assignment from God. It is to be a beacon of light to those around you, even as you pass through some dark and muddy waters. Even as you fight just to survive some of the more terrible storms that you will encounter, God wants you to be a lighthouse of hope, joy, peace, comfort, safety and rest. Remember that God is on your side. Do not ever forget that.

In this book, I will discuss the events of the three particular biblical storms that, I believe, sum up the majority of storms any person will face. I will bring many non-traditional points to light and show you how a complete understanding of the passages will bring a new and fresh understanding to you. In bringing you my opinions, you will discover truths that can make an eternal impact on your life. Not only will I dissect each storm from a biblical perspective, but I will also delve into the geology, geography, meteorology and archaeology surrounding each story for the purpose of giving you as complete an understanding of each storm as I am able.

My prayer is that you, the reader, will lay this book on the nightstand beside your bed and refer to it whenever troubles arise. My hope is that you can glean from the pages that follow some semblance of order and clarity with which to deal with your particular storm or battle. My belief is that, if you are open to what the Spirit of God would like to show you, you can become more informed and have better success predicting, avoiding and dealing with the storms of life. My excitement is that you would become so good in this new field of spiritual meteorology that you could help others around you to learn, survive and succeed in passing through their storms better. My desire is that you would use this manual as a motivation to become closer to the Almighty God, to recognize just how much Jesus Christ gave to you in His Holy Word, and to live out your destiny by not becoming bitter and brokenhearted from the storms you have encountered. My heart is for you to win, pure and simple.

It is my hope that you will take this book, read it, use it and pass it along. I thank you sincerely for purchasing a copy and would ask that you would use the words that I have written, together with a God-given opportunity, to speak into the lives of those around you. The words contained herein are not about me or even you, but they are about God, doing His will, and helping those around you to see Him in all of His glory. Thank you again, and God Bless You.

Stan Jordan

PS: If you would like to share your own storm stories with me, request prayer or arrange a speaking engagement, feel free to contact me at stanleyjordan@hotmail.com—please type "Prevailing Winds" in the Subject line.

Section One

SETTING THE STAGE

1

THE EARLY SHOW

One of the oldest concepts that permeates history and literature is that God uses the weather to punish His children. That concept has been used to belittle millions of people over the ages and to destroy multitudinous lives. Another more modern concept of Christianity is that the devil is behind all of the foul treachery imposed by weather related events. Again, this misconception has ruined countless lives. The truth is that the weather is a natural and sometimes unpredictable phenomenon that we are only beginning to understand. It is a system God developed millennia ago in order to caress the earth and bring about her beauty. Although we have nothing to do with the natural courses of our earthly weather, we often do have something to do with the weather in our lives. It is therefore conceivable that we are mostly responsible for the storms that hit our lives. Moreover, since we are more responsible for them than anyone else is, we should learn how to prevent their arrival and prepare for their vociferousness.

A storm can be defined as follows: a violent atmospheric disturbance that is accompanied by wind, rain, sleet, hail, snow or thunder and lightning; an outburst of a direct, furious or tumultuous force; a sudden, raging, angry attempt to assault and capture a stronghold or fortified place with the intent of captivating it completely. While these storms are the natural disasters (hurricanes, floods, blizzards, tsunamis, etc.) that we read about in the newspapers and hear about on our television sets, there are also spiritual storms that can be far more treacherous. In our case, we can relate the storms of life to the savageries that come against us. The phrase "the storms of life" could be defined as any of the following: a sickness or a disease that attacks our body or the body of a loved one; a rocky marriage, a divorce or any other failed relationship; a layoff from work or the loss of a job or major contract; overdue bills, bankruptcy or some other financial crisis in which more is owed than can be paid; a legal challenge or the accusation of wrongdoing; an arrest, incarceration or the potential loss of basic civil freedoms; the death of a loved one; any moral failure; war, terrorist attacks or social chaos; a wayward child, spouse or other family member; succumbing to the demands of alcohol and/or drugs; an accident or the loss of a limb or sensory input devices (i.e. eyes-sight, ears-hearing, etc.); any rumor, misquotation or other verbal attack about us or those we love; fire, theft or any physical natural disaster; emotional bondage or mental breakdowns; murder, rape or any other violations of the human body; an unwanted pregnancy, miscarriage or the abortion of a child; clinical depression, abnormal anxiety attacks or the loss of the ability to cope with life. (Note: Throughout the rest of this book I will refer to these types of storms as the spiritual storms of life, although they could just as easily be termed the emotional or personal storms of life.)

It is this uncontrollable weather, these unalterable storms, that dictates to us the when and where of its arrival. And, while there are none of us who can manipulate the weather, there are a select few who understand some of its intricate complexities. Fewer still is the number of men and women who can accurately predict it consistently. Meteorologists try to interpret the signs and predict what will occur next, but they often miss the mark miserably—a mistake we should not repeat. Even with the professionals' use of sophisticated computers and fancy mathematical formulas that base tomorrow's weather upon today's events extrapolated into the future, few meteorologists are as accurate as we need them to be. This brings us face to face with the reality that we cannot beat severe weather or even use it to our advantage. It is what it is and it does what it wants, regardless of whether or not we understand or approve of it. Even though we have come a long way from the simple forecasts of earlier days, which were more akin to "backcasts" due to the fact that they basically recounted what had already happened, we have not come far enough down that road in God's eyes. We know that we cannot completely eliminate the conflagrations that erupt in our tinderbox, but we can prevent some of them.

In understanding the nature of the weather and how storms form, meteorologists have been able to develop better warning systems for people in the path of dangerous weather. These warning systems have helped save lives. Although we would like to believe that we are invincible and do not need warnings or protection from the storms, the fact is that we cannot handle them or bear their full force alone. The weather ultimately influences how each of us lives our lives. It helps us to determine our daily movements as to what we do or do not do, what we plan or postpone, where and when we travel, and how we plant and harvest. It even helps shape our outlook on life. This event we term "the weather" is a most powerful force that we seem unable to buck against; therefore, we must learn to cope with its fury better than we currently are. Maybe we can trick it or learn from it and seek proper shelter before it arrives. If there is only one rule that we can live by, then we should let ours be the old adage that intimates that "An ounce of prevention is worth a pound of cure." In other words, it is cheaper and easier to prevent something bad (a storm in our case) than it is to rid ourselves of it or to fix it after the fact.

The storms of life that we face are serious and intent on destroying us. Some of us feel that if we ignore them long enough they will go away on their own, while others sit idle and deny that they are there at all. Attitudes like that are dangerous. Although the struggles that we are discussing are not the norm in life, they are more common than most would like to admit. Of the many difficulties in life that we may experience, the storms we are examining in this book are unique, terrifying, deafening and unusual. How often do we see something brewing on the horizon and then ignore it, thinking that our faith can overcome anything? More often than not, we see the storm and hear its song as it plays upon the masts, the ropes, the sails and the water. We know what it will do to our lives and those around us, and yet we do nothing. Even as it first touches our ship, we sit and blithely accept its wicked kicks. As Shakespeare so aptly describes us:

NORTHUMBERLAND

His noble kinsman: most degenerate king!
But, lords, we hear this fearful tempest sing,
Yet seek no shelter to avoid the storm;
We see the wind sit sore upon our sails,
And yet we strike not, but securely perish.

LORD ROSS

We see the very wreck that we must suffer;
And unavoided is the danger now,
For suffering so the causes of our wreck.[2]

In light of these facts, we need to understand more completely the nature of the storms of life and how they relate to us. Of equal importance, however, is how we apply the principles found in the Word of God to those storms that we must face down. We will discuss and dissect three biblical storms and will uncover, in the process, some truths that can help us weather the next storm that arrives at our address.

In the first section of this book, we will look at preventative measures to take to avoid many of the storms that come to our lives, and how to weather the storms that we are already experiencing. We will also look at what to do after the storms have passed. The major emphasis of this section will be on prevention. One key in dealing with the challenges of life is that the more we can prevent, the better off our ship will be. Nevertheless, for those that we are not able to or did not prevent, we will look at some productive behaviors that we should practice and some non-productive behaviors that we should avoid during the storms of life.

In the second part of this book (the middle three sections), we will examine three biblical storms in detail. Dissecting each story together will allow us to experience how truth can peel back the layers of deceit that have been pulled over our eyes. In each discussion, we will uncover a number of lessons to be learned and how the attitudes of the cast can hinder or help. I will attempt to provide a complete sense of mood and setting from which we can unearth rubies of great price. Some of the tools we will use as we dig into each story are: historical information, geographic settings and their related importance, economic data—if it proves pertinent—and archaeological details. In the end, we will tie these all together with a unique perspective that will hopefully change the way we think.

In the last section of this book, we will tie up all of our loose ends and set the reader upon a course of true discovery and discernment. When we put the final pieces of the puzzle together, it will give the reader the assurance and confidence that she can actually avoid some storms in life. For those storms that cannot be avoided, the reader will know that he can make it through them as a better person. In the end, we will encourage the reader to set up a plan of attack and to follow through with the lessons of this book.

The Oklahoma Climatological Survey defines prevailing winds as "the wind direction most commonly observed during a given period."[3] For our discussion, I would like to embellish that definition. We can define life's prevailing winds as any circumstance moving toward us from a particular direction that possesses greater strength and influence than we do, and that has the capacity to disrupt the regularity of our lives or to destroy anything in its path. These winds then descend upon our lives with an overwhelming force and the single-minded intent of gaining complete victory by establishing their superiority over us. Storms in our lives come to overpower us, to overtake us, to overwhelm us, and ultimately to destroy us.

The storms of life come at us for many reasons, and we must realize that. There is no single reason why they attack. Most of the time, it is important to know why the storm has come. Every time it is of the utmost importance that we know what to do now that the storm has descended upon us. This book attempts to explore the storms of life and how we should react to them. It is by no means an exploration into or an explanation of all of the storms of life, or of the Bible; however, it is an in-depth look into what I believe are the three main categories of storms in life.

No book on storms, most would argue, could be complete without an engaging look into Job's experiences; but I believe that many of the lessons Job had to learn also needed to be learned by Paul as well. Indeed, the Job-type of storm is the one that would immediately come to the forefront of most people's minds. Satan wanted to toy with Job and make him turn from God. He desired to sift him as wheat, to destroy his faith, and God allowed him nearly complete access to Job's life. The Lord granted the Devil many privileges as it pertained to Job, but he could not take his life. I believe that this type of storm brutalizes some people, but it would not come to the lives of most. My reasoning for this is as follows: God declared to Satan that Job was the most upright man upon the earth. There was "none like him on the earth, a blameless and upright man, one who [reverently] fears God and abstains from and shuns evil [because it is wrong]" (Job 1:8 AMP). This assessment of Job's life by God puts him into a most exclusive club; a club that most of us will never darken the doors of. It would be arrogant of us to believe that God grants that kind of access to the life of the everyday woman or man. It is simply not a Biblical precedent. That is why I only reference some aspects of Job's storm and have declined to include his story as one of the storms that we will explore in these pages. With many similarities between Job's storm and Paul's storm, I have included their common lessons.

Each of us will encounter multiple storms during our lifetime as we meander along life's path. Some of these will approach with the sultry saunter of a harlot; others will strike with a sudden, blinding ferocity rarely encountered on the high seas. Still other storms will turn marginal weather systems into nightmares of death and destruction with a slow and steady gait. There are at least three ways to react to these storms in our lives. It is up to us to determine which approach is necessary for the specific storm we are in at that particular time.

On Any Other Ordinary Day

With the sun peering over the horizon, the day breaks clear and bright and is filled with the possibilities that each dawn brings. Majestic mountains ascend into the heavens and deep, sun-soaked valleys prevail upon the lower landscape. With the natural beauty that surrounds us, we feel reassured that this day will be no different from the day before. We sense control in the regularity of the mundane, and it numbs our awareness. Little do we realize that the events of this day will push us to the escarpment of disaster. The choices we make will alter the direction of our lives forever. Poor choices may kill us and good choices will save us, for a storm will suddenly be upon us. This storm will force us to choose, and this day will defy everything mundane that we have ever grown accustomed to.

Everything is great. Life is good. Captain and crew are in the boat, and all is well. We are sailing along, enjoying the day, the water, the wildlife, the fishing and the outdoors. We are staffing the rudder, checking our maps, plotting our course and listening to the weather report–all under sunny, blue skies. Sea gulls are flying overhead, and fish are jumping from the water and nearly landing in our boat. Our hold is full of food and possessions. On deck we have our family and a few good friends. It is a perfect, calm day with the whisper of a breeze caressing our cheeks. There are no waves and there is no fear.

Then, without warning, the sky darkens as a strong wind picks up, blowing black clouds in from the west–the very direction that we are heading. In an instant, the light breeze turns into the violent blast like that from a jet engine. The sustained wind speed tops forty knots with gusts in excess of sixty knots. The sea is churning with a purpose, and that purpose is to destroy our boat and to drown all who are aboard. Waves smash relentlessly against the hull while throwing tons on water across the deck of the ship. Our boat teeters atop the cresting waves as her keel acts like the blade of a plow, peeling furrows out of salty soil.

We glance around at our instruments and then across the deck as another wave deposits it burden upon us and takes our boat deeper into the abyss. Our boat is sinking. She is going down and we have few options left. The choices that we make in the next few moments will either justify us or condemn us. If we choose to act according to what God has said, then we will live; however, if we allow our desperation to bow to the resolve of the storm, then it will prevail against us. It is our choice alone to make.

Our first reaction is to save ourselves. Grabbing buckets and starting the bilge pump, together we bail the water from the craft. Throwing everything overboard that could drag us down seems like another good idea, so we lighten the load enough so that we can ride over the waves with more buoyancy. Quickly we run and batten down all of the hatches. We hunker down as we attempt to guide our boat through the storm safely. In our mind, the only way to make it through is out of sheer determination and hard work. Several critical elements will assure our survival. The first is remaining patient and rolling with the waves. The second is in positioning our boat correctly; we must face into the storm. Our instincts and gut feelings will need to be trusted. Successfully surviving this storm will require that we ride it out. It is in this type of storm that we determine that sometimes we've got to learn the discipline, perseverance and trust associated with walking through our problems and on to the other side.

Our second reaction may be to scream at the storm and to tell it just who the boss is–GOD. As we stand up on the prow of the boat, we gather all of the courage we can muster and tell this storm to stop. We quell the fear rising in our throat and take command of the situation, telling the storm to be still and silent. Come hell or high water, there will be no storm on our watch. This storm is going to obey our voice. An inner strength rises up within us and gives us the strength to know that, with some storms in life, we have to learn to have the faith and boldness to speak to our problems and watch them melt away.

Our final reaction may be one of sheer frustration. On the verge of giving up, exhausted from fruitless bailing and hoarse from screaming, we suddenly remember our wayward passenger. This passenger arrived suspiciously at the last port of call; however, he is now nowhere to be found. We send the crew searching for him (as if they need that added distraction) to see if maybe he can explain what is going on. He did say that he was a "man of God" (that should read *former* man of God) and that he was running away from his maker. After the crew finds him, they drag him topside for a heated discussion. What he tells us leaves us bewildered. As this passenger sits before us, we must make an impossibly difficult decision. Now that we have rowed until our arms feel like they will fall off, we must accept the fact that he was correct. We must listen to God's transgressive son and do what he says even though his proposal is ridiculous. The decision is unanimous and we decide to throw this man overboard to his death. It is the most damning decision any of us have ever made. Murder is now our common brother. Without any other advantageous avenues of rescue apparent, we are left with the sickening choice about which there is no other alternative. In this storm, we must learn to have the discernment and fortitude to throw overboard whatever is sinking our ship. This takes intrepidity and courage that many can never muster; bravado will never suffice.

The key to surviving any of the storms of life is discernment. Without it, we will be lost and finished as we continually make the wrong choices. This could be disastrous. For a clearer understanding of what discernment is, let us look into the definition and then apply this understanding to a person of discernment. Discernment can be defined as the act, art or process of sifting or separating something mentally from another so as to investigate, examine, scrutinize, question, test or prove its reliability and truthfulness. It is to recognize something as being separate or different and to be aware, through our senses, of the significance of a word, act or situation. In short, discernment is to perceive something that is obscure or has been concealed.

A person of discernment, then, has a keen understanding and insight into any particular situation into which she may find herself thrust. She may obtain the details from her environment by her attentiveness and/or by the accumulation of information she obtains through her senses (both physical and spiritual), and can then use this knowledge to discriminate as to the secret cause or concealed truth about a particular situation. This person of discernment is able to be sure and fixed in her opinion and understanding due to her ability to distinguish between the options. She can then make appropriate decisions based upon that judgment. When faced with a new situation, she may recognize a distinctive trait from prior knowledge or experience that may assist her in her assessment of the circumstances surrounding her. She may not possess all of the facts, but she can use any acquired knowledge to make wise judgments in real-world situations. Given information, the person of discernment is then able to make the best and right choice.

Discernment comes to us in many ways. Sometimes it comes from experience or diligent study, while at other times we obtain it from keen observation and awareness of the events that take place around us. Yet at other times we partake of discernment's fruit from an unsettling thought, impression or feeling that God places in our hearts or it is borne out of a vision or a dream. How we obtain our discernment is irrelevant; what matters most is that we get it. Many people consider discernment to be something super spiritual and unobtainable to all but the spiritually elite. Others unwittingly call it intuition, which is an inaccurate portrayal. In terms of intuition, discernment could be thought of as "Intuition Plus." The plus is the spiritual side that

I have been stressing. Nevertheless, it is simply as I have stated above, no more and no less. It is critical that we possess it.

We must remember that life requires something of us. It is required that we take action or we will not survive—not making it through the storms without major devastation or loss of life. Whether we bail, speak or toss, we have to do something. As participants in life, we are neither idle spectators heckling the superstars on the field, nor armchair quarterbacks with nothing to lose. Shouting plays at the coach on TV from the comfort of our living room is cheap and easy, and to think that we can call the plays better than the he is arrogant. If we were thrust into the role of a coach with everything on the line, or as a general in the heat of battle, we would quickly change our pretentious tune. Screaming from the sidelines is easy. It costs us nothing to criticize the President and his entourage in Washington for what we perceive to be the lousy job that they are doing, but we would do no better if the job of running an entire country or heading up disaster relief efforts were given to us. Working within the confines of disaster is difficult, bloody and muddy. No one enjoys it, and nearly no one thrives upon its rigor mortis. Most of us can barely handle our single, sole, solitary life, but when someone else fails to make our grade we instantly turn into the answer man. What we must do is not easy, but we must perform our duties while on the field of life and stop criticizing others when it is their turn to play. It is unacceptable and suicidal to sit this one out and hope for a better storm next time. We must play our part no matter how ugly it gets because there may be no next time, and no one else will do it for us. God will do His part, and that is all.

Dealing with a storm is like opening a safety deposit box. It requires two keys. Without both keys, the box will not open. Without both parts, there is no solution; we are left without any hope of survival. In addition, as epoxy's two parts are, once mixed there is a limited setup time before they harden forever. The two keys we need to have are, first, to know why the storm has come and what the proper course of action is that will take us through it (discernment). Second, we must make the tough decisions necessary for survival (courage). We only have a certain amount of time to act properly. If we do not act or if we hesitate in our reactions, then the results will be devastating. Well-intentioned people who have the right reactions and plans, but who implement them far too late in the game for them to do any good, regularly miss proper timing.

For the quarterback to unexpectedly come alive in the last two minutes of the fourth quarter and start throwing long-yard-age, hail-Mary touchdowns may be too little too late if his team is down by forty points. Unlike professional athletes, we cannot afford to play around. This is life, and this is real. We will not get the chance to replay this down, this game or this season. We do not get a coach's challenge where we can demand an instant replay, multiple points-of-view or slow motion ruling from the referee that may overturn our penalty. If we are counting on that type of safety net, then we have been deceived somewhere along life's path. No such safety net exists. Rulings and practices such as these are incorporated into the fabric of our public sports for the sake of good sportsmanship, and to attempt to compensate for the bad calls that most referees make. Life gives us no such niceties. The choices that we have made we are generally stuck with, both good and bad. That is why we must choose wisely and timely. Choosing our way with discernment during the ungentle-ness of life will bring us home.

The second key or critical quality that we must possess is courage. Courage can be defined as that quality and firmness of spirit that enables us to face any fear or difficult decisions with full possession of our own powers, with a full assurance and firm determination that the reward kept continually in view shall be obtained and with an unbroken spirit that is unshaken in purpose and belief.

When presented with the opportunity to beat the storms of life, we must not miss our opportunity to act–but we can if we are not vigilant. In order to do what looks impossible, we must possess a courage that cannot be feigned. To endure what looks unending and to stand tall when all around us are giants is fundamental. We may not be as fortunate as Paul and the men on board the Alexandrian ship; we may not escape with our lives. This is critical, and this is real life at its worst. The choices we make will be the difference between a shipwrecked life and a good story. One thing is for certain: we must choose to do something. As the old saying goes, "An idle mind is the Devil's playground," and so idleness in the midst of the storms of life is a prescription for reckless disaster.

As a final note of summary, let us look at the U.S. Army Survival Handbook. In it, soldiers are instructed in the art of survival in desperate combat situations (not unlike life's storms). It is imperative that we learn the skills necessary to survive the storms of life now while the weather is calm and sunny. There is little chance that we will make it through the storms alive or without major devastation if we deploy into the tempest with little knowledge of basic survival skills. We must learn now how to handle whatever wickedness the storm may hurl at us, test and train as if we were entering the worst battle of life tomorrow, and remember to keep our wits about us when we enter the fray. Discernment and preparedness are our keys to survival. Let us not forget that, ever.

S	Size Up the Situation.
U	Use All Your Senses.
R	Remember Where You Are.
V	Vanquish Fear and Panic.
I	Improvise.
V	Value Living.
A	Act Like the Natives.
L	Live by Your Wits, *But for Now,* Learn Basic Skills[4]

3

LATE BREAKING NEWS

Storms have become an international phenomenon in recent years. The Weather Channel stepped up and hit a grand slam on storms and now nearly every media outlet has its own spin on the action. In the media we have storm related programming and daily weather reports in hundreds of daily and weekend newspapers as well as thousands of radio[5] and TV stations[6] [7], and most, if not all, of them have at least the potential for predicting or reporting the weather. The federal government has enormous interests in weather related phenomenon which includes the National Oceanic and Atmospheric Administration (NOAA), the National Center for Atmospheric Research, the Office of Naval Research's Coupled Boundary Layers and Air-Sea Transfer program (CBLAST), the Federal Emergency Management Agency (FEMA), the National Weather Service (NWS) and the Air-Sea Interaction Tower (along with many other weather related agencies). We have even taken it as far as requiring storm ready certifications, early warning systems, emergency evacuation plans and temporary shelter locations for municipalities that are located in areas prone to the worst kinds of natural devastation.

Today's meteorologists have everything available in storm tracking gear from Triple-Doppler Radar and sophisticated prediction software to various government agencies and Internet websites that disseminate climatological information. All told, the annual monetary value alone dedicated to the tracking, understanding and reporting of storms worldwide is astronomical. The NWS alone has a total annual budget of around $700 million (US dollars)[8], and FEMA has been responsible for doling out hundreds of billions of dollars in emergency relief funds[9].

Estimating the annual worldwide monetary impact related to the prediction and understanding of storms and natural disasters and the loss-of-use incurred would be nearly impossible, but the total cost to the world community would easily reach into the billions of dollars and thousands of man-hours. In addition to that, we can add the hundreds of billions of dollars and hundreds of thousands of man-hours spent in cleaning up and rebuilding our world after the weather has wreaked havoc upon the land. In fact, we have such a fascination with stormy weather that we have created an entire industry dedicated to tracking storms and reporting their devastation. In addition, as if that was not enough, there is a relatively new field opening up known as space meteorology. There are even some universities involved in this new field, such as Boston University with its new Center for Integrated Space Weather Modeling, which are developing brand new curriculums and spending millions of dollars on building space weather monitoring facilities. Predicting the weather has just taken its leap beyond the boundaries of earth!

It is clear that we are fascinated with a good storm and even more so with a devastating one, as long as it happens somewhere else. Of course, besides all of the technologically advanced weather prediction and tracking equipment we have available today, eyewitness accounts are still the most mesmerizing. The storm chasers and multiple storm survivors are the people who get the television interviews rather than the guy who calibrates the Doppler radar equipment. Some seem to thrive on the exhilaration of being in the middle of the storm and at its mercy. Others actually get their fifteen minutes of fame because of the storms that they have witnessed firsthand and survived or, better yet, have video footage of—for those of this latter kind, it may even prove to be a financial windfall of sorts. Yet for all of our fascination with storms and natural disasters, we are still in the dark ages when it comes to the storms that attack our personal lives.

If a poll were to be taken, most people would be able to describe what storm is approaching the area, where the jet stream is currently running, and what the approaching storm's expected impact might be. Yet we are still regularly blindsided by each storm that hits our personal lives. This should not be. It seems that we spend no time at all studying the events in our lives in order to predict any upcoming storms. Instead, we spend most of our time finding out the weather for tomorrow's backyard bar-b-q or next week's golfing event. Some of us spend hours watching the weather channel, especially in the wintertime, so that we can plan our trips around a storm's predicted path. Yet we do not even spend five minutes looking at the events barreling down upon our lives. I know some people who will not even travel in the winter for fear of snow, ice, wind, rain or some other perceived evil winter weather event—even if it means that they hurt the ones they love or are unavailable when they are needed the most. They allow the weather to paralyze them during its inclemency. Even after all of this, the question still begs asking: why is it that for all of this fascination with and preparedness for natural storms, and with an entire industry dedicated to predicting and understanding them, do we not better forecast the storms of life?

One reason may be that it takes too much work for most of us to bother. We cannot just click on The Weather Channel and get the forecast for our life. It is not that simple. There is no website where we can type in an ID and password to obtain a personalized report of what lies ahead in our life. Neither is there a toll-free number with people standing by to help us figure it all out nor are there any "Get out of this storm FREE" cards. When disasters do befall us and we are devastated, we typically run to the man of God for answers; however, the truth is that God wants us to speak directly to us so that we can be prepared ahead of time for the storms that may come. Yes, we should seek wise counsel during the storms of life, but God wants to help us avoid some onslaughts and to be better prepared to face the ones that we must walk through. As children of God, we do not always know the whys and why-nots of life's storms. What we must realize is that God alone is omniscient, and that He has promised to lead us and guide us if we will let Him.

Gordon MacDonald relates the role of an effective father to the recreational sport of canoeing in his book "The Effective Father."[10] He indicates that an effective father must continually keep one eye looking downriver in life in order to avoid potential deadly situations, or to prepare to make difficult decisions. This is the same with the storms of life. We should keep one eye looking downriver all of the time so that we can spot dangerous rapids, waterfalls, or fallen trees and branches in the river. Once spotted, we can then determine whether we should get the boat out of the water or if we can safely navigate these waters that lie ahead. Invariably we fall victim to a coup de main, subsequently letting the atrocities of life take control. Should we let this continue? We most certainly should not. Yes, there will be storms that come out of nowhere that we could not predict even if we had the best prediction equipment available. But we can see most storms coming a mile away if we are looking in the right direction.

The Bible says that the rain falls upon the just and the unjust, so let it now be settled that difficulties will arise. Of this, there should be no doubt. John admonishes in the Book of Revelation that if we have ears, then we should hear. To this I would add that if we have eyes, a nose, hands or a tongue, then let us see, smell, feel and taste. Predicting the storms of life will require us to use all of our senses, including our spiritual ones. Sometimes the sign of life's severities will come in the look of the clouds looming ahead, while at other times there will be a certain scent in the air that we recognize. Strange noises or the rumbling of thunder may often be the triggering events that will subtly announce the storm's approach. And certainly, sometimes there will be nothing tangible at all, only an inkling or a premonition of something afoot. We cannot predict all of life's storms, but we can predict many of them if we will use the God-given senses, both natural and spiritual, that we possess. If we are constantly listening for the water rushing over rocks and watching for its foamy froth, then we can, at least most of the time, predict the approaching rapids and get our boat out of the water before it is too late—before we are thrust headlong into a situation that we cannot possibly handle well.

All combat takes action in order for us to survive. Inaction spells disaster every time. We cannot simply sit inside and hope that the terrorisms will pass over our lives without touching us in any way. It is imperative that we come to the table prepared to do some work–hard, gritty, nasty work if need be. Our motto should be that we are ready and that we will survive. Allowing the wind and the waves to prevail over us unchallenged is unacceptable. The attitude that we must fight to retain is that we will become better and not bitter during life's storms.

GOD, COULD YOU PLEASE STAND UP?

When a storm arises, we often cry out for God to show up on the scene and rescue us, but what we often forget is His modus operandi. In the Old Testament, when God showed up, He often arrived in the midst of wind, fire, lightning, thunder, smoke and shaking. God often made a big entrance. So when we ask Him to show up in our lives, why do we not expect to be shaken up a little bit? And why is it that we always blame the shake-ups on the devil? Maybe we are not in a storm at all; it could be just a sun shower. It is possible that the mix up in the weather is God moving on our behalf; however, it is also probable that we had a hand in the aggressions that have come against us. This is why discernment is so critical. Not all storms are as they appear. A windy day is not a storm. Snow flurries are not a storm, and so we should not become hysterical with every breeze that blows. The storms of life that we are talking about are when the furiousness of evil breaks loose and the floodgates open unhindered upon us.

Why is our first reaction to a storm typically to blame it on someone else, namely the devil or some demonic spirit? Is it really so hard to believe that we could be the one to blame? Confined in our thinking to finger pointing when it comes to the arrival of the hostilities of life, we rarely hear that this storm may be of our own doing. Always Satan is our scapegoat. Even when we sin, he endures most of the blame. There is an old saying that declares, "The greatest trick the devil ever played was in convincing people that he did not exist." I say that "the greatest trick man has ever played is in blaming the devil for everything bad that happens." Weak in nature, we are unable to place the burden squarely upon our own shoulders. When faced with certain disaster, we bind, loose, pray against, curse, kick and scream, but we rarely think that the storm is due to our lack of awareness or ill preparedness or sin.

The true but difficult fact is this: sometimes the storms of life are our own fault. Sometimes we were just too busy to see the storm clouds approaching or too foolish not to get our family in under cover. Maybe what we need most is a change of understanding. How can we pray for God to help us out of our storm when it is we ourselves who caused this tumultuous violence? A startling revelation is found in the fact that at these times we may be praying against ourselves. Honest and intelligent reflection would be better predecessors to prayer than our shortsighted assumption that we have been wronged. Instead of presuming that it is the devil's fault, maybe practicing discernment–the ability to see beyond the obvious–would be a better first course of action. We first need to figure out the reason for the storm's arrival, and second need to hear how to survive its brutal assault.

When the rapacious gales assault us and we realize that we are at their mercy, one of our reactions is to control whatever we can that is within our grasp. Now control can be good, or it can be bad. Any attempt at control is good when we control ourselves, our attitudes, and our behaviors, keeping them lined up with the standards of God. However, when we try to exercise manipulative control over those around us or under us, especially our children or business or family members, we cross the line into bad. Thinking that any outlet or venting is justifiable, we end up taking out our frustrations with the storm upon those we love the most; we then use this to control others. Control over lesser people makes us feel powerful, and control over the storm makes us appear venerable. We become a hero of the faith with a platform from which we can launch a ministry or manipulate people's pocketbooks. In using our superior faith and understanding, we have performed where others could not. It is during these vulnerable moments that we realize we cannot control the storms. As God bows His head and covers His eyes with a sad hand, we then venomously proceed in striking out at whoever is most accessible. How pathetic we sometimes become when faced with difficulties in life.

Another of our familiar reactions to the storms of life is to run and seek shelter. We dodge this way and that, running through puddles and jumping over curbs as we attempt to avoid the weather and protect our designer clothes from becoming soaked and ruined. In short, we try to duck out of the storm into any alcove, doorway or anything that will prevent it from further destroying our plans. The problem with this type of behavior lies in where we seek shelter. When an atmospheric disturbance unexpectedly pounds down upon us, we will take shelter in anything that promises to shield us from the storm's fury. Jesus' disciples sought shelter in their own fear; Jonah sought shelter in his disobedience; and the men on the Alexandrian ship sought shelter in their own intelligence and experience. How often do we react in a similar fashion? What we should do is seek *proper* shelter, not just any shelter.

Most of us will naturally gravitate to one familiar behavior or habit when bad weather arrives because we have become accustomed to it sheltering us. This shelter may be a job, an unbiblical idea, denial, self-abuse, indifference, a lie, drugs, alcohol, depression, or despair. A shelter is anything that offers us protection from the storm, even if that protection is only perceived. It is not uncommon for it to be so well disguised that we do not even recognize it for what it actually is. When tumultuous winds blow, we fail when we do not assess the situation for its inherent uniqueness and, rather, react flippantly to it per our usual course of action (or inaction). Most of us will seek shelter outside of God every time, and this is inexcusable.

We could run to God when the challenges arise, but we glibly profess that we can handle them ourselves. Knowing where to run (or at least where not to run) should be rudimentary, but growing up is hard to do. The shelter under the shadow of the Almighty is an ideal place in which to weather the storms, but we typically run and hide in something less stringent. Buying into the lie of suitable shelter at no cost, we scurry everywhere but where we should. It is true that God requires a price for the shelter He provides, but, though His shelter is most expensive, it is also the best.

While each of us will encounter at least one storm, what matters most is how we handle them, not how few or how many we encounter. Every struggle in life should teach us something. It is tragic to face them only to come through unchanged. When storms arise, we do not need arrogance; we need discernment. We need people who recognize what is taking place and who know how to proceed. In writing to the Philippian church, Paul spoke of the discernment we need.

And this is my prayer: that your love may abound more and more in knowledge and depth of insight, so that you may be able to discern what is best and may be pure and blameless until the day of Christ, filled with the fruit of righteousness that comes through Jesus Christ—to the glory and praise of God. (Philippians 1:9–11 NIV)

Sometimes what is best is for us to go through the storm. It is not always best to attempt to pray them away. If oysters could pray away every grain of sand that would enter their shell, then we would never know the beauty of pearls. Likewise, if we could pray away every negative circumstance that arises, we would miss most of the beautiful lessons that life has to teach us. Imagine the jewels that we can form through the adversity of tackling life's storms the right way. Moreover, imagine the pain and disillusionment we can avoid by properly understanding the realities of life.

THE PATH OF DESTRUCTION

All storms cause damage, some more massive and widespread than others. In our world today, the extent of the damage is measured in property damage, loss of use, casualties, insurance claims, and the need for federal or international aid to rebuild after the storms have passed. Let us look at what storms have been up to in the world in recent years.

• March, 1999: Insurance companies have paid out $91.8 billion in losses from weather-related natural disasters in the 1990s so far, close to four times the weather-related claims handed out during the entire decade of the 1980s. . . . At $15 billion, weather-related insured losses in 1998 were second only to the $25 billion recorded in 1992, according to the recently compiled estimates from the German reinsurance company Munich Re.[11]

• March, 1999: According to NOAA research . . . the U.S. has already seen 37 "billion-dollar storms" since 1980–31 of them since 1988–totaling $160 billion in damages.[12]

• November, 1999: Did you know that in the U.S., hurricanes, floods, and tornadoes cause an average $9.2 billion in damage each year? Or that of the 30 most powerful hurricanes since 1900, more than 40 percent of the total damage occurred in southeast Florida?[13]

• 1992: Aug. 22–26, Bahamas, southern Fla., and La.: Hurricane Andrew left 26 dead and more than 100,000 homes destroyed or damaged. With total U.S. damages estimated at $26.5 billion, it is the most costly hurricane in U.S. history.[14]

• Late Summer/Fall, 2004: After a nearly unbroken succession of hurricanes in the Caribbean and typhoons in Asia, the global insurance industry is doing its books, with 50 billion dollars (40.3 billion euros) in economic losses and 20–35 billion dollars in insured losses expected so far. These estimates, made by Munich Re, the biggest reinsurer in the world, take into account hurricanes Charley, Frances, Ivan and Jeanne in the Caribbean and southeastern United States, as well as the Songba and Chaba typhoons in the Pacific region.[15]

• Spring, 2005: U.S. ex-presidents Bill Clinton and George Bush ended a tour of four tsunami-hit nations with a visit to the Maldives and said 11.5 billion dollars was needed for reconstruction across the Indian Ocean. [This is in reference to the tsunami that hit 11 nations in Asia and Africa on December 26, 2004 and killed nearly 300,000 people. Although the human loss is tragic and the economic figures are staggering, imagine how much higher both would have been had this tsunami hit a more developed area of the world, like New York City.][16]

• September, 2005: The devastation that lays in the wake of Hurricane Katrina will topple all US records for natural disasters as many estimate the insured damages alone will escalate past 100 billion dollars. The final tally for rebuilding the devastated Gulf Coast region could balloon to between 200 and 300 billion dollars—making it by far the costliest natural disaster to ever strike the US in terms of its economic impact. This is in addition to the more than 1,000 dead due to the hurricane and the unprecedented evacuation of an entire city of nearly 500,000 people.[17]

• September, 2005: Quickly following in Hurricane Katrina's path, Hurricane Rita pushed an already devastated region further into despair with what experts estimate could be total damages of six billion dollars or more.[18]

• September, 2005: According to the Insurance Information Institute, MSNBC's research and recent projections for the economic impact of Hurricane Rita, all of the top ten costliest hurricanes to hit the US have occurred since 1989 with combined total insured losses of over $100 billion dollars.[19]

NOTE: This list includes figures gathered through October 1, 2005.

Insurers can calculate the fiscal costs of natural storms, but no one on earth is able to quantify the amount of personal and psychological damage done due to the trespasses of spiritual weather. Most of these conflicts that everyday people suffer through will never be recorded or reported. It is difficult for us to imagine the sleepless nights spent due to a child in trouble, the despair embraced due to the deluge of pink slips handed out every year, the pain endured by the parents of children with disease or mental illness, or the abuse that drugs and alcohol bring to the lives of innocent family members. What is more difficult still is to equate those psychological traumas with dollars and cents. As I have stated before, this is an impossible proposition. So why is it that we care so much about the natural weather and yet do not care at all about the storms of life? Why is it that for all of the money spent in the world each year that seemingly few people are concerned with preparing for the inevitable incursions to which we will fall prey? Only after we have been sucker-punched and knocked down do we start to question the weather's motives.

If we are honest, it is not hard to imagine the shipwrecks that could have been avoided had people kept their eyes on the waters ahead. We can be sure that thousands of families could have better prepared for or avoided life's storms by applying the lessons of this book to their personal lives. For example, imagine how many more homes in South Florida could have survived Hurricane Andrew's onslaught had they been built to a higher building standard. Or imagine how many lives would be unaffected if people did not build their farms in flood plains or erect entire cities below sea level. Were people not so apt to build their dream homes in areas prone to landslides and mudslides, earthquakes, forest fires, or hurricanes, tsunamis and typhoons, then the world would be spared much loss. My point is that we cannot carry these natural mistakes over into our personal lives. We must decide to plan better. The bearer of bad news and the naysayer are not people to flippantly disregard. They just may be more enlightened and of a more informed status than we are.

Our reaction to negative news is surprising. Should someone approach us and say, "Hey, do you see those clouds up ahead, and do you feel the rain pounding down upon your head? Do you see the wind uprooting those trees and smashing them against your house? You might want to take cover because this storm is dangerous," we would brashly turn and reply, "No, God won't let that storm affect me. I am His child and I have a covenant with Him. You just do not see as I do through the eyes of faith. Living in fear must be terrifying for you." My response to a situation like this is to say, "No, there really is a storm approaching." I do not know why these misguided interpretations of biblical thought persist. What will inevitably take place if we continue to ignore reality is that one day we will awaken to a situation far beyond our control and worse than we could have imagined. In addition, on that particular day, God just might not bail us out. He might let us suffer through humiliation and loss based upon our lack of discernment and slothfulness. In that case, we can know that the storm will not be of His doing but of our own. It is at these times when we become enamored with our own superior understanding of God that we cannot accept truth from those around us, and that we are most prone to failure.

We have been trained that we should guard against those

who would lead us astray, and so we should. But in our zeal, we have taken this line of thinking too far. Many of us will no longer listen to anyone who may say something that we perceive as negative because of false teachings we have heard. Instead we have glamorized a gospel filled with fame and fortune, and have glossed over the harder points of Scripture. Falsehood should be rejected no matter who is teaching it; but on the other hand, truth should be heeded no matter what its source. Truth's packaging has nothing to do with its inerrancy. If we disagree, then we can simply consider Balaam's donkey. God's truth came to Balaam wrapped in a furry, four-legged beast that stubbornly refused his master's bidding. We should not judge truth's messenger quite as harshly as he did.

Due to the egos of many who would have us listen only to them, their lop-sided teachings have grown into doctrines of disregard that have stymied the spiritual growth of a generation of Christians. As members of a particular movement that enjoys some temporary success, they use this success to validate their errant views and to convince us to ignore sound doctrines that have existed for hundreds of years. What are the errant views? That we can pass through life unharmed and can speak any storm away. Some even claim that they have received these doctrines as a new revelation. The danger inherent in listening to only one person (or group/denomination) for our truth can be readily seen in such examples as the branch Davidians of Waco, Texas, and the poor souls involved with Jim Jones and the Jonestown massacre.

One of the dangers we all face is when we become too selective in deciding from whom we will accept truth. This is at no time in history truer than in today's church-going member-ship. Flamboyant elocutionists reeducate us into believing that they are the designated oracles of God while they monopolize the minds of their followers. We limit where truth can come in, often accepting it only from card-carrying members of our denomination, or from the pages of national newspapers. How-ever, God requires us to hear, know, and accept truth however it comes to us. We are required to speak to one another in hymns, psalms, and spiritual songs and to bear one another's burdens, confess our faults one to another, and pray for one another. In other words, we are to have a close, open channel of communication with each other with no delineation of spiritual hierarchies. We must be able to hear from God through the channels He has placed around us in order to survive the atrocities of life. And yet, as much as we must be open to God's truth from whatever source it arrives, we should be vigilant and reject all that is not truth from these same channels. It is a confusing and difficult road to navigate; yet it is a road that must be traversed.

6

METEOROLOGY 101

There are four ingredients that interact and give us our weather. These four ingredients are as follows: Solar energy, air, water and the earth. How, where and why these four elements interact is how we get our weather patterns and events. The resultant activity, our weather, influences how we all live our lives. It determines when we plant and harvest, what will and will not grow in any given locale, and what size the harvest will be. The weather moves kings, priests, princes and paupers. Having no regard for us at all, it strikes where it wills with whatever force it can muster. Under its uncontrollable force, not houses or barns, nor land and vegetation can withstand it. Ultimately the weather can and will erode away anything that man can build. We would be foolish not to respect its determination. Whether we like it or not, we must all face the fact that the weather is to some extent our master. Due to this interrelationship with the weather, I will shallowly delve into some of the more basic practices and understanding of meteorology with the belief that the principles discussed will better help us understand the storms in our lives.

Natural storms are like battles in the sky between warm and cold air masses. In a similar manner, opposing spiritual forces often clash within our lives causing severe emotional weather. Each different air mass in our atmosphere has a different temperature, air pressure and humidity level. When two of these collide it causes the air within each mass to move and equalize, thus causing changes within them to occur. Sometimes these changes are more violent and drastic than at other times, and this is what gives each storm its own unique character. Moreover, while each weather event has unique parameters defining its relative strength and intensity, all storms are beneficial in some way.

BENEFITS OF STORMS AND/OR SEVERE WEATHER:

• Storms clean and cool the air.

• Storms carry life-giving water from oceans and lakes, rivers and streams, and deposit it onto the thirsty land.

• Storms fix nitrogen in the air (by way of the accompanying lightning) so that it is available for plants and animals.

• Storms replenish local water tables and underground aquifers.

• Storms (thunderstorms in particular) are the only form of precipitation in some parts of the earth, and without them the years of drought would be unending.

• Storms (hurricanes, typhoons, etc.) cause such upheaval in the ocean that the phytoplankton (the base of the marine food chain) bloom in huge numbers, and thus create a feeding frenzy for the zoo-plankton and other sea creatures all the way up the marine food chain.

Most people think that we could do without all forms of severe weather, but these folks are shortsighted and ill informed. One man's tragic storm may be another man's answer to prayer. For example: Dew upon the ground is looked upon by most people as magnificent, gentle moisture. However, these same people look at the large, ominous storm clouds in the sky as foreboding and dangerous. The interesting part is that both dew and clouds are formed by the same phenomenon—condensation. One is viewed as gentle and the other is viewed as menacing, when the truth is that they are the same. The only difference is in perspective and location. Condensation on the ground (dew) is considered good, while condensation in the sky (clouds) is considered bad.

In order to predict the weather, we must understand it. In order to understand it, we must have a way to quantify it. Every weatherman has certain tools at her disposal to assist in building weather models, understanding the state of the atmosphere, and hopefully, in accurately predicting the weather for a given area.

WEATHER PREDICTION TOOLS

• Radar.

• Detailed and up-to-the-minute images from weather satellites.

• Weather balloons (daily released from weather stations throughout the world).

• Research vessels traversing the world's bodies of water.

• Specially designed weather aircraft (many of which fly through storms in order to gather information).

• Weather readings collected from the huge fleet of commercial airliners that circumnavigate the world daily.

• Private weather service firms, which compile weather related data.

• Human observations.

• Barometers (instruments that measure atmospheric pressure).

• Thermometers (instruments that measure atmospheric temperature).

• Hygrometers (instruments that measure the atmospheric moisture levels).

• The eleven-year cycle of sunspot activity (The Solar Cycle).

• Computer generated weather models formed by complex mathematical calculations.

• Data from an entire network of weather buoys and C-MAN stations located around the world (C-MAN—Coastal Marine Automated Network Station).20

All of these tools put together make up the vast and complex array of observation posts that help us piece together the status of the earth's weather. It is from this vast array of information that each meteorologist calculates her weather pattern predictions for her own locale. In fact, it is the very premise of meteorology that states that by understanding and keen observation we can accurately predict the weather. In a similar fashion, we have a host of tools at our disposal from which we should be able to become more accurate predictors of the storms of life. We will discuss these tools later.

There are further key concepts of meteorology that will help us gain the upper hand on our own life's weather patterns. One of the most important is the understanding that, basically, tomorrow's weather depends only upon today's weather. With this in mind, scientists now use computer programs to solve a system of complex numerical equations that analyze the current weather (from a variety of sources as listed above) in order to predict the future weather. This may seem like an unlikely way to predict the weather, but it has allowed meteorologists in the last few years to become more accurate predictors of local weather phenomena. We must keep this concept in mind as it relates to our own lives. Many times our future storms broadcast telltale signs, as to their imminent arrival, days or months in advance. If we would only analyze those signs, then we could predict some of tomorrow's weather. This would help us become better prepared for those future disasters that will try to knock us out of life's arena.

Another key concept that will assist us lies in understanding where our weather systems begin. The atmospheric changes that dictate the earth's weather first occur in the upper layers of our atmosphere. What this means is that in order to understand and predict the weather, a meteorologist must know what is going on, say, 20,000 feet or more above the earth's surface. This information is far more important than what is currently happening on or near the ground. Our vantage point, unfortunately, is often confined to near-earth locations. We simply cannot usually see that high in the air—without help, that is. This is why we must rely upon our heavenly Father and His holy word while in continued prayer and supplication. It is only then that we will gain that upper perspective and will see the weather to come, as well as those storms that are already pummeling our lives. God's advanced knowledge is what will prepare us to face the coming dilemmas.

A third key concept is in understanding the nature of storms and the weather in general. Meteorologists are not simply interested in or satisfied with predicting when and where a storm may occur. They are most interested in how storm systems develop into marauding tempests. Their goal is to understand completely the why, where and how of a weather system, and to use this knowledge to prevent storms from occurring in the first place. One of the first steps in understanding these weather systems comes with understanding the basis of pressure systems.

"A low, or a *low pressure area* [system], is a region of rising atmospheric air. Active weather on Earth is defined by the presence of lows, which generally produce clouds, strong winds, and precipitation [sometimes severe]."[21]

"A high, or a *high pressure area* [system], is a region where the atmospheric pressure is greatest with relation to the surrounding area."[22] Thus "Highs are frequently associated with light winds and . . . clear, cool [and mild] weather. ."[23]

In reference to high and low pressure systems, it is interesting to note the often misunderstood idea in Christianity that high pressure situations make us more prone to attacks. and that low pressure situations are the most ideal. This could not be any more misleading. It is most often during those areas of low pressure when we form fatal bad habits and make our worst decisions in life–decisions that will ultimately lead to the killer storms of our century. The real crux is that we must continue to make right decisions no matter what the pressure is around us or upon us. These correct choices are critical for our comfort and survival.

Recently I asked a meteorologist a question, and his answer proves starkly apropos to our discussion. The following two-part question was posed to Donald Rosenfeld at the website Allexperts.com: "What would you say is the single most important step that you take each and every time you sit down to develop a weather forecast? What aspect of predicting storms is most critical?"

His answers are awesome: "I review past trends. Predicting storms is most impacted by estimates of future upper air patterns." As I've been stressing all along, the key to knowing the future weather depends upon two critical elements. First, knowing and reviewing the weather of the past (days or weeks), and second, estimating what the upper level air patterns are going to do next. How key it is for us to remember and review the storms of our past (and not only those storms in our past, but those that have struck the lives of those around us), to be completely familiar with their particular nuances, and then to get God's upper perspective on what is coming after the storm. In other words, we must have discernment. What a beautiful gift discernment can be when we exercise and develop it fully.

The question has been asked of me, "So what does all of this meteorological mumbo-jumbo have to do with life?" Well, that is easy to answer. It has everything to do with life. We can take these principles of meteorology and apply them to our personal lives, and if we do, then we will have better success in predicting and avoiding some storms. If we can become more proactive in life, and if we can discern the spiritual weather around us, then we will begin to develop a better feel for the existing conditions and will be more likely to see unpleasant weather approaching. Once we have this preventative mindset, this level of discernment, then we can peer into the areas of our life and look for warning signs of battles to come. Let me give a more practical example. A man who is armed with the knowledge that immoral sexual issues have been an ongoing struggle in his family for generations can know that this is a struggle he must prepare for and defend against before it even hints at arrival. Another example is that if there have been perennial money problems for members of a particular woman's ancestral strain, then this may be an area in her life that, too, is prone to weakness. It is to these areas of our own dark closets that we must venture in order to change what may be a long line of generational curses. The saying that bad or good runs in a family is true, as much as modern Christians would like to think differently.

A popular, albeit blatantly untrue pet doctrine within today's religious culture is that once we become born again and have a new daddy, our old struggles are over with. This is spiritual ignorance and misguided bliss all wrapped up into one neat, little, deceptive package. The thought is that now that we are card-carrying members of our church, the sins of our fathers will no longer be around to haunt or visit us. This is untrue. How easy life would be if we could simply darken the door of a church, and thus have our earthly moral struggles abated. Truth, however, is more demanding than that. Even though we may be born again, we must continually beat down the doors of our own whited sepulchers and drag out all skeletal inhabitants from within. We can and will be visited by the ancestral sins of our family lines, so we may as well face that fact now. Predicting which of these attacks will come and preparing for their arrivals are pivotal points in surviving the rapaciousness of life.

How can we predict the storms of life, and why, exactly, do they occur? Well, let us look at these:

THE REASONS WHY A STORM COMES:

• The devil brings it.

• God brings it.

• We cause it ourselves.

• Someone near or with us causes it.

• No one in particular causes it; the storm comes of its own accord.

STORM PREDICTION TOOLS (NOT AN ALL-INCLUSIVE LIST):

• Some storms are just not predictable in any sense of the word.

• When we run away from our responsibility. (Jonah 1:3)

• When we set sail during the wrong season. (Acts 27)

• When someone warns us of an approaching storm. (Acts 27)

• Discernment and/or a clear word from God. (Numbers 22:12)

• A vision or dream that warns us of events to come. (Genesis 41:1–8)

• The examples of those around us and the storms that they have faced.

• When a couple is in deeply divided disagreement about a moral, spiritual or familial issue thus causing their house to be divided. (Matthew 12:25–29)

• When we allow sin to reside on board our ship—either our own sin (Jonah) or by being unequally yoked with unbelievers. (2 Corinthians 6:14–18)

• The Bible—the written Word of God.

In the movie "Proof of Life," Meg Ryan's character, Alice Bowman, says this when talking about the difficulties we often encounter in life. (I paraphrase), "Things don't happen for a reason. They just happen." Storms often do not have a real reason why they have shown up, they just do. The Bible says that the rain falls on the just and the unjust; however, it is not enough during a storm to simply think that this is the case. Of course, some storms in life come for no apparent reason, but many more are due to our own fault or that of another person. We often have a picture of ourselves that is untrue to reality as we paint ourselves with the same brush used to illustrate the fathers of the faith. Often our pride and arrogance, which are rooted in our dim understanding of scripture, are the most habitual precipitators of our own foul weather. Having been correctly taught that because of Christ we are justified and can enter into the throne room of God unhindered, we then falsely conclude that we have the right to demand our own way out of our mess. This, however, is untrue and is diametrically opposed to Christ's request that His father's will be done and not His own. Even though we are heirs together with Christ, we would do better to remember Isaiah's words: "Then said I, Woe is me! For I am undone *and* ruined, because I am a man of unclean lips, and I dwell in the midst of a people of unclean lips; for my eyes have seen the King, the Lord of hosts!" (Isaiah 6:5 AMP). We are, after all, still human, and we have many frailties and shortcomings that may never get fully fixed until we leave this world and enter the next.

Some preach that we should never ask why, and I both agree and disagree with that line of thinking. When confronted by a storm of life, we must continually ask why it has visited, no matter how much it hurts, until we have ascertained that the tempest's fury is of no fault of our own. If it is our fault, then we should repent and change directions; however, if we determine that we did nothing to facilitate its maddening arrival, then we need not ask why any longer. We should never assume that we have done nothing to cause the whirlwind. Our first assumption must normally be that either we caused the storm or someone around us caused it. Due to our sinful nature, it is guilty until proven innocent rather than the other way around.

There are many who claim the promises of God as they confess, profess, and try to deny their way out of the storms of life while lost in a maze of eternally positive possibilities. Some even practice this to the denial of reality and relevant scriptural principles. As valid as positive confession is, we often fail to realize the validity of low-dose negativity. Dr. James Dobson said it well when he stated that,

"Admittedly, positive thinking can be a good thing. People who are naturally upbeat are more pleasant to be around and they seem to get much more out of life. They are also more productive than those who are routinely 'down' and discouraged. But negative thinking has its advantages too. It is negative thinking that leads me to buckle my seat belt when I get in a car . . . [and] It's negative thinking that causes me to buy life insurance . . . [and] It's negative thinking that encourages me to avoid behavior that could be addictive—such as using illicit drugs, alcohol, or pornography. There are millions of other examples of what might be called 'beneficial negatives.' The bottom line is that there is power in any kind of legitimate thinking. Indeed, if a person only allows himself to read or hear positive messages, he will have to skip over at least half of the Scriptures. [Even] Jesus said some of the most profoundly negative words that have ever been uttered."[24]

Being positive does have its advantages, but looking critically at the circumstances around us is of more value than we may think. Yes, we must always maintain a positive attitude (although there will be many times that we will not be able to); however, to confess our will over something that is in God's power to control is foolhardy. Moreover, even where positive confession has its place and is filled with power, we must realize that the supernatural, miraculous act does not come from our own reserve but from God's awesome limitlessness. What may appear to us to be Satan's machinations may actually be God's maneuverings. It can fairly be assumed that Balaam perceived his situation as negative, but we know that it was positive. Despite his sin and disobedience, God used his crooked voice to bless the children of Israel. He tried to beat the donkey out of the way of his will, but his striking could not succeed. Biblical stories such as this are fun for us to read and study, but our vision becomes cloudy when similar situations strike our own lives. Do we think that our reasoning sways God? When these fomentations hit too close to home for us to handle, we portray them as ruthless attacks that are to be prayed, confessed, or believed away.

I recently read a book by d.c. Talk entitled "Jesus Freaks." In it, the authors recount the heart wrenching stories of many martyrs for Christ. As I pondered the stories, I was struck with a disturbing thought. Many today teach that this type of sacrifice could be avoided if only we had enough faith. They convince us that all uncomfortable circumstances can be "faithed" away. The truth, however, is that all of these martyrs gladly gave up their lives when faced with these unmitigated eradications. There is not one story that reports any desire to pray the storm away. This is a slap in the face to those who would attempt to confess their way out of temporary and light afflictions. It is silly how we try to tie life up into these neat little packages, but this is reality and those strings just will not hold.

All of those we will study about in this book (Paul, Jesus' disciples and Jonah) had an unshakable knowledge of God's sovereignty, something that is quickly becoming lost in today's charismatic circles. Even though miracles and deliverance are well-ensconced biblical objectives, they knew that they could not escape life unscathed. This opposes the teachings today that would have us believe that we are in control, that we are the masters of our own destiny and that we are little gods. Those who promote these teachings confuse instances in the Bible where people had encounters with God and where their faith appropriated a timely miracle with a divine relinquishing of control. These miracles occurred at specially appointed times when God had provided an opportunity for the supernatural to overrule the natural, but that does not mean that we can demand a miracle any time we choose or get out of life's difficulties because they are uncomfortable. Biblical stories of the supernatural manifestation of God's power merely indicate that, at certain moments in life, He has given us an opportunity to reach into eternity and grab a handful to bring back with us to the present. That is it. We must never believe that we can control life or God. Our job is to live and learn. His job is to rule. We will rule with Him, eventually, but not now, and only then under His direction.

God has not relinquished control to us, who only see in part and know in part. That would be a foolish mistake on His part. He still maintains complete control as He should, and we dare not ever forget that. This is why the men of these storms did not ask why their storms had come, for they already knew. They knew it was either because God wanted it or because they or someone around them thrust them into that situation. Armed with that knowledge, they then tried to deal with their tempests as best they could; some did well and others did not. The disciples fell flat on their faces. Jonah ran away like a spoiled child. Paul steadily walked through to the end. We should read their harrowing accounts, learn from both their successes and failures and then put this newly acquired understanding into practice. In addition, although we have a duty to deal well with the storms in our own lives, we further have a responsibility to warn others of the storms that may be approaching their lives. Such a mandate is not so easy to do tactfully, but it is nevertheless necessary. We are, after all and in a way, God's meteorologists and should report the weather to all who will tune in to our station.

REPORTING LIVE FROM THE MARINA

Speaking symbolically, we are all on a boat of sorts in our lives, and actually may be on several boats at the same time. These boats could be a marriage, family or job, a church, ministry or related group, a business or business dealing, any social club or league, any mechanical means of transportation, a fraternity or other college affiliation or our very life itself. To help us better understand the symbolic correlation, we will look at various physical boats and boat operators. In so doing, we will be able to more clearly see what they might represent and how they relate to us. The descriptions will assist us in gaining a more keen understanding of how the storms of life relate to the various boats in which we reside.

A SHIP MAY REPRESENT:

• A sole means of support. This boat represents a way to make a living, a way to buy what we desire, and it provides us with a sense of security and strength and dignity. (Isaiah 23:14; Ezekiel 27:26, 29; Luke 5:2)

• A means of transportation. This boat transports us around the circles of life. (Matthew 9:1)

• Anything that we use to influence others with. This would include a pulpit, leadership role or place of prominence in an organization, business or ministry. (Matthew 13:2)

• A tool of war. This would include any post, position or place of influence with which we harm another. (Numbers 24:24)

• A way of life, and everything included in a lifestyle or a family. This would include anything that represents all or part of our earthly possessions. (Matthew 4:18–22)

• A cargo hauler or any vessel designed for the sole purpose of accumulating wealth or supplying necessary provisions. This boat would include a business, organization, ministry or charity. (2 Chronicles 9:21; Psalm 107:23; Proverbs 31:14; Acts 21:2–5)

• A means of escape. This boat would be anything we use to distance ourselves from reality or an uncomfortable situation including lies, destructive habits and elaborate fantasies. (Matthew 14:13; Jonah 1:3)

• A place of captivity. This boat could represent anything from a job to a family to a career to a church. It is important because we all find ourselves held captive in situations that we cannot, and in some cases should not, be released from. (Acts 27:6)

• A way of thinking. This boat could represent any doctrine, philosophical approach, religion or thought process to which we may find ourselves bound. This is critical because we all have patterns of thinking that often hold us back, keep us down or otherwise control the way we live.

THOSE WHO UTILIZE THE BOATS OF LIFE:

• The utilitarian. This person's boat is a small motorboat, rowboat, catamaran, canoe or kayak. It is strictly for practicality. The reason this person is out on the water is in order to do what needs to be done on or across the water.

• The weekend yuppie. This person's boat is a large powerboat or sailboat. It is strictly for pleasure. The reason this person (along with family or friends) is out on the water is to forget about the doldrums of the workweek and to escape the demands of life.

• The rich businessperson. This person's boat is a large yacht or a small oceangoing vessel. It is strictly for pride. The reason this person is out on the water is to revel in being a status symbol, to flaunt success, and to make appearances.

• The captain/pilot. This person's boat is any private or commercial vessel that is captained by someone other than the owner, and is in the service sector. It is strictly about transportation, work and timing. The reason this person is out on the water is to ferry local passengers or to transport cargo to nearby ports of call.

• The overseas shipper. This person's boat is an oceangoing container ship, tanker, or cruise ship. It is strictly about traversing the seas and making money. The reason this person is out on the water is to transport ore, oil, goods or people to and from worldwide ports of call and to do so in the most efficient, cost effective fashion available.

• The deckhand or crewperson. This person's boat is owned and operated by others who retain full control and final authority. It is strictly about service. The reason this person is out on the water is to serve aboard the ship of another and to fulfill the wishes of the captain and/or owner.

Storm Watch

What has recently become fashionable in difficult times is to proclaim that Satan has desired to sift us as wheat as Jesus informed Peter, but God forbid that we encounter even a portion of what he endured for Christ's sake. In our thinking, we often align ourselves with the shining examples of biblical lore. It puffs our feathers up when we believe that we are similar to Job in our hour of suffering, but most of us will never equal God's assessment of Job's life—that he was the most upright in all the earth. Job's harassment is unique or at least uncommon, but the value of his story is nonetheless important as it details some practical examples of behavior. Along with Job's story, we will reference below some other behaviors (both productive and non-productive) that will help us to maintain our course with God. (These lists are not exclusive or all encompassing.)

Productive Behaviors:

• We should hold fast to our blameless uprightness. This is elsewhere translated integrity. It means that Job was completely righteous, a finished product who was well rounded and balanced in his attitudes and dealings in life. We should strive for this quality and maintain our own integrity. (Job 2:9)

• We should listen to the voice of God and godly counsel only. (Job 38:1–Job 42:9)

• We should speak of God that which is right. (Job 42:7b)

• We should cast down any thoughts and imaginations that would try to exalt themselves against the knowledge of God and take them captive in our minds. This means that we can overpower the evil, fleshly nature with God's help and defeat it before it can ruin us. (2 Corinthians 10:5)

• We should confess our sins one to another. (James 5:16)

• We should ask of God with right motives. (James 4:1–3)

• We should not lose our hope. (Acts 27:23–25)

• We should lay our hand upon our mouth, if need be, to keep it closed so that we do not speak more evil upon ourselves. After all, the Bible does say that even a fool is thought wise if he shuts his mouth. (Job 2:10; Job 40:4; Proverbs 17:28)

UNPRODUCTIVE BEHAVIORS:

• Cursing God, charging Him foolishly, or otherwise sinning with our lips. (Job 1:22; 2:9, 10)

• Allowing ourselves to think that the calamity we have witnessed in the lives of those around us cannot possibly touch us as well. (Job 4:3–5)

• Listening to the accusations of well-intentioned yet scripturally unsound friends. (Job 4:1–Job 37:24)

• Fighting, blame placing, posturing, or lashing out at those who are in the storm with us or are standing on the sidelines watching us. Avoiding this type of childish behavior is always appropriate.

• Falling apart, freaking out, or otherwise losing our composure during our storms. This type of behavior, although popular, is unacceptable. (Mark 4:38–40)

Lingering at the table of negativity and supposition. Discussing at length the details of what is taking place and speculating as to its cause only promotes unhealthy questioning in the midst of life's struggles. There will come a time after the storm when we can more objectively reflect on the storm and gain keen insight into its details; however, during the storm is not that time. (Job 4:1–Job 37:24)

We must trust that God wants us to be blessed. God wants us to keep our boat and our belongings, but if we do not obey and act as He says we should, we may lose it all. Alternatively, like Job, God may allow it all to be taken away from us so that that which is within us may shine forth, and then it will all be returned to us, plus more. What is critical is our discernment of the situation. It is what will help us to determine why the storm has arrived and how we should respond. One pitfall that we must avoid is the lie that there is only one correct response to all storms.

Therefore, when the question is posed, "How do we know which response we need to have to our storm?" we can be confident and know that the answer lies in how closely we have been listening to God. Some tools will come in handy for us as we attempt to ascertain the girth of the storm and its potential impact upon our lives.

IN ORDER TO SUCCESSFULLY DEAL WITH EVERY BRUTAL CATACLYSM THAT MAY ARISE, WE MUST SEEK OUT AND PARTICIPATE IN THE FOLLOWING BEHAVIORS:

• Discernment or Intuition Plus.

• Prayer to God and no one else.

• Wise and godly counsel from mature, well-seasoned and trusted individuals.

• Common sense and knowledge, without which wisdom cannot exist.

• Past personal experiences, or those related to us by others that give us insight into our current situation.

• Examining the storm's responses to our actions. This one is a bit tricky, but let me explain. We cannot let the circumstances of life trick us or convince us that we are all right; neither can we let the false calm trick us into thinking that we have done the right thing. Equally important is not allowing ourselves to think that the storm's unresponsiveness to our cries means that we have done the wrong thing. This is why we must discern the proper response and then perform it until it works; however, when we repeatedly respond to a storm with a course of action and it does not work, then maybe we need to admit that we missed it and should seek God's face for the right solution or course of action.

9

INEFFECTIVE USE OF FAITH

Contrary to popular opinion, we can neither shout every mountain down nor command every squall to cease. We cannot faith our way out of every atmospheric upheaval, and we cannot dance our way clear of every venomous terrorism. These confessions do not always produce the way we would like them to. Hearing is one thing, but listening is another. If we think that all storms of life can be erased by an excessive use of faith, we are mistaken. That is a myth. The stark truth is that faith is over-stressed to the point where it becomes just another glamour toy we have acquired. Sometimes our vehement proposal of faith is ineffective because it is the wrong solution—period. At other times, though, it is the only option.

Recently I heard of a man who lived in the South. The region he lived in was experiencing a devastating drought, and all of the farmers around him had lost their crops. Yet he had lush, green fields that displayed no signs of trouble. This farmer's green fields extended throughout his property and right up to his fence posts, but beyond the posts, the land was barren and desolate. It lay as a parched reminder of the severe drought that had decimated the area's agricultural lands that year. The reason why this man had green fields? His fields were spared because he listened to God. He had felt the Lord prompt him to borrow the anointing oil from his pastor and to anoint every fencepost on his property, so he did. Together they prayed and believed that God would supernaturally care for his crops. The great thing is that God caused a heavy dew to settle on this man's property each night that caused his crops to remain healthy. Amidst swirling accusations of secret underground wells and irrigation systems, water ban violations and illegally hauling water in from out-of-state, this farmer reaped a bountiful harvest while the crops of his fellow farmers were non-existent.

The point I am making here is this. Upon hearing that story told by a minister friend of mine, I was struck by one thing: most people who hear this will think that they can apply this principle to every storm that they are in and everything will turn out fine. Well, my friend, I have to be honest. That is not true. This was a valid move for this man because God prompted him to follow that course of action. What this farmer did is not the answer to all of life's problems. It might not even work for this man again if there were to be another situation like that a few years down the road. The countless embroilments in life that erupt due to a myriad of pressures all have different solutions and lessons to be learned. A mountain of faith will not always take us through. Sometimes we have to have that dogged, determined, stubborn faith that helps us walk on, even as we stumble across the valley's hot and rocky floor with ragged, bloody feet. It is a simple concept that we often fail to remember when life gets windy and rough. During the storms of life, God promised that, "When you pass through the waters, I will be with you, and through the rivers, they will not overwhelm you. When you walk through the fire, you will not be burned *or* scorched, nor will the flame kindle upon you" (Isaiah 43: 2 AMP). He has promised to be with us, and we must take comfort in that.

In another time long ago, a storm arose throughout the land after Joseph became second in command in all of Egypt. When faced with a drought that stretched out seven years, did Joseph anoint the fence posts and thus escape the effects of the drought? No. Egypt and Israel both succumbed to the drought just like all of the other nations, despite the fact that God's man was in charge of Egypt, and Israel was the land of God's own people. The redeeming quality in all of this is that Joseph had listened to God before the drought and had hoarded year's worth of grain in the barns of Egypt–more than enough grain needed for Egypt to survive. He had listened to God and had done according to His word. Joseph practiced discernment and had the solution in place before the problem (storm) ever arose. Again, I hesitate to relate these stories because so many people today think that one solution that worked for "Joe Somebody" will work in their situation. This is a lie. People tend to apply these laws or principles as haphazardly as they spread their favorite jelly on their morning toast.

There is a question hidden within in this story. Why did not anyone in Israel know of this storm of drought before it happened? They were, after all, the very children of God. Is it not more than interesting that a pharaoh of Egypt was the one to hear and not a prophet of God? This shows us that the warning signs can be heard by any of us if we are listening, Christian or not. Pharaoh may not have been able to interpret the dream, but he is the one whom was given the dream. He also knew that he had a responsibility to get the dream interpreted so that he could understand it—ahh, there is that annoying discernment issue again. The supreme leader of Egypt did not blame the dream on bad pizza or an excess of junk food before bedtime, or on Satan trying to steal his faith and joy and victory. Frivolity did not become a pharaoh, so he knew that this was a message that he must heed. This should be a wake-up call to all of us. We should not be so quick to ignore the warning signs that God may be sending us, no matter where they come from. In addition, we should not be so quick to think that Satan will not take advantage of a storm in our lives to try to take us out completely.

Even when Satan is not responsible for the turbulence in our lives, he will still try to throw us off our course. When he perceives that we will not turn from God despite the severity of the weather, we need not be duped into thinking that he has given up and gone home, or that he is standing idly by and watching with tears streaming down his pitiful face. He will attack any vein that he thinks will bleed. Satan easily tricks us through some unholy oracles when we are at the mercy of the wind. However, we have to be as wise as serpents and realize that the solutions to the storms of life are as numerous as are the causes. Discerning judgment is our key to unlocking the door. Hearing that solution from God and implementing it is what will save us.

In order to fully understand the storms that we are studying, we must understand as much of the background, customs and the nature of the storms as we can. That way we can attempt to experience the message from as close to first hand as possible. If we take only one part or do not understand any of the culture and history, then we miss the nuances and revelations that Jesus spoke about in Mark 4:11–13. As we put our hand to this difficult task, we will unearth many jewels that the casual observer would not even know existed. Jesus called the nugget-laden stories of which He was so fond parables. Since He knew that most could not or would not choose to comprehend what He said, Jesus cloaked the true meaning of His teachings within parables–meanings that need to be mined out of the soil of His Word. Although the Bible says that He explained everything fully to His disciples, there was still work to be done to understand these parables fully. We must understand that truth freely given is not appreciated as much as that which has to be labored for. If we must work to haul it up from beneath the surface with our own hands, then that truth will forever change us. Jesus wanted His disciples to understand Him fully, and He wants no less from us.

Section Two

JESUS AND THE DISCIPLES

THE STORY

On another occasion, Jesus began to teach beside the lake near Capernaum, and a bigger crowd than ever gathered around Him. The crowd was so large that, in order to teach them more effectively, He sat in a boat a little way out from the shore. Now with the entire crowd facing him, He used this pulpit to continue to teach His doctrine by using parables (illustrations or comparisons put beside truths to explain them) and stories. Jesus spoke as much of the Word to the crowd as they were able to hear and to comprehend and to understand; however, He did not tell them anything without presenting it to them as a parable. In contrast to this, He privately explained everything fully to His disciples (those who were peculiarly His own, His close followers and the twelve disciples). That is to say that He explained the hidden meanings wrapped within the fabric of the parables.

On that same evening after He had finished teaching this great crowd that had gathered at the seashore, He said to his disciples, "Let us now leave this place and go over to the other side of the lake" (presumably to catch fish). So the disciples took Jesus' suggestion and, after leaving the throng, joined Him in the boat in which He had been sitting for most of the day. They left just as they were and without any previous preparations, food or coats, even though they would be traveling unprotected over the open waters in the middle of the winter. Together with other small fishing boats from Capernaum, Jesus and the disciples set sail for the sardine fishing grounds of Kursi.

Some time after they had set sail, a furious and violent

storm of hurricane proportions arose on the sea. The storm suddenly fell down upon them from Mount Hermon (from up on the Golan Heights, northeast of the lake) in the form of cyclonic gusts and was accompanied by a violent upheaval beneath the sea, similar to a tsunami. This storm's fury was so intense that an unending line of waves beat against the short sides, breaking over them and filling the boat with enough water to sink it. But during this entire encounter, Jesus, who was no doubt weary from teaching the crowd, remained asleep on a leather cushion lying on the rower's bench in the stern of the boat. When they found Him resting, their natural understanding caused them to panic. They quickly woke their Lord and rebuked Him saying, "Master, rescue and preserve us. Do you not care that we are drowning? Why are you not helping us get out of this storm? At least you could get up and help row. It doesn't appear that you care at all about us or our well being, but would rather sleep lazily upon that cushion while the rest of us risk death by drowning in an attempt to right this ship."

And He, the Master and Son of God, responded to their rebuke with a most powerful and pointed rebuke of His own, saying, "You are cowards! How dare you rebuke Me when it is you that need the reproof. Why are you so timid and fearful? How is it that you have been with Me and witnessed My many miracles and still have no faith; no firmly relying trust in Me? Can you not recall My teaching on the mountainside where I taught you about the Be-Attitudes and instructed you not to worry about your life? Do you not remember when I told you that your heavenly Father feeds the birds of the air and clothes the lilies and grasses in the fields? It was at this point that you should have realized that I am the God over nature itself, including this storm. Where then is your confidence in Me, the Son of God, and in My veracity (My unwillingness to tell lies), and in My honesty and truthfulness and integrity? I told you that he who has an ear let him hear, and I admonished you to give extreme care and thought and study to the truth that you hear. If you let My truth fall into the good ground of your heart, then it will produce a bountiful crop in your life. Do you actually think that I would let you drown in a ship while I am here with you? And even if so, don't you believe that I care the most about you, My dear children and that I would take you with Me to a better place? Did I not help the Father number every hair upon your heads? I truly wish that you would not just hear My words but that you would also grasp their meaning and comprehend the full measure of what I have said."

With His rebuke uttered, He got up from His cushion, stood firm and tall against the cyclonic gusts, rebuked the wind and said to the sea, "Hush now! Be still and muzzled!" And the wind ceased and sank to rest as if exhausted by its own beating, and there was immediately and without any pause a great and wonderful calm (a perfect peacefulness) in the sea around them. This caused the disciples to gasp, as they were stunned with bewildered wonder. What Jesus had just done shook them to the core. They had had no premonition as to what He was going to do, and after He performed this miracle, they were dumbstruck with awe. No longer did they fear the storm (obviously because it was gone), but they now marveled at Jesus and were filled with great awe. That choking fear was now intensified in the unbelievable power Jesus displayed, and they feared Him exceedingly and as much or more so than they had previously feared the storm. After they had gathered some measure of composure over their emotions, they said to each other, "What kind of man is this that we have been traveling with, that even the wind and sea obey Him? Could it be that we have misjudged and misunderstood He who we have walked with? He surely is the God over all of creation. This man, this God, deserves our obedience for He cares deeply for us. [Adaptation of Mark 4:1–41].[25]

Home Port

*"the port in which a vessel is registered
or permanently based."*[26]

Mark 4:1a
Again Jesus began to teach beside the lake. (AMP)

What makes this story so intriguing is the background information not made available in the biblical text. It is critical that we possess at least a basic knowledge of the disciples and their craft in order to completely understand the nuances of this story. After we have acquired this knowledge, we can then revisit the account and draw some relevant life lessons from it.

On this day, Jesus began to teach His gospel at a location near Capernaum. At that time, Capernaum was the most important city located on the northwestern shore of the Sea of Galilee and was also the nearest in that area to the Jordan River. Jesus centered His ministry in Capernaum and performed a great number of miracles in and around the city.[27] Although Capernaum is never mentioned in the Old Testament and was cursed by Jesus for its unbelief in the New Testament (Matthew 11:23–24), it still was a significant enough place for Jesus to use as His headquarters instead of His hometown of Nazareth.[28] It was always large enough to be called a city and was apparently more than just a spot on the map. We can surmise this after learning that it had its own synagogue, a permanent office of taxation, a group of itinerant tax collectors[29], a customs station[30], and a Roman centurion who commanded a company of between 50 and 100 men[31] who were garrisoned there. Capernaum, it seems, was at the center of the hustle and bustle of the day around the Sea of Galilee.

The Sea of Galilee, approximately twenty-one kilometers long and eleven kilometers wide, is variously known as Yam Kinneret (its modern, Hebrew name), which is usually shortened to Kinneret, the Sea of Chinnereth or Chinneroth (in the Old Testament) and as the Lake of Gennesaret or Gennesareth[32] and the Sea of Tiberias (in the New Testament). It is approximately 211 meters below sea level and is surrounded by hills.[33]

The economic and political importance held in ancient times by the Sea of Galilee and the surrounding towns was influential enough to entice a large population to live in close proximity to her sweet, prosperous and sometimes dangerous waters. Josephus recorded that there were over 230 fishing boats that regularly worked the waters of the Sea of Galilee during the first century,[34] and according to Shelley Wachsmann, "Then, as now, the lake swarmed with a living supply of swimming and swarming protein packaged in silvery scales. Thus the Sea of Galilee was an important source for food" [not only for the immediate area and Israel, in general, but also for other more distant shores].[35] A continual southerly flow of the Jordan River through the Sea of Galilee caused her waters to be so sweet that they produced fish by the hundreds of tons annually, which in turn caused her fisheries to become famous throughout the entire Roman Empire. The three groups of edible fish that created and sustained this economic bounty were the musht, biny (or barbels) and the sardines.[36] This flourishing export trade is what put Israel on the map both politically and economically.[37] It is no wonder then that a large portion of Christ's ministry was carried out on and around this lake. In fact, research has shown that during Jesus' time and "in spite of the steep hillsides around the lake, nine cities of 15,000 population or more thrived in the first century as part of an almost continuous belt of settlements around the lake."[38] These settlements did not exist independently of each other, either, but they traded with each other across the lake. In this respect, these New Testament cities became a vitally interconnected ring of trade that formed a web of commerce encircling and criss-crossing the lake.

Cast Off

"Letting go the lines to a mooring, wharf, dock, buoy or another ship in order to move away."[39]

Mark 4:35, 36

On that same day [when] evening had come, He said to them, Let us go over to the other side [of the lake]. And leaving the throng, they took Him with them, [just] as He was, in the boat [in which He was sitting]. And other boats were with Him. (AMP)

As our story opens, we find Jesus and His disciples surrounded by a throng (arguably at least a few hundred people). Having just mystified them with His indelible teachings, He then suggests to His followers that they depart from this port city and head off to the other side of the lake. An important perspective that will prove useful is gained when we realize whom Jesus did not invite along for the trip. He did not invite any of the crowd to join them. Did Jesus know what lay ahead of them? Had He already envisioned the demoniac? Was He secretly preparing Himself to deal with the strong demonic forces He would soon encounter? Would the crowd have drained His aura even more than His disciples' lack of faith? Of these questions, I have no firm answer except to say that Jesus surely knew what was ahead and obviously did not need or want an entire crowd gathering around Him on this most important mission. Knowing the sensitivity He possessed to virtue flowing out of Him, I am convinced that He could not allow a potentially draining crowd to distract

Him in the District of the Gerasenes.

What this shows us is that we must exercise great caution in who we allow into our boat. We cannot ever appear stand-offish; however, we cannot allow ourselves to continually rub shoulders with those whose only aim is to drag us down in life and suck us dry of faith. In this instance, though, it is likely true that Judas was aboard the boat as well, but what we must also remember is that we are not Jesus incarnate. Life is not a game and we must act with extreme care when allowing other people access to our boat, even when it is in the name of rehabilitation, pity or compassion. There are a few, select people who have the ability to maintain close contact with those in sin and in direct disobedience of God without becoming tainted or compromised. This is not a situation where most of us would shine, though, and it is not even advisable for the strong and gifted however necessary it may sometimes appear. Jesus was one who could handle it without being dragged down, but most of us could not. I am not recommending that the church remove itself from those hurting and in need around us, but what I am saying is that we must not allow them to reside in our boat with us. We can and should minister to the lost, disobedient and dying, but we do not need to become members of their inner sanctum. The Bible says that we are to avoid the very appearance of evil, let alone lie in bed with it on board our ship. When we are confronted with this type of a situation, the deterioration of events is predictable, dependable and tragic.

The question has been posed to me, "Why would Jesus suggest that they leave so late in the day and in the middle of the winter?" It is from the long-time fisherman Mendel Nun that we learn at least part of that answer. He recounts that on this particular occasion, " . . . the boat of Jesus' disciples was on its way, together with other fishing boats from Capernaum, to the sardine fishing ground of Kursi, where work in the winter starts before sunset . . . [and continues throughout the night]. The distance between Capernaum and Gergesa (Kursi) is only eight kilometers . . . [and] fishermen, cautious by nature, were not in the habit, particularly in the dangerous winter season . . ." of traveling much further that that on the lake.[40] *(See Map 1: The Sea of Galilee in the First Century a.d.)* With this knowledge in hand, it is obvious and understandable why Jesus and the disciples left Capernaum when they did, and it was in order to arrive in Kursi in time to fish for sardines. It was something they may have done a hundred times before, and there would have been no cause for alarm by His suggestion.

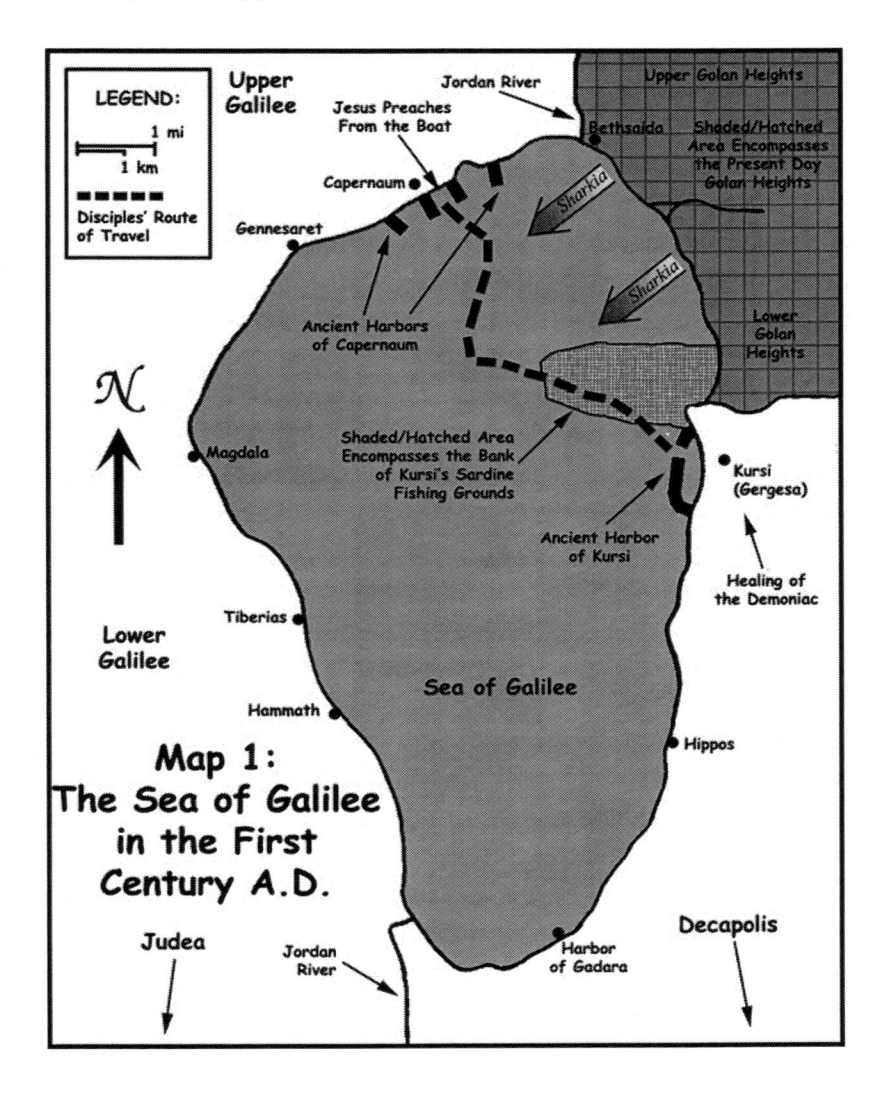

LEGEND:

1 mi

1 km

Disciples' Route of Travel

Upper Galilee

Jesus Preaches From the Boat

Jordan River

Upper Golan Heights

Bethsaida

Shaded/Hatched Area Encompasses the Present Day Golan Heights

Capernaum

Gennesaret

Ancient Harbors of Capernaum

Sharkia

Sharkia

Lower Golan Heights

N

Magdala

Shaded/Hatched Area Encompasses the Bank of Kursi's Sardine Fishing Grounds

Ancient Harbor of Kursi

Kursi (Gergesa)

Healing of the Demoniac

Tiberias

Lower Galilee

Hammath

Sea of Galilee

Hippos

Map 1: The Sea of Galilee in the First Century A.D.

Judea

Jordan River

Harbor of Gadara

Decapolis

The communities surrounding the Sea of Galilee were dependent upon the fishing industry, and of the three main groups of edible fish that were found in the Sea of Galilee, it was the sardine that took on the world, so to speak. During this era, fresh sardines were an important part of the Jewish diet, and pickled sardines were widely distributed to many distant lands. Strabo, the first century Roman historian, notes that the Sea of Galilee provided the best fish for salting and that the town of Magdala (Migdal) was the center of this fish pickling industry.[41] In fact the Kinneret sardine, found in huge schools on the eastern side of the lake near the bank of Kursi (which, incidentally, has always been the best sardine fishing ground in that sea),[42] is still of considerable economic importance.[43] We can then speculate that Jesus, who most likely had other demands on His mind as well, was simply suggesting that they go and fish; however, it is also entirely possible that He, knowing that nothing short of a sardine fishing trip would get these men to leave for Kursi and ultimately the region of the Gerasenes, suggested fishing simply as a way to get the men moving.

These disciple fishermen, the sea mariners' landlocked cousins, were equally as physically tough and mentally able as those who sailed the oceans and were probably not much different than fishermen are today. An ancient fisherman's life would have required a strong mind and body, copious amounts of manual labor, incredible physical stamina and the ability to endure long, lonely, dangerous and sometimes frustrating hours at sea. A typical day would have required the fishermen to methodically throw out nets from their boat (in excess of two hundred pounds each when empty), haul the nets to shore (adding several hundred pounds to their weight when filled with fish), wash and sew torn nets, row their boat through all manner of weather, repair damaged or decaying parts of their boat and, finally, transport and offload the fish from the boat to wherever they stored, processed and sold their catch. Along with the physical components of their day, these fishermen would also have needed to be savvy meteorologists in order to predict and stay out of treacherous weather, and competent oceanographers, needing to be experts on the sea's depths, beds, animals, plants and prime fishing locations in order to be commercially successful. In finishing out this examination of the fishermen, let us look at a short list of some typical fishermen traits.

• They are dedicated. Successful fishermen start their day long before others are awake and can often be found setting their gear or hauling their nets and traps aboard long before daylight has come. And since most fishing is seasonal, they have a limited time in which to catch as many fish as possible. What this means is that fishermen must work every possible day of the prime fishing season, including days of inclement and uncomfortable weather, in order to make their desired or necessary level of income. It is likely that most fishermen make great money for six to nine months out of the year, but it is also likely that many of these same fishermen may have little or no additional income for the remaining three to six months of the year.

• They are independent. Most people who have chosen fishing as their vocation have done so because they want to be on their own. A fisherman wants the freedom to choose what to do and when to do it, not having work hours set by someone above them. For those who work for a skipper or a captain, they enjoy the freedom in choosing their assignments. They work by the trip, job or season and do not have a firm, long-term commitment to one particular vessel or owner. They come and go as they please (or as the money demands) and may work aboard several different vessels during their career (as well as possibly venturing forth with their own vessels at times).

• They are enterprising. Successful commercial fishermen are interested in making money, lots of money. Though many of them kick against governmental stipulations, reduced catch sizes, and mandated moratoriums, they continue to make enough money to remain in operation because of their drive and initiative, oftentimes having many proverbial irons in the fire. Many of these fishermen may hold part ownership in a local marina or other fishing vessels, operate a fish market or participate in alternative fishing ventures including diving for sea urchins or scallops and digging clams. Most of their activities revolve around fishing and are geared towards making money and building a successful business.

• They are tough. A fisherman puts in long hours performing monotonous, strenuous work diving or hauling in traps or nets or setting out gear. Injury often takes a back seat when there is work to be done because there may be no one else to do the job. Having neither comfortable health plans nor sick days and neither paid vacations nor disability insurance policies, fishermen have to fish even when they don't feel like it. Not only must they fish through injury and loss, they must also maintain the gear and the boat and the business's books in the spare time sandwiched between fishing trips. This toughness, however, is not relegated solely to the physical realm. Mentally these mariners are tough as well, having had to deal with the deaths of many close friends, facing tougher fishing restrictions each year while attempting to maintain the size and liquidity of their business, and having to spend long, lonely hours out at sea while sometimes not bringing home an acceptable catch.

• They live. Stereotypical fishermen do not gain their reputations from fictional characters spun into existence by fat, balding authors sitting in underground cubicles with no ventilation, who have neither seen the ocean nor smelt its salty brine. No, they have gained their infamous reputations from being exactly as they are, alive—vividly alive. Fishermen live life to its fullest and make no bones about any dealings they may be involved in. And when they are not plying the waters, fishing for scaled creatures of the deep, they can often be found partying with as much vigor as they fish with.

• They are macho. Leaning heavily upon their experience and determination, fishermen often believe that these qualities alone will get them through any situation, no matter how hopeless. Many will even ignore marine forecasts and play down whatever impending doom they may be facing, believing more in their own machismo than in the misplaced fear of others, especially women. They are forceful and domineering and, for the most part, have faced down many hellish storms that would have crippled the weak. Every successful return trip from sea adds to their self-assurance and further validates their perceived superior abilities.

• They are risk takers. Fishermen may be risk takers either by choice or by necessity. They live or die by their ability to catch fish. Their businesses succeed or fail according to their capacity to consistently deliver a marketable catch. If they do not catch fish, then they do not eat or pay their bills. Often this complicates what might look to others to be easy decisions. For instance, fishermen may feel compelled to fish in more severe forms of weather (and thus take greater risks than the normal person) because there are bills to be paid and no other means by which to pay them. This may cause them to take risks that place them into more dangerous situations than the average person. They also may simply love what they do so much that they are willing to take chances fishing (sometimes calculated and sometimes with reckless abandon) rather than suffer a decades-long death facing a computer keyboard and monitor.

In speaking of the fisherman's trade, it is important that we look at some of the more intricate details of their gear in order to get a full understanding and appreciation for their craft, and ultimately of them. In a time when many people peer over the rims of their designer glasses and gaze condescendingly towards fishermen in general, it is important that we have a change of attitude regarding these disciples. Many feel that fishermen are inherently stupid or intellectually inferior, and so they have chosen fishing as a profession because they could not make it elsewhere. I pray that the details presented in this section will erase all superiority we may feel over fishermen. Fishermen are neither dumb nor inferior to other professionals in any way. In fact, in some ways fishermen are superior in their understanding of nature and the elements and of commerce and camaraderie than the general public.

As we will see, certain parts of the ancient fisherman's gear were technological marvels of the day and did not change in form or function until the mid-twentieth century, something that cannot be said of our more modern inventions, which seem to "improve" daily. The production of some of the items they used regularly, stone anchors for instance, still leaves modern scholars scratching their heads as to how they were fashioned. Thus we will see that a first century fisherman was not dumb (nor are they today), as some would lead us to believe. They may have been rough and they may have been crude, but they were definitely tough, smart and resourceful. We often tend to look down upon these men that Jesus chose as being simple in the sense of intellectual inferiority when compared to our modern-day standards, but this attitude can be harbored only by those who must breathe the diseased air of superiority in order to survive. Nothing could be more misleading than to think of these disciples in that regard.

THE DISCIPLES AND THEIR CRAFT

The most common boats in use in Jesus' time on the Sea of Galilee were craft most suited for fishing on a small lake, and, although they were used mainly for fishing, they were also used for general communications and travel across the lake.[44] The vessels were not large by any standard. In fact, as Mark relates to us in his gospel, an unusually large catch of fish enclosed by a single net was nearly enough to capsize two of them. Obviously, there were no powerboats sporting large inboard motors in those days, so their main means of propulsion was nature-based. While wind power would have been the most prevalent and preferred method of propulsion, " . . . they were [also] regularly equipped with oars [in order] to enable them to progress . . . in the heavy storms, which occasionally sweep across the lake."[45]

We cannot know for sure what the size of their ship was, but we can make an educated estimation. Mendel Nun's book on ancient stone anchors gives us some insight into the types of boats that existed during that time. Nun writes that,

During periods when the lake was surrounded by thriving settlements [such as in Jesus' time], hundreds of boats of various sizes plied it [sic] waters. From written and iconographic sources, we may assume that most of these were small fishing craft, about five meters long and capable of carrying up to six people. Larger boats, manned by four or five sailors, are mentioned by Josephus Flavius. These boats, which had four oars and a sail, were about seven to nine meters long, and could carry ten to fifteen passengers, or freight of equivalent weight. Ancient sources do not tell us of larger boats on the Sea of Galilee, and anchors found do not provide evidence for these.[46]

In our story we read that, on this particular evening, there were many other men and boats together with Jesus and His disciples venturing forth to Kursi. It appears that the boat Jesus was on carried most of the twelve disciples in it (although the Bible doesn't gives us the exact number) as well as anchors, nets, weights of various kinds, miscellaneous tools and other fishing gear, oars and sails. Thus, we can be reasonably sure that their boat was one of these larger boats, commonly known as a trammel boat, which was approximately twenty-five feet long, twelve feet wide and with four-foot high sides. Therefore, as they set sail along the deepening shadows cast across the surface of the lake by the setting sun, let us pause to examine some of the objects found aboard this boat, objects that will further point to the fact that these disciples were hard-working, intelligent, highly motivated, concerned individuals who were at the top of their craft.

In our exploration into the gear stowed on board these boats, let us first examine the types of anchors that would have been in use for boats of this size. Mendel Nun informs us that there is considerable archaeological evidence that supports the fact that even small boats like the one carrying Jesus and His disciples carried anchors and, further, would have had at least one spare on board as well."[47] Most of the anchors that would come to mind today bear little resemblance to those that were in use during this era in and around the Sea of Galilee. And, although there were many anchors of advanced design (in reference to combination iron, wood and lead anchors) being used elsewhere in the world at that time, there is no historical or archaeological evidence of these types of anchors ever being in use on the Sea of Galilee. The anchors they did use were simple stone anchors. There is little doubt that they could have used composite anchors since the technology did exist at that time, but such anchors were expensive to manufacture, and so were most likely either too costly or too inconvenient for these inland mariners to possess. It appears quite natural that throughout the years and often pressured by a lack of ready cash, the owners of these small trammel boats would have continued to use stone anchors—anchors which were always there for the taking and cost them nothing other than the time it took to gather and fashion them. All of the anchors found in the Sea of Galilee region have been stone weight anchors, and there have been no pieces of composite anchors ever discovered there.[48]

Of the hundreds of these stone anchors that have been recovered from the sea and her surrounding shores, " . . . the great majority of boat anchors used in the Sea of Galilee were made of basalt . . ."[49] which is the softest, most common stone found in the region (although others made of limestone and flint have also been found). And even though these stone anchors were heavy and worked adequately, they would have been more awkward to handle and less likely to hold well than their technologically advanced composite cousins, which were in widespread use in the Mediterranean Sea. The stone anchors likely found in this boat along with

Jesus and the disciples would have been in the fifteen to twenty-five kilogram (35–60 pound) range,[50] and thus further substantiates the supposition that Jesus and the disciples were traveling in a trammel boat.

The anchors the disciples used were made from stone, but the question that remains to be answered is this: How did they get a rope to remain around the stones so that they could be used as an anchor and not lost? The answer to that is simple. The ancient mariners did not tie a rope around the stones, but instead, they drilled holes through the stones so a rope could pass through the hole and tie back onto itself. Upon first appearance these stone anchors, with a hole bored through their top center portion, look a lot like what we might envision as a large, bulbous, primitive earring. And, "If we inspect the hole, we note that it generally has a bi-conical form. That is, it was drilled from both sides: on each outer start, the aperture is larger and diminishes in size until both holes meet at the halfway point. [Thus] the hole resembles two cones."[51] Truly, these men were not dumb by any stretch of the imagination.

Next, we will examine the different types of net the fishermen used, which were works of art in both form and function. Catching fish on the Sea of Galilee was no easy task, as it required finesse and strenuous effort as well as specific nets for each type of fishing to be performed. For a moment, let us consider the dragnet.

The dragnet [seine] is made of netting shaped like a long wall, 250 to 300 meters long, 3 to 4 meters high at its "wings" and 8 meters high at the center. The foot rope [sic] is weighted with sinkers, and the head rope has cork floats. The dragnet is spread a hundred meters or more from the shore and parallel to it, and hauled toward the shore . . . by a team of 16 men for larger nets, or a smaller team for smaller nets.[52] . . . As the net comes near the shore, the skipper takes the boat and when necessary dives from it to lift the foot-rope [sic] over possible obstacles such as stones protruding from the bottom . . . This continues until all the ropes are out of the water. Then the fishermen sit down in the shallow water and haul the net [in] until it is piled up on the shore . . . and a good catch may bring in hundreds of kilos [of fish].[53] . . . The whole operation takes an hour or more [and] after this operation is completed and the fish sorted, the net again arranged on the stern, and the ropes coiled and placed in the boat, the work starts over again at another location, and may be repeated as often as eight times during a day's fishing.[54]

The next type of net we will consider is the cast-net. "The cast-net is circular, measuring from 6 to 8 meters in diameter, with bars of lead attached to the edge, and used by a single fisherman."[55] A cast-net can be used from the shore or in shallow water, or it can be thrown from a boat into deeper waters. This net is thrown with force out into the water, where it falls like a parachute and sinks to the bottom. The fisherman then dives down to the bottom and retrieves the net and the catch (which could easily exceed the man's own body weight). This is all done while holding his breath.

The last type of net that we will look at is the trammel net. The trammel net was generally never used alone but was nearly always used with at least five units attached to each other. With each unit measuring approximately thirty-five meters in length and two meters in height, this entire system would have been well over 150 meters in length.[56] The fishermen would quietly lower this trammel net system into the water during the early evening so that it formed a wide, sweeping curve whose ends each nearly touched the shore.[57] With the middle parts of the net system bulging in an arc hundreds of feet from shore, the entire system of nets would then be hauled in, and the fish disentangled one by one, by hand.[58] This procedure would not normally take place once a day, but would usually be repeated ten to fifteen times during a night's work. This type of brute-force effort could expect to bring fifty to one hundred kilograms of fish in during a night's work; however, some veteran fishermen may remember more memorable hauls of as much as half a ton.[59]

As we can clearly see, the physical demand upon the

fisherman's body was incredible. Daily he endured long hours of strenuous labor in order to corral the scaly creatures scattered in large schools beneath the surface of the water. Though these fishermen were strong and resilient, we should not limit our admiration of them to their physical abilities alone. We should also realize that they were smart, possessed some technologically advanced knowledge and were experts at reading the weather. They used these powers of observation along with their experience in order to estimate the best times and locations to fish. And since their success as commercial fishermen depended to a great extent upon the efficiency of their nets, as well as their abilities to locate fish, it is also important that we take a brief look into some of the finer details of the particular nets they would have used.

The fishing nets used in and around the Sea of Galilee were made of organic fibers, which is why there have been very few fragments of these ancient nets ever recovered near the lake; however, there is at least one piece of netting that was found in a cave near the town of Ein Gedi that was made of linen. Each net was a finely woven work of art that resembled a large, intricately crocheted doily. After the grueling hours of each fishing trip had passed, these nets were washed, inspected for damage and then hung out on walls or poles in order to dry. Any damage that was found in a net would have been repaired immediately so as not to affect the catch of the next trip. The item that assisted in this task of net repair was the netting needle, which was made of bone, bronze, wood or metal and measured ten to thirty centimeters in length.[60]

Finally, a net would simply float around in the water if it had nothing to hold it down or pull it towards the bottom of the lake. The fishermen on the Sea of Galilee ingeniously used stone sinkers along the bottom of each net (in order to drag the net down and thus create a wall of net) as well as net anchors (which kept the nets in place). These stone sinkers, we would assume, would have been made of some heavy variety of stone to make them more efficient and for that we would be correct.

However, another assumption we might make is that they used soft stones for this task, since they needed to have holes drilled through them, and for that we would be incorrect. Often, the ancient fishermen picked flint (the hardest stone) as their stone of choice for this task since it is higher in durability and specific gravity than the others available. What is not clear, however, is how they were able to drill the holes through flint since the only mineral harder than flint is diamond, and none of that has yet been found in the Sea of Galilee region.[61] Therefore, " . . . it appears that ancient man possessed the knowledge, the tools, and the patience"[62] to perform this task, all of which we apparently no longer have.

Taken Aback

"A dangerous situation where the wind is on the wrong side of the sails pressing them back against the mast and forcing the ship astern."[63]

Mark 4:37
And a furious storm of wind [of hurricane proportions] arose, and the waves kept beating into the boat, so that it was already becoming filled. (AMP)

The Storm, a Common Sharkia

As we shall learn, storms on the Sea of Galilee were not uncommon, and this is why this incident with Jesus and the disciples is so puzzling. These were weather conditions that these fishermen must have dealt with many times before. They had probably even heard of worse events from their fathers, grandfathers, uncles or cousins from the time that they were small children. A fisherman on the Sea of Galilee could not let down his guard but, because they would suddenly appear, had to constantly be on the lookout for signs of these storms, which could endanger the boat, the crew and the catch.[64]

The climate in Israel is the typical Mediterranean climate. It is characterized by long, hot, dry summers and short, cool, rainy winters. Rainfall is spread unevenly over the land of Israel, and often the annual precipitation is concentrated in violent storms that cause erosion and flooding.[65] This is due to the fact that surrounding the lake are " . . . steep cliffs and sharply rising mountains . . . [which] . . . rise to the Golan Heights and the fertile Hauran plateau . . . [and] . . . As a result of this formation, cool winds frequently rush down these slopes and unexpectedly stir up violent storms on the warm surface of the lake."[66] *(See Map 1: The Sea of Galilee in the First Century a.d.)* In speaking of this stormy event, which we are exploring, Nun informs us that "This is an accurate and detailed description of an eastern storm on the Kinneret. It fits precisely the tales of contemporary fishermen who have sailed to fish for sardines at Kursi and were caught in transit by the well-known eastern storm, called 'Sharkia' in Arabic ('shark,' as we know, means east in Arabic)."[67]

As we see, Shelley Wachsmann agrees and further states that

As is abundantly clear when one reads the Gospels, the Sea of Galilee can be fickle, and the possibility of sudden and dangerous storms exists. In antiquity, sailing on the Mediterranean Sea was seasonal, limited for the most part to the summer months, when storms were rare and the skies were clear. Because of the relatively short distances in the Kinneret, however, seafaring continued throughout the winter months. There is a daily order to the winds during the summer and fall around the Sea of Galilee. In the winter months, the weather system is more chaotic, and the winds have a tendency to shift, blowing first from one direction and then the other. It is also during the winter that the sharkia comes howling down from the Golan Heights to stir up the Kinneret, raising waves that pound the western side of the lake. Sharkias come at a frequency of about once every two weeks and generally last for about three days.[68]

The sharkia, a quick and dangerous storm, is part of the seasonal fabric of weather surrounding the Sea of Galilee. What the disciples encountered was a particularly ferocious sharkia that may have had a contributing geological factor involved in its onset about which we have no specific record.

GEOGRAPHICAL AND GEOLOGICAL CONCERNS

The Sea of Galilee is located near the northern end of one the longest and deepest scars in the earth's surface. This scar is known as a geological rift, or fault line, and is locally known as the Jordan Rift Valley.[69] This rift is currently one of the most important rifts known to geologists. The Jordan Rift Valley occupies a small portion of the giant Syrian-East African Rift (or the Great Rift Valley), which extends from North Syria to central Mozambique (and beyond) and is nearly 6,500 kilometers long *(See Map 2: Middle East/African Geological Fault Lines & Crustal Plate Boundaries)*. In Israel the Jordan Rift Valley, traditionally a North-South transport corridor crossed by many important East-West trade routes[70], is dominated by the Jordan River, Lake Tiberias (Sea of Galilee) and the Dead Sea.[71]

Due in large part to crustal plate activity, this region has been geologically unstable throughout its existence. This fact has most likely contributed to many tectonic plate related events (i.e. geological fault lines, tremors, earthquakes, tsunamis, etc.). This geologic instability may even have been the indirect cause of the disappearance of an entire New Testament town and may help explain just why the disciples were so scared. "The New Testament tells us that Bethsaida is where Jesus fed the five thousand, cured the blind man, and walked on the water. Yet, as compared to other sites of religious significance, very few people have visited or even heard of Bethsaida. The city was likely destroyed by a tsunami from the Sea of Galilee in the second century c.e. (common era)."[72] Even though Bethsaida was destroyed well after the disciples' deaths, it is probable that the tsunami that wiped her off the map was not the first of its kind in this region. If the disciples were aware of this type of activity, whether by personal experience or as part of the fabric of fisherman's lore, it is likely that any particularly hostile lake activity would have been viewed with the type of hopeless fear displayed by the disciples. It appears to me that their fear was more irrational than it should have been and is therefore likely that, though this storm was a sharkia, it may also have had the character of something more sinister. It is with this knowledge then that we can understand why the disciples would have reacted as vehemently as they did in rebuking the Master.

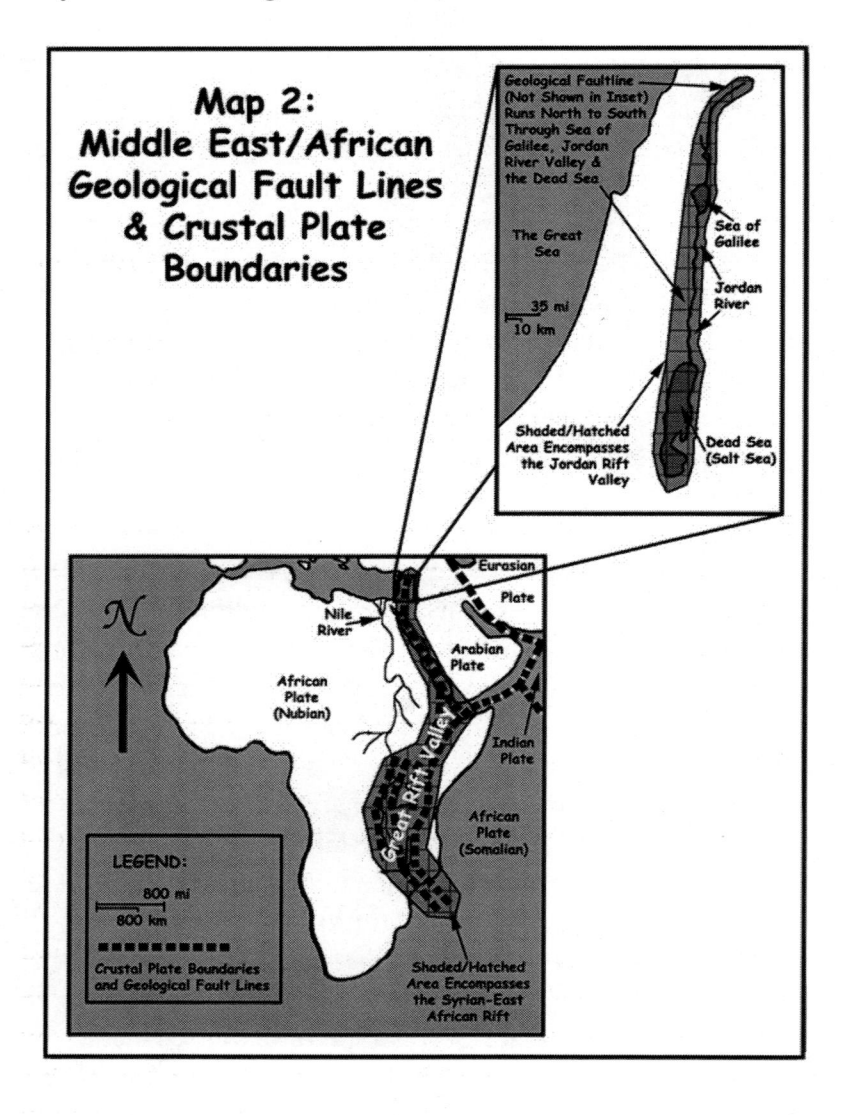

5

AYE, AYE, WE'LL TOE THE LINE

"Aye is old English for 'yes.' The seaman's reply, 'Aye aye, sir,'
means, 'I understand and I will obey.'"[73]
"Toe the line—When called to line up at attention, the ship's
crew would form up with their toes touching
a seam in the deck planking.'"[74]

Mark 4:38–41

But He [Himself] was in the stern [of the boat], asleep on the [leather] cushion; and they awoke Him and said to Him, Master, do You not care that we are perishing? And He arose and rebuked the wind and said to the sea, Hush now! Be still (muzzled)! And the wind ceased (sank to rest as if exhausted by its beating) and there was [immediately] a great calm (a perfect peacefulness). He said to them, Why are you so timid and fearful? How is it that you have no faith (no firmly relying trust)? And they were filled with great awe and feared exceedingly and said one to another, Who then is this, that even wind and sea obey Him? (AMP)

The content of Jesus' teachings, which we will not detail fully, before this storm is revealing. Jesus summed it up to the crowd when He challenged them with this: "He who has ears to hear should listen, but let him also consider and comprehend the hidden meanings of which I am speaking." He wanted them to get it. The teaching was aimed at sparking the listeners to hear, understand, comprehend and put it into practice those truths that he was teaching in order that they might bear fruit. What Jesus wanted was for His words to make a difference in their lives. Without the reality of His truth, they would remain unchanged forever. In light of this, maybe the storm was a lesson to the disciples from God above or maybe it was a small test designed to show them where they were spiritually. It was, after all, Jesus who suggested the trip in the first place.

Before the storm, Jesus had been teaching about the parable of the sower. The disciples were under the mistaken impression that they had understood what He was saying, but it is clear that they had not. Often we are like them in that we believe we have grasped the full meaning of God's word when we have barely scratched the surface. Unlike the good ground, their hearts were similar to the stony ground that received the seed of His teachings but were immediately offended once the afflictions arose. They actually thought that He would abandon them to death. How ludicrous this appears when we consider that He was yet aboard their vessel. Hearing His words did not produce good fruit or a lasting harvest in their hearts, but it produced only a weed that was easily plucked out.

Jesus had told them earlier that there was nothing hidden that would not become known. In other words, their hidden or buried attitudes and handicaps, which they pretended were not there, would indeed be revealed. The secrets that they held inside their hearts would not remain hidden. We, too, should heed this warning from Christ that our own hidden attitudes and agendas will suffer the same sudden exposure when the worst of life falls down upon us. Who the disciples were would become known, as will our true nature. If only they had realized just how quickly their lack was going to be revealed, maybe they would have been more honest and prepared. Faith might well have arisen within them if only they had grasped His truth and realized that He had been talking about them. It would do us well to realize that He is still saying this to us.

In Psalm 89:9 we learn that "You rule the raging of the sea; when its waves arise; you still them." (AMP) And in Psalm 107:23–30 we read

Some go down to the sea and travel over it in ships to do business in great waters; these see the works of the Lord and His wonders in the deep. For He commands and raises up the stormy wind, which lifts up the waves of the sea. [Those aboard] mount up to the heavens, they go down again to the deeps; their courage melts away because of their plight. They reel to and fro and stagger like a drunken man and are at their wits' end [all their wisdom has come to nothing]. Then they cry to the Lord in their trouble, and He brings them out of their distresses. He hushes the storm to a calm and to a gentle whisper, so that the waves of the sea are still. Then the men are glad because of the calm, and He brings them to their desired haven. (AMP)

The disciples should have been familiar with the Psalms if not most of the Old Testament, and they should have known of God's power over the sea. But it does not appear that the disciples could figure this out. They knew that God was in control and that Jesus was the Son of God, yet they questioned whether He cared enough not to let them drown. Surely they must have been able to figure out that He was not going to let Himself die and that the chances were pretty good that, since they were with Him, they would not die either. But it seems that all of their logic must have escaped them as their panicked emotions took over. How often do we let the storm confuse us and talk us out of what we already know about the character and nature of God?

These men were sailing with Jesus and doing fine when suddenly the storm assaulted them. They may have been laughing and talking amongst themselves or discussing the teachings of the past day. Without warning, it hastened its arrival until they were blindsided with wind, waves and fear. It appears to have been a regular meteorological event, and there is no indication of disobedience to blame. So the question is, "Why were these men afraid?" Typically, as life rages around us, we become the most fearful when we know that we have sinned. Not often do we panic when we have acted righteously or obeyed the voice of God completely; however, the disciples, who daily fished these waters and who had most likely witnessed sharkias before, rebuked the Christ when confronted with disaster. It is bone chilling when we consider how they woke Him and spoke to Him. They did not speak with reverent and worshipful fear. The followers of Christ, His closest friends and witnesses, lashed out at Him like He was an ordinary man.

In bringing this point home to where we live, I pose these questions: "When our storms hit, how do we react? Do we, with a disconcerting fear striking at our heart, look helplessly to God and begin to rebuke our Creator? And when we turn to look for help, are those with us in a similar state of mind?" The answers are that many times we completely lose control and are in desperate need for someone to help us out. At times, we struggle to the back of our boat only to find our pastor sleeping. Incredulously we may look at him and, for a second, feel like slapping him awake. How could someone sleep at a time like this? We have seen him cast out devils, heal many people and raise the dead, but we had no idea that he was as callous as to sleep during our most desperate hour. Recklessly abandoning all of the control we have left, we decide to shake him awake screaming, "Hey, man," over the howling wind and crashing waves, "what are you doing sleeping? Don't you care about us at all? How can you sleep when our very lives are at stake here? Get up and help us! What is wrong with you anyways? Do something, do anything at all, but don't just lie there and sleep." At this point, we are so consumed with our own situation that we have not even considered those in the boats near us. What of their plight? It seems that during out tempests' butchery we are rarely concerned about others. Instead of it being all about God, it is all about us; we want our own flesh to be rescued. The situation is this: With our rebuke of Christ, we try to arise and play God, demanding that He help save us. We may have just come from a church service where the minister was teaching in parables and then later had a private leadership meeting in which he explained the hidden meaning of those parables. He may have explained to us the parable of the sower, the parable of the lamp on a stand, the parable of the growing seed and the parable of the mustard seed and then told us the secret to the kingdom of God, but we obviously did not get it. True, we are still babes in Christ, but God does not excuse our lack of faith due to the newness of our experience. In addition, if He will not excuse the young in Christ, then He certainly will not excuse those who have been around for years.

Obviously, when Jesus got up and rebuked the wind and the waves, and the seas immediately became calm, it took the disciples as completely by surprise as it would us. They were not expecting Him to do that. We cannot be sure what the disciples wanted Him to do after they woke Him up, but calming the storm with His words was certainly not something they had swimming in the back of their minds. This is obvious by the surprise they expressed when He performed the miracle. They may have wanted Him to get up and help bail water, or they may even have wanted Him to grab an oar and start rowing, but to dare to expect that He could tell the storm to stop and that it would obey was beyond their comprehension at this point. What Jesus wanted was for them to do as He had done. He wanted them to exercise their faith and to put into practice what He had been teaching them. But in order to do that, the disciples needed to lay aside the technological marvels in their gear, abandon their hope in their equipment and experience, and to reach out beyond themselves and command the storm to cease. Was it too much to ask of them at this time? No, but still they could not because of fear.

The entire point of Jesus' rebuke was that the disciples did not think that He cared about them. They did not believe that He would keep them from harm. This is probably the hardest thing in the world for us to come to grips with: the fact that Jesus Christ, the Son of the Almighty God of the universe, loves us deeply and is daily concerned about us, our affairs and our well-being. How can we become convinced of this, convinced enough so that it will make a difference in our daily walk? For some it comes in an instant when they become born again, while for others it only comes after years of experiences in Christianity. This knowing may never come for some because they fail to develop an intimate relationship with God. Somehow, though, we must become convinced of the fact of Christ's intimate love for us—despite and regardless of the situations we may have to face down.

We cannot make the assumption, like these disciples did, that God does not care for us and that He will let us drown during the pillaging warfare of life. Though we may not come through the storms the way we would like, and though we may lose some belongings along the way or botch our escape, we must always trust in the most crucial fact of Christ's love. He has an undying devotion to the believer's cause and He loves us both simply and most complicatedly. God loves us as He loved David, the man after God's own heart, and He loves us as He loved Jonah, the bigot prophet who ran from the call of God only to be rescued by His loving heavenly Father. God's love is extended to us as it was to Peter, who denied Him, and to Paul, who persecuted and killed Christians. Yet God used one to found the church and the other to write most of the New Testament. Christ's love for us is as intimate as when John lay on His bosom. The love of God is bound to follow us with an unselfish commitment for our long-term happiness. Temporal issues are not always of major concern to Him because He has eternity in mind. This is the place where the disciples fell down the most that day. The lesson that we must take most to heart is that Jesus Christ loves us. We must become convinced of that. Jesus chided and rebuked His disciples for their lack of faith in who He was. His rebuke was not for the absence of their powerful, earth-moving, storm-stopping faith, but for their lack of faith in Him and His character.

This story reminds me of one familiar to both the modern day Christian as well as the disciples on board this boat with Jesus. It hearkens back to the time when the Philistines amassed at Socoh to do battle against Saul and the men of Israel, who were concentrated in the Valley of Elah. Here both sides stood, eyeing each other from opposing mountainsides and sizing up each other's offensive potential, as well as their defensive prowess. Israel may have had visions of grandeur earlier in the week as they gathered their weapons, sharpened their swords and marched to the place of battle, but what happened next nearly brought them to their knees in surrender.

A large Philistine named Goliath stepped out from the tents of the camp and delivered his ungodly monologue, challenging the men of God to put up or shut up. He jeered and taunted them and cursed their God from his perch while he strutted around the Philistine camp. He was nearly ten feet tall and carried a helmet, armor and sword that weighed nearly as much as another grown man. This apparently disturbed the Israelites to the point that when his short harangue was over, they were immediately dismayed and filled with terror. God's own people were locked up with fear.

During all of this, the Israelites stood around conferring with one another as to what exactly should be done. Should they give up or run headlong into a suicidal battle, or should they send for reinforcements? Running away had a pleasant ring to it as well. I am sure that none of them got much sleep as this went on for days. Finally, someone stands up and declares that this has gone far enough. That someone, however, is not the one that anyone expected. It was not Saul, whom the Bible describes as a head taller than the rest of his people (1 Samuel 9:2b), and it was not the Israelites' greatest and best warrior either. Their oldest and most experienced fighters were as afraid as the rookies in the army were. The man who stepped forward was a teenaged boy named David. When all of the men in the army who bore the responsibility of fighting displayed the same paralyzing fear, this young boy jumped to the forefront.

When David stepped onto the scene, he asked why someone was not willing to face the uncircumcised Philistine and cut him down. What he was asking was this: Were there no warriors in the entire company of the army who would stand up in the name of the Lord and fight? Was there nothing so important for them to do that even one of them would take the chance and step onto the field with this behemoth? Would someone have the boldness to stand up and declare, "Thus says the Lord"? The Israelites allowed Goliath's power, size, prowess and notoriety to intimidate them to the point of inaction. They allowed themselves to be caught in the death grips of fear even though he had not touched the hair on the head of even one of them. This is, unfortunately, the same situation we find the disciples in when this storm rocked their world. Even more unfortunate is that we, too, stand dazed with fear when life's menacing storms repeatedly threaten to overpower us.

This storm and its many predecessors were allowed to threaten the disciples. The stories that were told and retold throughout the years, and the recounting of horrific details of tragic situations of old had taken ahold of their hearts. Though they had the Son of the God of the universe on board their boat, they were over-influenced by the bark of the storm. Its fury spoke to them in a way that got on the inside because to them, Jesus and His power were still on the outside. Had the disciples believed what Jesus had been teaching, they would have reacted much differently. Even if they had not known exactly what to do, they should have at least had a holy indignation well up inside their throats. Jesus wanted the disciples to step up and to speak up and to allow their knowledge of God to dictate to them that something had to be done, that this storm could not proceed. Had they accomplished this they would have entered into a new realm of possibility with God and would have experienced a new boldness, authority, determination and purpose that they had never dreamed of before.

Jesus wanted the disciples to act like David the teenage phenom had acted. David's shining moment was not in striking Goliath down with a stone; nor was it in his chopping Goliath's head off, though both were equally impressive feats given his inexperience in battle. David's encomium was that he allowed God's righteous anger to well up on his inside and produce actions of righteousness on the outside. David's everlasting tribute is that he would not allow fear to rule him. Jesus wanted the same for His disciples; however, He would have to wait for them to step up until a later date. The great thing here is that, though Jesus was disappointed by His disciples' inaction and paralyzing fear, He calmed the storm for them and gave them another chance. (Actually, more than one of them would need several future chances to get it right, and most of them eventually did). This should be an encouragement to us all. If we blow it in our decisive moment, then we should not despair and give up hope. The Christ who redeemed us will give us another chance to prove ourselves. We can then be more prepared and motivated for our next encounter with life's furious onslaughts.

The key is not always necessarily that we win but that we participate. The key for us is that we act, that we at least try to shout this storm down. Even when the disciples finally did get some chutzpah later on and attempted to cast out some demons and failed, Jesus did not get angry. He simply instructed them that some kinds of demons could only come out by prayer and fasting. What am I saying? I am trying to get it into our spirits that if we try with all of our heart and still fail, it is better than not trying at all. I think that by the time another test came about and the disciples at least tried to cast this demon out, Jesus was pleased with their effort, even though it proved ineffective. God can work with our effort, even if it's in the wrong direction or not quite up to par. But what He cannot work with is inaction based upon fear, intimidation, terror and fright. To Him this spells N·O·T H·E·A·R·I·N·G. That is not the way to become effective in the kingdom of God.

The main difference between Jesus and the disciples during this storm was that the disciples allowed the storm within, while to Jesus, it was still without. They had allowed this raging storm to penetrate their hearts and shake them to the core, something that may have become instilled in them by years of experiencing similar situations. When they yelled at and rebuked Jesus, it was just as they would have done to anyone who was found sleeping at a time like that. They allowed the storm to come in and to take control; this was their mistake. However, to Jesus the storm was simply that, a storm. He could sleep freely because

He knew it was external. The storm may have been outside and pressing Him, but it was not inside and shaking His beliefs.

Our lesson here is this: Like the disciples, we are not novices and we know what to do during the storms of life. We have been taught and schooled and have learned how to make it through the storms safely by watching how our ancestors have done it. Having been in trying situations before, we should be mature enough and have gained enough knowledge, wisdom and faith to face this bombardment and say "Enough!" But oh, we of little faith. Instead, we allow the storm to come in and take over our lives. Even though we know better, we do not keep the storm in perspective and treat it as what it is, a storm. Instead of standing up in the midst of this storm with faith and confidence and courage and authority, we have cowered in the back of our situation and relinquished control to the sea itself. We should be ashamed of ourselves. We could have done better. As babes in Christ, we should heed Paul's warning.

We have much to say about this, but it is hard to explain because you are slow to learn. In fact, though by this time you ought to be teachers, you need someone to teach you the elementary truths of God's work all over again. You need milk, not solid food! Anyone who lives on milk, being still an infant, is not acquainted with the teaching about righteousness. But solid food is for the mature, who by constant use have trained themselves to distinguish good from evil. (Hebrews 5:11–14—NIV)

Sometimes when life's maddening infernos threaten us, we have to act like Jesus did and ignore what makes sense in order to do what is right. It is often that we have to stand up and do what might look crazy to others. Even the great faith healers of yesteryear had to battle this troubling dilemma. We question whether we should do the sensible or the fanatic when at times the only way out of our storm is to do what looks downright ridiculous. For example: dipping in a dirty river seven times (2 Kings 5:1–14) or spitting in the dirt and making a mud-poultice with which to restore a blind man's sight (John 9:1–7). The point is that in this type of storm, we must draw the proverbial line in the sand and tell the storm that it cannot cross. Standing tall, we must speak in faith and declare that the end of the storm is here and now. It is a God-moment, and we will bask in God's goodness when it is over. This is not about us, though; it is about God. There is no power that is resident inside of us other than that higher power of God, which is supernaturally and infinitely more powerful than anything here on earth. In fact, it is so otherworldly that it can defy any natural law that exists. During this type of storm, we have a divine appointment to act, and we should not meet our nemesis with anything but the faith and determination to see God's glory and power made manifest in our situation.

There are many ways in which we can speak to our storms, but they must all flow out of a right relationship with God. Unless we are closely listening to His voice, then we will not know what to speak; however, if we remain intimately His friend, then He may give us the words to speak that will melt our storm's ferocity. These words of mountain-moving power may come through the gift of faith, a word of wisdom, or a word of knowledge as described in Paul's letter to the Corinthians, or they may arise out of a special time of prayer and fasting. Another avenue down which God can command His word to us is from our daily Bible readings or through wise and godly counsel. Whatever storm may arise and whatever words of faith we must speak, the knowledge that we are following God's course of action, and not our own, should always precede our stand of faith.

The interesting thing about this storm is that first the disciples feared the storm and thought that they would be drowned by it, and then they feared Jesus after He rebuked it. There are many times in life when we act due to fear, and this is wrong. Equally as wrong are the times in life when we do not act due to fear. First, we fear the problem and then we fear the solution. We must not let fear cast us back and forth and dictate our life's decisions.

Most Christians today are more consumed with what is going into a person's mind than with what is coming out of his life. We draw generalized conclusions that do not stand up under scrutiny. What most of us do not seem to understand is what Jesus revealed in the book of Matthew. Jesus urged His disciples to grasp and comprehend the truth that "It is not what goes into the mouth of a man that makes him unclean and defiled, but what comes out of the mouth; this makes a man unclean and defiles [him]. For out of the heart come evil thoughts (reasonings and disputings and designs) . . . [and] these are what make a man unclean and defile [him]" (Matthew 15:11,19a, 20a AMP). That which comes out of us is of critical importance to God, and this is nowhere more relevant than when we are in the middle of a battle. What comes out must be good and not evil. It must be part of the solution and not more of the problem; it must be more of faith and less of fiction. Getting out of the storm will not happen with negativity, doubt and depressing thoughts. Becoming a survivor, which seems to have become just another media-blitzed cliché, is all about having the right attitude no matter how dumb or stupid it may seem and by having courage, discernment and faith. Should we let the storm within? No. However, if we do, then we must not let it produce words, thoughts and actions of despair that come out.

The thing that matters to God is how much of His word we put into practice, not how many church services we attend, sermons we hear, or Bible verses we memorize. In order to conquer, we must do; we must put what His word says into practice. Crying will not do it. Flocking to the altars at church and weeping will not do it either. But acting upon the Word will. We cannot be cleansed by our penance. The problem is that most of us think that outward displays of repentance will wipe our slate clean and bring about the end of our storms, but this is false. The truth is that jumping and shouting, howling and wailing, and beating ourselves with sticks or crawling up stairs on broken glass are all equally as ineffective. We must act upon God's word and do what He has said. It is what comes out of us that matters, and if what comes out does not pass muster, then it was not worth it after all.

As our story continues, Jesus asks us to go to the other side of the lake, and we proudly suggest that He ride with us. We are so accommodating, and though our boat is small, it is familiar to us. We have been in it hundreds of times during our tenure on these waters. We have fished on this sea with our fathers, and now we fish here with our sons. Actually, our houses line the shores of the lake like chickens roosting on a branch at night. Spring, summer, fall and winter, we have been out here on these waters for it all–the good, the bad and the ugly. This lake has a tendency to give rise to some sudden, ferocious storms, and we have weathered a lot of them in our lifetime. We have heard our fathers and uncles for years recount the stories of the storms that they have endured on this lake. Sitting around the campfire at night after a hard day's work, the stories have flowed like water from an artesian well. One story gives rise to another as each man tries to remember a storm that was worse than that depicted in the last story recounted; and so it continues. The stories of narrow escapes and gut wrenching loss drift long into the night until no one wants to go to sea again. Stories of men who collapsed onto shore after giving all they had fighting the storm, only to give up to the swells and let themselves and their vessel be smashed headlong onto the rocks of some distant shore. All of us admit that we have known a man or two who have not made it through some of the more ferocious storms this lake has spawned. Some storms have acted as if they were toying with the boats, while others have mercilessly pursued their victims. The worst, though, seemed resolved to utterly destroy both boat and crew, never relenting until they successfully pound these small vessels and their passengers into the sea floor, never to be raised again.

But for all of our stories or horror, we have all made it through to laugh and talk about our most feared storms, which still cause us to shiver when alone in the darkness of the night. These storms have made even the most strapping men cry like babies and plead to their gods for mercy and rescue. Unwavering in purpose, these storms have struck fear into our hearts and have pompously declared themselves as omens for anyone who would dare extract a living from this lake. Continually reborn in the stories of those lucky enough to survive their fury, these storms have lived on throughout the decades. It is one of these storms that we are now fighting. We can now relate fully to the fear described in our own father's quivering voice as he told us of the one that almost took his life. But we are lean and strong, and we know our boat better than he did. Having practiced our emergency drills, we know our seamanship and survival skills are as good as the next person's are. After all, we are professional fishermen, and we and our crew have been here before. The man sleeping in the rear of our boat had received little attention during our voyage until this storm arose. Now, when the furies of hell are breaking forth upon us and we have forgotten all except what is currently taking place, we lose control and question whether God is going to let us drown. What a shame. We are yellow with a streak that will run through our progeny if we do not change our attitudes now. The question we must answer is, "Will we change?"

Upon further contemplation of the disciples' situation, I must now pose an intriguing question. "Would the disciples have gone ahead with the trip had they known what was coming? And will we?" Revealed in His simple suggestion to cross over is the fact that there was no question as to the why or the whether. The disciples simply said, "Yes." When we start to predict the unmitigated whirlwinds that will swirl around our lives, will we go when Jesus speaks, even when we know of the malignities that lay ahead? We must come to the place where we can honestly say, "Yes, I will go because God said and no matter what the storm dishes out I will survive." In this will be a true test of our maturity in Christ that can become a shining testimony to those around us. At times like this, we must rely on the truth that lets us know that, "We are assured and know that [God being a partner in their labor] all things work together and are [fitting into a plan] for good to and for those who love God and are called according to [His] design and purpose"

(Romans 8:28 AMP). Walking into calamity when we know it is coming is something we have been trained not to do, but sometimes it is the right thing to do regardless of the outcome.

It is at this point that I would like to digress a little and explore an important and pertinent question posed in the previous paragraphs, and that is, would the disciples have been as willing and eager to make this trip (or would they have made it at all) had they known about the storm before they departed from Capernaum. This is a difficult proposition to face in any age. Many today know of the inherent dangers involved in what they do. Racecar drivers know that they might not make it to the next pit stop alive. White-water rafters and storm surge kayakers know that one misstep could cause a blow to the head that would end their life. Test pilots know that every time they strap themselves into their cockpits it could be their last, wild ride. And almost every parent alive knows that the morning kisses they give to their children could be their last. In short, we all know that today could be the day that our luck runs out, but we continue to live and make choices that could very well lead us into the final battle of our life. We know full well that today could be the day that the killer storm invades our space and wreaks its own unique form of havoc upon our life.

In light of this, let us turn our gaze briefly to Noah to learn what a remarkable man he was and what insight his life can give to our story. It is Noah who willingly went into the storm that God told him was coming. Noah was forced neither to listen to God nor to obey His requests. He could have involved himself in the rampant violence and perversions of the day, or groped for power like the others around him. He could have laughed at the Lord's warning. Let us face it, no one had ever even heard of rain before, not to mention floodwaters that may have been in excess of 30,000 feet above today's known sea level. Actually, the Bible mentions no specific explanation to Noah about what rain was or what these waters from the deep were going to be. Noah, however, wisely chose to listen to God and to obey Him. Not to do so would have been the end of humanity.

CHART 1: NOAH AND THE GREAT FLOOD

Chapter Reference	Commentary
Genesis 6:13, 17; 7:4	In these verses, Noah is informed by God of the storm that is to come upon the earth. God also shares with Noah how bad this storm is going to be, explaining in graphic detail all that will take place.
Genesis 6:14-16, 19-21; 7:2-3	In these verses, God tells Noah in specific detail how he and his family are to prepare for the upcoming storm. He lays out a course of action for Noah to follow. God lets Noah know that he will have to do something himself in order to be prepared to face this storm.
Genesis 6:18; 7:1	In these verses, God tells Noah where his place of safety from the storm will be, but he does not tell Noah how long this storm will last. Noah can hide during this storm, but only in the place of God's choosing. The place of God's choosing and provision requires a tremendous effort on Noah's part. An ark (ship) like Noah builds will not exist for many millennia hereafter. What he is asked to build is beyond every wild imagination. He may possess a builder's skills, but this ark is like no boat ever built before. It requires work, dedication, attention to details and decisive action—possibly to the abandonment of other activities, vices or pleasures. Noah will have to drop some of his priorities and rearrange his wish list in order to complete this project on time.
Genesis 6:22; 7:5	Noah, ever the blameless and righteous man of God, carries out the instructions of the Lord to the letter, even though he knows exactly what he will be walking into. He gives his family members no vote that we are told of and does not ask for other opinions. He simply gets busy doing what God has said and distances himself from the people around him—he has to because soon they will all be destroyed. However, through it all he will survive.
Genesis 7:6-24; 8:1-14	In these verses, God righteously unleashes the most dreadful storm the world has ever known. Noah and his family are required to go through this

	storm (enduring its onslaught and wreckage for one year and ten days). They have done all that the Lord commanded; they have done all that they could do. Though their lives are spared, they lose everything that they owned and nearly everything that they valued and treasured on the Earth. God vows to be with them and to establish a covenant with Noah, but in this process, Noah and his family have to leave 600 years worth of accumulated possessions behind. They lose their houses, barns, land, animals, precious possessions, friends, extended family and neighbors, tools and money. Nowhere in this story of incredible detail is there any mention of them saving any of their possessions—so we must infer that they did not. They will make it out alive, but only with the clothes on their backs. They must leave it to the Lord to make up for what they had to abandon.
Genesis 8:15-22	In these verses, the storm has finally passed. Noah and his family are allowed to step out from their place of safety and provision and into a land where nothing much exists.
Genesis 9:1-17	In these verses, God makes his blessing known and He establishes an eternal covenant with Noah. God swears never to flood the earth again. He has required his blameless one to walk through an unimaginable storm, but now all the beasts and creatures of the earth and air and seas will fear Noah and his sons.
Genesis 9:18-29	In these verses, Noah and his descendants are now left to get back to work and to rebuild civilization itself. Everything will begin afresh and anew. Nothing remains of humanity except them, and so it must all be created again. Noah and his sons are now given the ultimate task and responsibility, and one of the greatest bequeathals of power and dominion ever given to a man or a family (none other except Adam and Eve). They are commanded to replenish and revitalize the Earth.

We see in Genesis chapters six through nine an incredible example in the life of Noah as it relates to the storms of life *(See Chart 1: Noah and the Great Flood)*. In this chart, I have given a brief explanation and overview of his most powerful faith. As we see from his story, God may request that we follow a path that is flooded with dangerous waters. God may tell us that we will be required to go through a storm, but may not give us any further details as to the storm's severity, duration or the losses involved. He may even appear to be asleep while we are nearly drowning and have lost control of our vessel. In being fully prepared, we must fix it firmly in ours minds now, before the aggressions advance, that He does indeed love and care for us. Though many times His actions are unexplainable and His concern is barely perceptible, His eternal love for us remains. Our attitudes towards God and the storm must reflect righteousness and truth. We must not allow ourselves to feed attitudes that will only harm us and possibly sink our ship. Instead we must plant and nurture those most virtuous attitudes and hold fast to our conviction that God, indeed, is in complete control—whether we like it or not and whether we approve of it or not.

Again, we may ask, "Who were these fishermen, the disciples of Jesus?" At first glance it is easy to criticize them for their fear, especially after considering Jesus' chastisement of them. But upon a deeper understanding and some delicate extrication, we can see the picture a little more clearly now. Did the disciples panic and display a lack faith? Yes, and Jesus said so. Nevertheless, let us not forget what they did correctly. First, they never questioned whether going to the other side was right or not, even after the storm had kicked up. Second, they did not throw anything overboard and thus did not lose any of their belongings or gear. Finally, when they did run, they at least ran in the right direction and to the right person for help, Jesus.

Often our reactions are the opposite of these. First, we look around to find something to throw overboard. Second, we run to everyone except Jesus for help. Frenzied, we reach for that which is moveable and trust in those who see as dimly as we do. The disciples may not have reacted as well as they could have, but they also most certainly did not act as poorly as they could have. Sometimes this is the difference between life and death, of survival or devastation. It is important that we analyze what we did wrong and what we did right. Then we can shore up those right attitudes and actions and work on changing the poor ones that need honing. We can always strive to do better, but should not become completely discouraged when we at least partially behaved well.

Why were the disciples so scared? Well, they were on a small boat in the middle of a large body of water with a vicious storm attacking them—who would not be scared? Even the most seasoned fishermen get scared of the weather and the water at times, especially when it seems to be seeking them out for personal retribution. On the disciples' boat, there were no below-deck quarters, no bunkhouse, no radar, no emergency beacon buoys, no helicopter rescues and no cell phones, bilge pumps or life preservers. The boat was medium sized for the day and probably a little crowded, and they were just plain not happy with this turn of events after hearing the Son of God minister for the entire day. Attacks should not come directly upon the heels of a church service or spiritual victory, but they can and often do. We are often dismayed in our greatest moments of strength when we turn and find that we have been blindsided by the worst atmospheric concoction ever imagined.

The disciples were so used to rowing out of storms by sheer determination and exhausting effort that Jesus remaining asleep in the back of the boat frustrated them. When they awoke Him and questioned whether He cared, they were actually rebuking him. It was not a casual word either. This was a strong and sharp criticism of His inaction. The disciples were expressing their severe disapproval. They probably even glared at Him with that expression of blame that we sometimes get when someone does not do something we think that they ought to. The disciples found fault with Jesus' position during the storm. To them, He should have been vertical and helping. To Him, they should have had more faith in His intentions. During this exchange, the disciples may have even questioned whether or not He was lazy. They obviously questioned His love and probably His loyalty. What they probably really meant to say, "Hey, why aren't you helping us?" They certainly did not expect Him to calm the storm. On the contrary, they probably expected Him to help them row.

When we go to cross to the other side and the storm comes up, we often question whether we made the right choice or not. This is why we must know that God orders our steps. Note that the disciples questioned whether God cared, but they did not question whether their going was right or not. Why? It is because it was His idea to go to the other side. That is how our lives should be. We should only move and go when it is His idea; otherwise, we should remain firmly planted. With that fact settled, we have one less thing to question when the storms of life do arise and descend upon us.

The attitude that we must have to make it through the storms of life looks like this: We are going over come what may. If we die, so be it; if we make it, great. But we are going through this thing or we are going to die trying. This attitude was prevalent in the early church. Consider the martyrs of the first centuries. Some even cried out, "Let me light the fire," when they were bound upon the top of their own bonfire pile. They were not afraid of death as we are. They defied the fears in their own hearts. We must defy the storm and not give in to it. We may lose this battle, but we need not lose our self-respect or our courage.

Section Three

JONAH AND THE PHOENICIAN CREW

1

THE STORY

And so it was that while Jonah, the son of Amittai, was lying prostrate before God that they conversed about his next prophetic assignment. It was during this conversation that God clearly communicated His thoughts and feelings concerning the Assyrian nation to Jonah. Not wanting him to misunderstand, God gave special emphasis to the contents of His commands as He intimated to Jonah His wish to show mercy to the Assyrians if they would repent. Jonah argued back that if that was the case then he did not want to go because he knew that God would show them too much kindness. As Jonah childishly refused to go, God spoke to him saying, "Now stand up and get ready to travel as my prophet to Nineveh for it is a city of great importance in Assyria with a large population of people who do not yet know me. I want you to proclaim to its inhabitants this message that I have given to you, and I want you to deliver it clearly, distinctly and forcefully. Tell them that their city will be overthrown because their evil attitudes and actions are contrary to my very nature, and then invite them to repent. They do not understand that their acts have become habitual compulsions that will cause them to be destroyed. Enlighten them to this reality; that I have declared a death-sentence against not only their city but their entire nation as well. Inform them that these wicked malefactions that they embody are in full view of my righteous eyes and that because of that, I have pronounced this judgment upon them."

But instead of obeying God, Jonah stood up from his prostrate position, driven by his ingrained repugnance of the

Assyrian nation and all that they stood for, and made hurried preparations to leave immediately as if to avoid some perceived unpleasantness. He was so disgusted with what God was asking him to do that he rejected God's attitude and sentiments towards the Assyrians and instead decided to run away to Tarshish (which was considered the most distant and remote of the Phoenician trading places known during that time). So Jonah left his home in Gath-Hepher and traveled about two day's journey to the port city of Joppa, and, after searching, finally located a ship that was bound for Tarshish and was ready to leave. He then hired that boat and crew and paid them the money they required to transport him to Tarshish. With a sigh of relief, he then stepped down from the dock and onto the ship, somehow foolishly thinking that by leaving his home and the area he might actually run away from God's face and the gaze of His eyes. Jonah believed that he could simply abandon his life as a prophet and the dictates of God and escape without incident.

Not many days after the ship had left port, the Lord hurled a great windstorm (similar to a hurricane) down upon the sea that continued to grow in size and power as the grueling hours wore on. During this time, the anger of the storm caused such a strong, furious and turbulent upheaval in the sea that, in confederation with the wind and rain, the waves were tearing the ship apart from every side. This unexpected and particularly hostile storm caused the sailors to be terrified. Each man cried out of his distress to his own idol god for rescue. The crew, now irresolute because of this disaster, threw with violent force the equipment, containers, cargo and tackle that were in the ship into the sea in order to lighten their load and ride out the storm. Moreover, during all of this, Jonah, who had gone down below the deck and into the hold of the ship where the cargo was stored, remained deep in a dead sleep upon the dunnage and appeared to be unconscious.

So the captain, leaving his post on deck, ventured below into the holds of the ship to locate the missing passenger. Upon finding Jonah nearly unconscious in a deep slumber, he violently shook him until he woke up and screamed, "What is the matter with you? How can you remain so sound asleep at a time like this? Get up now and call upon your God, and maybe that will turn His mind steadily toward us so that He may take pity on us and let us not die." The sailors, now panicked with fright, were now sure that someone on board was to blame for this savagery. They convinced each other to gather together and cast lots, thus determining who the guilty party was and why this disastrous storm had come upon them. So they cast their lots and the lot fell on Jonah, indicating that he was responsible. They then begged and pleaded with him, shouting, "Please tell us why this disaster has come upon us. What is your occupation that God takes such an interest in you? What kind of a place did you come from that God wants you not to leave? And what is your country and nationality?" Jonah replied, "I am a Hebrew, and I respectfully and reverently fear and worship Yahweh, the one true God, the God of the heavens and of the earth and who created the sea that we are in and the dry land that we departed from."

This revelation caused the men to be seized with a terrible yet reverential fear. They said to him, "What is this thing that you have done? How could you do such a thing? If your God is in complete control of all of this, then why did you think that you could run from Him?" For the men knew both by keen perception and by the matter being communicated directly to them that Jonah had attempted to flee from the very face of Jehovah God. Jonah had told them earlier that he was giving up on the life of a prophet for God and would be relocating to a more distant shore. Then the sailors asked Jonah, "What now should we do to you so that these wicked waves and howling winds may subside and be calm for us? Is there anything that we can we do to you so that we can survive?" The reason they asked this of him was because all along the sea had continued to grow more and more violently tempestuous, almost as if it was demanding a sacrifice. Then Jonah said to them, "Pick me up and throw me down into the sea with violent force where I will die. The sea will then become calm for you, for I know that it is because of my disobedience that this terrible storm has descended upon you. Your only hope of survival is to sacrifice my life."

But in spite of all that Jonah told the sailors, they were neither sure if what he was telling them was the truth, nor could they bear the thought of taking the life of someone that they thought might be an innocent man. So they got back behind the oars of the ship and rowed hard, pulling and pushing upon them with all of their might while trying to bring the ship back to shore by the valiance of their efforts. Their vain attempt to wrest the boat from the clutches of the storm proved fruitless because the sea continued to grow in strength and agitate violently against them. What none of them realized was that the storm was being driven by a force other than nature, a force that neither they nor Jonah could overpower either by might or by flight. Finally, they gave up their rowing, exhausted from their worthless efforts, and pleaded with the Lord, begging Him to hear them and answer their appeals for help. They cried, "We ask You earnestly, O Lord, and we implore You not to make us die because of this man's sin and disobedience. We beg You not to hold us responsible for his death though we are going to cast him into the sea. For You, O Lord, have done as You saw fit. You have felt great favor in sending this storm against Your wayward son for Your own good reasons."

After this, they picked Jonah up and hurled him over the side of the ship and into the sea, and it immediately ceased from its roiling rage. Instantly the wind ceased its turbulent assault. The rain completely faltered in its hurling descent. Then the men reverently and worshipfully feared the Lord with great awe and respect and offered Him sacrifices while verbally consecrating themselves to His service. Now all along, the Lord had prepared a great fish and assigned it a specific place in the sea where it was to swallow Jonah whole and alive. It was in the dark, inward, stench filled parts of this giant fish that Jonah abode for three days and three nights (or the span of about 72 hours) [Adaptation of Jonah 1:1–17].[75]

BOATSWAIN'S WHISTLE

*"Boatswain's whistle or pipe - small metal whistle
with a characteristic sound, used to signal the
announcement of important messages."* [76]

Jonah 1:1,2
Now the word of the Lord came to Jonah son of Amittai, saying,
Arise, go to Nineveh, that great city, and proclaim against it, for
their wickedness has come up before Me. (AMP)

JONAH AND THE CONVERSATION WITH GOD

Sometimes there is nothing more unnerving for a man or woman of God than to have to deliver a prophetic message of doom. A hard message often causes us to become edgy and uncomfortable, questioning whether God really spoke to us, or whether it is our own thinking that has penned this monologue. For Jonah it appears to have been just the opposite. He was, as we will later see, eager to pronounce judgment upon the Assyrians; however, he knew too much about God's kindness to believe that it would end in Nineveh's destruction. Jonah would have appreciated God picking someone else for this task, but He did not. It is apparent that Jonah was in prayer and was waiting on God in the period immediately preceding this book. What is not apparent, until we study the original language, is Jonah's position. Upon deeper study, we realize that Jonah was lying in the prostrate position, as was probably a daily routine for him, and listening. His physical location, other than being in Gath-Hepher, is not apparent or important, but given his rotten attitude, what is impressive is that he was still listening to and hearing from God. When our failures hurt others deeply, the rare person will even consider speaking to us again. What makes this story intriguing is what God does here with Jonah. He speaks to Jonah and gives him this assignment even though He knows that Jonah will run away in disobedience. It is an exceptional God that we serve who would take the time to speak to a son that He knew would betray his office and the trust placed in him.

And so it was that God communicated this critical message for Nineveh to His man in Gath-Hepher through an interactive vision or dream (Jonah 1:1–2, 4:1–2; Numbers 12:5–8). Why He chose Jonah we don't know. Surely there were other prophets scattered about the country in that day that He could have chosen, and surely God knew the decaying condition of Jonah's heart. Clearly none of this took God by surprise. The schools of the prophets that Samuel had set up in Bethel, Jericho and Gilgal[77] were still in operation at this time, and it is likely that Jonah would have attended one of those schools. Although he appears out of obscurity, " . . . it has been observed that Jonah must have been a true man of God [at least at one time] to be called to the important mission to Nineveh. He evidently had proven himself in previous assignments to warrant his selection for this one."[78] There is a tiny part of me that wants to believe this previous statement, but the bigger part does not buy it. Jonah had not arrived at this sorry state overnight. His position before God, though he was still seeking God, was not one of glory or humility. God knew what Jonah's reaction to this assignment would be, but Jonah needed to see the true condition of his heart. Times of adversity will come to us all, but God will not allow our future disobedience to postpone the tests of life. The Lord gave him an opportunity to change but he rejected God's offering, choosing instead to spit in the face of His Creator. I believe that Jonah had to be tried and tested, and, along with whatever other reasons God had, that this is at least one that He had in mind when giving this assignment to the prophet.

THE DATE OF THE BOOK

At this point, fixing the approximate date of Jonah's account will be helpful in establishing some of the historical parameters surrounding this event. It appears that of all the Old Testament prophetic books, only two were written before the book of Jonah, those being Joel and Obadiah. Amos and Hosea were written near the time of Jonah, and the three may have been contemporaries for a few years. The date of the actual writing of the book of Jonah has been a topic of some debate, with some suggesting that it wasn't penned until after the destruction of Nineveh in 612 b.c.[79]; however, it is generally accepted that Jonah lived during the early to mid part of the eighth century b.c. We can use the biblical reference in II Kings 14:25 to assist with pinpointing the date of the story itself. Jeroboam restored Israel's border from the entrance of Hamath to the Dead Sea according to the word of the Lord, which He spoke through Jonah. Since we know that King Jereboam II (793–753 b.c.) is the king that this verse is referring to, it is then logical to infer that Jonah lived and prophesied at some time during his reign. Therefore, the date of the events in this book are generally placed somewhere between 790 b.c. and 750 b.c. As a detailed study of Assyrian history will also prove,

The period of Jonah can be fitted into [the] historical conditions at Nineveh under Semiramis, the queen regent, and her son Adad-Nirari III (810–782 b.c.) . . . Jonah preached either in the closing years of this reign or earlier in the reign of Assurdan III (771–754 b.c.). This period was favorable for Jonah's ministry. Whether the plagues recorded in Assyrian history in 765 and 759 b.c. and the total eclipse of 763 b.c., regarded as portents of divine wrath, prepared the Ninevites for his message is not known.[80]

What is known, however, is that the natural disasters and phenomenon, which occurred during this six-year period, are sure to have unsettled the Assyrian nation. These events would have created a psychological climate conducive to receiving Jonah's message. The Lord has been known to use what could be mistaken as the natural occurrences of the earth to His own benefit before. We see that it worked with Pharaoh, and so this type of approach might also have worked with the Assyrians.

It is more likely then that the time of Jonah's call and subsequent sequestering in Nineveh is closer to the middle of the eighth century b.c. Leon Wood writes that

> *It [the period of time around 760 b.c.] was a time of general discouragement in the country and even characterized by panic and fear. For one thing, little remained of Assyria's former great empire due to the ineptness of weak kings. Then a serious plague swept through the land in 765 b.c., taking the lives of many people. And finally a total eclipse of the sun transpired on June 15, 763 b.c., and this is known to have spread general fear. Because such conditions would have measurably contributed to the effectiveness of Jonah's ministry (and it was indeed effective), this latter date becomes a possibility and probably the more likely . . .* [81]

To fix the details of kingdoms and rulers during this period, refer to **Chart 2: Rulers and Prophets**. This chart will help us maintain a proper chronological perspective on what was taking place during this period.

Chart Note 1: Information for this chart was compiled from the following sources. [82 83 84 85 86 87]

Chart Note 2: **R** represents the kings who did right in the sight of the Lord.

Chart Note 3: **E** represents the kings who did evil in the sight of the Lord.

CHART 2: RULERS AND PROPHETS

Year B.C.	Israel's King	Prophet	Assyria's King	Judah's King
880	Omri 885-874 (E)	Azariah, Hanani	Ashurnasirpal II 883 – 859	Asa 911-870 (R)
870	Ahab 874-853 (E)	Jehu, Jahaziel, Elijah, Eliezer, Micaiah		Jehoshaphat 872-848 (R)
860	Ahaziah 853-852 (E)	Elijah	Shalmaneser III 858 – 824	Jehoram 848-841 (E)
850	Jehoram (Joram) 852-841 (E)	Obadiah		
840	Jehu 841-814 (E)	Elisha		Ahaziah 841 (E) Athaliah 841-835 (E)—the only woman ruler
830				Joash 835-796 (R)
820		Joel	Shamsi–Adad V 823 – 811	
810	Jehoahaz 814-798 (E)		Adad-Nirari III 810 – 783	
800		Zechariah (not the		

		author of OT book)		
790	Jehoash 798-782 **(E)**			Amaziah 796-767 **(R)** Azariah (Uzziah) 790-739 **(R)**
780	Jeroboam II 793-753 **(E)**		Shalmaneser IV 782 – 773	
770			Assurdan (Ashurdan) III 773 – 754	
760		Amos, Jonah Hosea		
750	Zechariah 753 **(E)** Shallum 752 (Reigned only one month) Menahem 752-742 **(E)**		Asshur-Nirari II (some indicate V) 754 – 745	Jotham 750-731 **(R)**
740	Pekahiah 742-740 **(E)** Pekah 752-732 **(E)**		Tiglath-Pileser III 745 – 727	
730	Hoshea 732-722 **(E)**	Isaiah Micah		Ahaz 735-715 **(R)**

The period from about 824 b.c. to 746 b.c., although filled with many ruthless rulers, is generally considered an era of weakness in the Assyrian kingdom due mostly to inept leadership and internal dissension—especially as the eighth century b.c. moved into its second quarter.[88] In fact, this period and its leaders are considered so insignificant that most scholars omit the names of the rulers of Assyria during this seventy-five year period, instead opting for the headline "Period of Weakness". This is precisely the period of time it is believed that Jonah delivered his message of imminent destruction to the Ninevites. It may be that as the kings of Assyria were becoming weaker politically that the kingdom would have been more open to a word from Israel's prophet than during a time of strength and military prowess. What is also likely as this period wound down is that the entire nation was involved in a national call to repentance that would have caused them to appear weaker than they had previously.

THE FERTILE CRESCENT

Ancient Mesopotamia (which means "between the rivers") lies at the heart of the Fertile Crescent, "a section of the Middle East . . . [that] is a rich food-growing area in a part of the world where most of the land is too dry for farming,"[89] and is mainly comprised of "rich Mesopotamian marshlands"[90] that developed over millennia during the annual spring floods. The Fertile Crescent extends like a crescent moon from the edge of the Sinai Peninsula, up the eastern Mediterranean coast through present day Israel, Lebanon and Syria. It then swings northeast around the Syrian Desert, east and southeast through the interior of Iraq, and finally ends at the mouth of the Tigris-Euphrates Rivers as they converge and empty into the Persian Gulf. *(See Map 3: The Fertile Crescent)* To the north of this crescent are the mountains of present day Turkey and the Plateau of Iran. It is in the heart of this rich, Mesopotamian heartland that the city of Nineveh was situated, proudly perched on the northern bank of the Tigris River directly across from present day Mosul in Iraq. Though at the time of Jonah's visit Calah was the official capital city of Assyria, Nineveh was known as the great city (Jonah 1:2). And it was this great city that was founded by Nimrod, a great-grandson of Noah (Genesis 10:8–12); the same Nimrod who, it is generally held, represents the moral and religious evil and rebellion that Babylon came to be known and cursed for. "Existing ruins show that Nineveh had acquired its greatest extent in the time of the Assyrian kings mentioned in the Old Testament. It was then that Jonah visited it, and that reports of its size and magnificence were carried to the West . . . [and] . . . it was then, too, that the wealth, luxury, and power of its inhabitants called forth the indignant protests of the prophets."[91]

Up until the first part of the ninth century b.c., the Assyrian capital had always been Assur, but "Assurnasirpal II . . . established a new capital city, Calah,"[92] and not even two centuries later we learn that "by the end of his reign, Sargon II moved Assyria's capital from Calah to . . . Nineveh."[93] Others disagree with this timeline and state that the city of Nineveh did not become the capital until later during the reign of Sargon's son, Sennacherib.[94] Suffice it to say that this city, though great and obviously important, was most definitely not the capital of Assyria during Jonah's time. Nineveh was probably the largest city in Assyria, but it would not become the capital until nearly fifty years after Jonah's message had already been delivered.

It should be stated here that most scholars believe that the term city was used loosely in reference to Nineveh and in a similar way in which it is used today in large urban areas. Most believe that the great city of Nineveh, biblically described as three days' journey, was approximately sixty miles in circumference. The distance described was including the outlying areas of the city referred to by modern society as suburbs. This can be compared to a similar description, say, of New York City. When speaking of NYC, most people are including the city in particular and the surrounding boroughs and areas in general that make up what might be more appropriately termed the "Greater New York City Area." It was indeed a tremendous place to live and would have boasted many amenities scattered around an area of approximately thirty square miles.

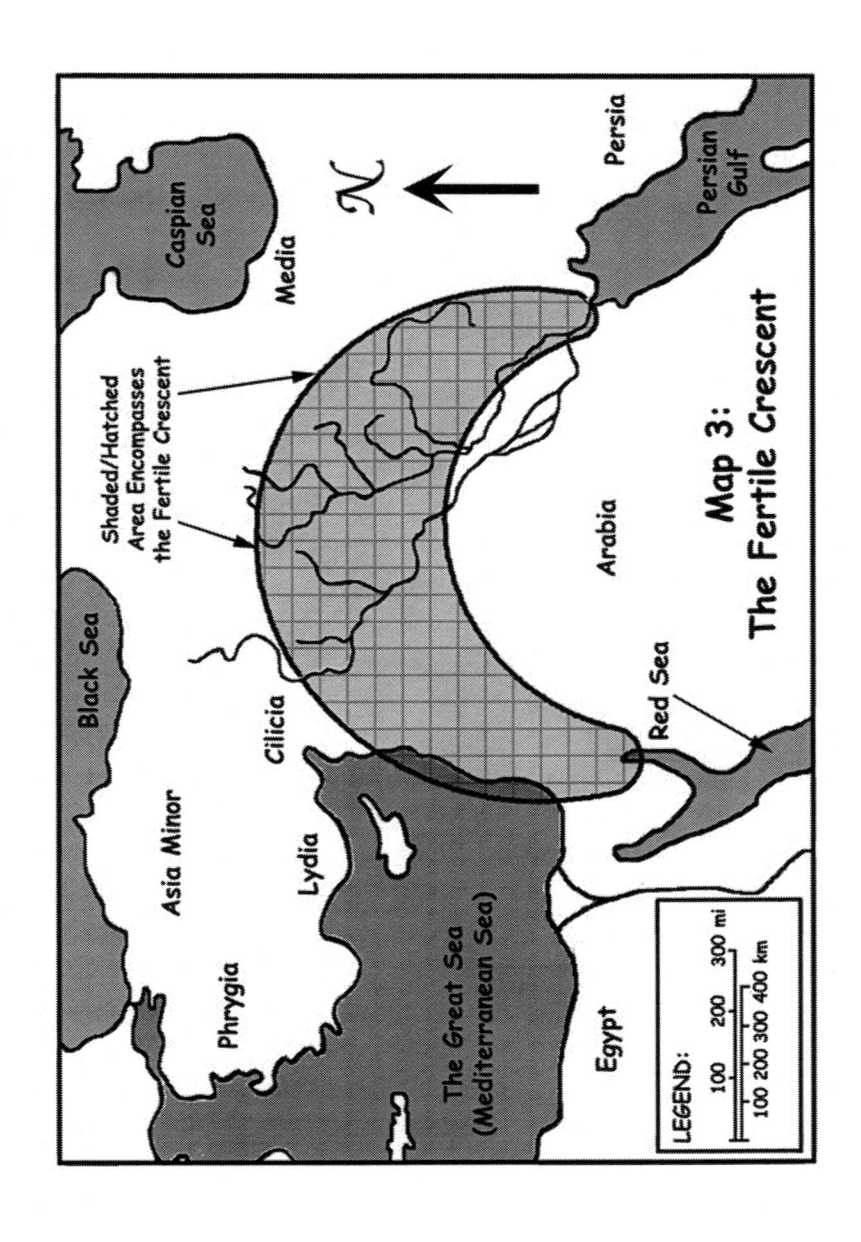

Map 3:
The Fertile Crescent

Upon the realization that Nineveh was not the capital of Assyria at this time, most people would initially ask, "Why Nineveh, then?" To this I can only answer, "I am not sure." It is possible that Nineveh, although not the actual geographic capital, was the cultural, social and financial center of Assyria, much like New York City is in the United States today. And, although the inhabitants of Nineveh repented at Jonah's message, the city would again take up its wicked ways that, by the close of the seventh century b.c., caused it to be overrun and nearly completely wiped from memory. What is interesting is that the city was so completely destroyed by the Medes and Babylonians, the inhabitants so completely murdered and taken captive, that not even a remnant remained to rebuild it. When this took place, Nineveh was so ruthlessly removed that modern day scholars did not believe it had ever existed until the mid-nineteenth century a.d. Up until that time, most had believed the existence of Nineveh to be a fanciful story spun by biblical authors not completely dissimilar to the story of Atlantis.

THE MIGHT THAT WAS ASSYRIA

"So just who were the Assyrians?" we might ask. Well, let us take a look. "Assyria was basically a land of farming villages and country towns, with a few, but only a few, major cities. Ashur, Nineveh, and Erbil, and perhaps Arrapkha, and these alone, were always substantial cities."[95] While other cities such as Calah did exist, they were not always great cities but, rather, rose up into influence for a time and then disappeared into nothingness. *(See Map 4: The Assyrian Empire)* The people fulfilled a variety of roles within their culture that varied from simple peasant farmers to artisans, craftspeople and tradespeople. The ancient Assyrians " . . . studied the stars and other heavenly bodies, (and) achieved important developments in mathematics, medicine, and architecture. They built cities, made advances in art and literature, and were the first people to develop a legal code . . ."[96] by which to govern their people and resolve conflicts. However, their advances were not limited to the sciences. As mighty warriors, they increased the breadth of the empire until it " . . . encompassed for the first time in history, within the realm of a single imperial domain, the whole of the 'Fertile Crescent.'"[97] For the study of this book and the purposes of understanding Jonah's story, it is this rapacious Assyrian army that we are most concerned with.

> *A century and a half of excavation . . . has revealed that . . . perhaps more than any other ancient nation, Assyria sustained itself through aggressive military raids, campaigns, and wars. And more often than not it treated those it conquered with a blood thirsty cruelty almost unique in humanity's recorded annals.*[98]

The Assyrian army was a force of professional soldiers who were fully trained in all areas of battle. Often they would lay waste to problematic cities as a show of force to deter the inhabitants around those cities from making the same mistake of daring to defy the king. Their might is recorded in many of the official archives, and their brutality is depicted in bas-reliefs and temple slabs recovered from archaeological sites. One bas-relief taken from an ancient Assyrian palace shows a group of soldiers returning home victorious after a battle carrying the heads of their enemies in their hands. Several of the soldiers even appear to be juggling the heads and tossing them back and forth to one another. What humiliation and fear must have struck into the hearts of the ancient Near East peoples.

Another report gives us insight into how ruthless the Assyrians were in battle. This account is regarding a revolt by rebels in the city of Suru on the lower Habur that Ashurnasirpal II went to suppress. Prior to laying it waste, he force-marched his own army to Suru over dirty, dusty roads during the summer's scorching heat in order to arrive quickly enough to suppress this uprising before it turned disastrous.

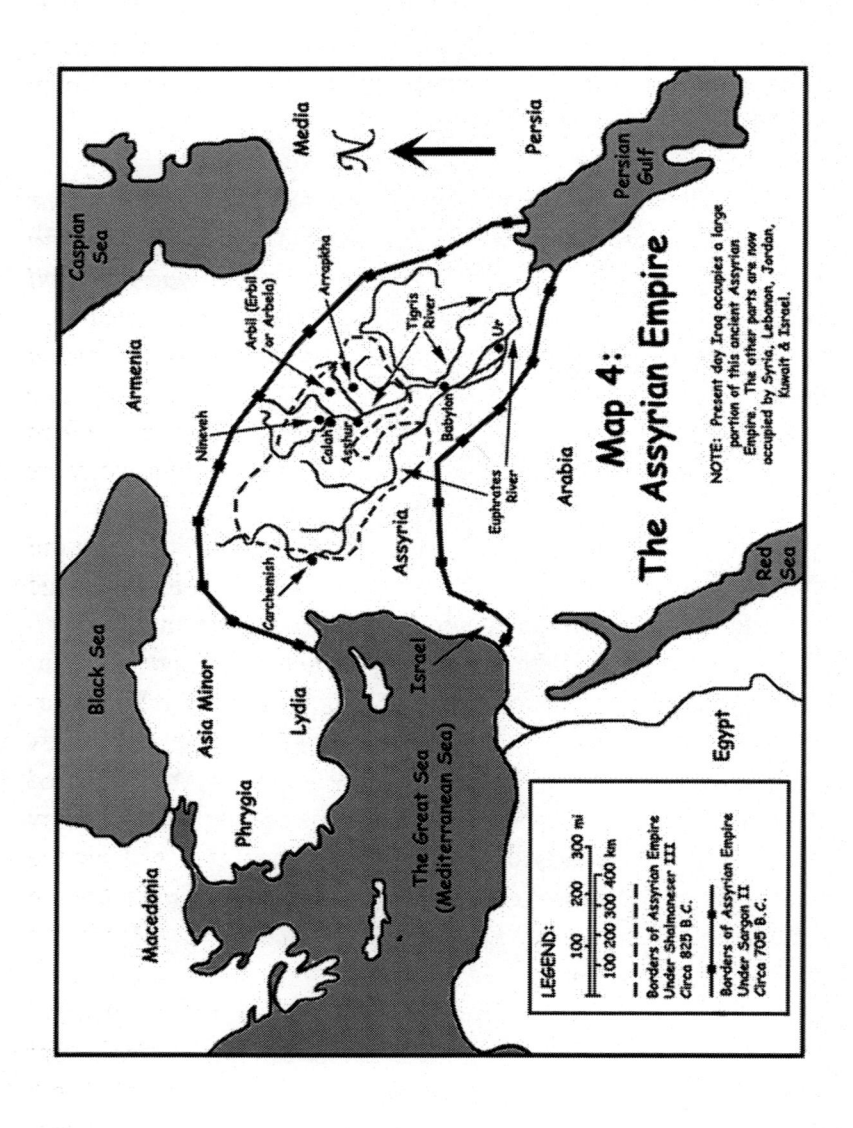

Map 4:
The Assyrian Empire

NOTE: Present day Iraq occupies a large portion of this ancient Assyrian Empire. The other parts are now occupied by Syria, Lebanon, Jordan, Kuwait & Israel.

LEGEND:

100   200   300 mi
100 200 300 400 km

Borders of Assyrian Empire
Under Shalmaneser III
Circa 825 B.C.

Borders of Assyrian Empire
Under Sargon II
Circa 705 B.C.

Ashurnasirpal II describes in some detail that the rebels [of Suru] were flayed [which was done while the victims were alive], impaled, beheaded, burnt alive, had their eyes put out, noses, fingers and ears cut off, and so on. To modern eyes, this grisly litany speaks of little more than sadistic excess. If, however, we are to place such behaviour in its historical context then a few pertinent observations need to be made. Whilst the relish with which Ashurnasirpal speaks of the punishments inflicted on his enemies finds no parallel in other royal annals, the rationale for such behaviour would have been understood and practised by earlier Assyrian monarchs and was to be a general feature of Assyrian policy until the fall of the empire. Indeed, the words of the prophet Nahum . . . are an explicit reference to the deliberate and cultivated Assyrian policy of "frightfulness." Notwithstanding that such behaviour has become synonymous in the popular mind with commonplace Assyrian policy, it is quite apparent from the annals that the kings were highly selective in their use of it.

In most cases when atrocities do occur it is consequent upon a vassal state renouncing the solemn oath of fealty to the king and the god Ashur, the punishment being viewed as the rightful chastisement of a rebellious subject. Such a policy was practised specifically to dissuade opposition to Assyrian rule by setting an example from which other potential rebels should draw the appropriate conclusions. In wartime a few intentional and selective atrocities were engineered so as to encourage the enemy to come to terms quickly, to avoid unnecessary battles. Thus the purpose of the policy was psychological, its principal object being to establish terror so as to convey a sense of powerlessness in the face of Assyrian arms.[99]

Obviously being sent to the Assyrians (Ninevites) upset Jonah. This anger he later displayed was justifiable in his mind for several reasons. We will discuss each of these reasons at length later in this section. Whatever the reasons were for Jonah's disapproval of God's command, it is sure that he knew intimately of these people and of their exploits, and it is surer still that this went against every theological idea that he was taught and every ideology he held dear. As a matter of course the ancient Assyrians " . . . indeed [practiced] consistently aggressive, pitiless, and often savage tactics and policies [and these tendencies] characterized all of the leaders of the new Assyria."[100] Again we read, in reference to Assurnasirpal II (ca 883–859 b.c.) and from the annals of one of his campaigns,

> *I captured the city; 600 of their warriors I put to the sword; 3000 captives I burned with fire; I did not leave a single one among them alive to serve as a hostage. Hulai, their governor, I captured alive. Their corpses I formed into pillars; their young men and maidens I burned in the fire. Hulai . . . I flayed, his skin I spread upon the wall of the city . . . [and] . . . the city I destroyed.*[101]

This type of treatment and contempt that the rulers of Assyria openly displayed towards their enemies was not something that was simply confined to one generation, either. These values were passed down through the generations and through the royal lines, so that we see that even the sons followed hard after their fathers' examples. "Such war tactics and techniques [as his father practiced] were applied with unusual energy and relentlessness by Assurnasirpal's son, Shalamaneser III (ca. 858–824 b.c.), who devoted fully thirty-one of his reign's nearly thirty-five years to vigourous military offensives."[102] It is clear then that though the Assyrians made immeasurable contributions to society in the areas of math, science and the arts, many of which were the seeds of common practices today, they were indeed consumed by the need to conquer and to conquer brutally and completely. Their most elemental beliefs seem to have rested upon an unwritten mandate to conquer. To this people and this city of influence (Nineveh— the Robber City[103]), Jonah was being sent so that God could, in Jonah's own words, show them too much mercy. Is it any wonder why he argued so strenuously against God's command? No. But even though his disapproval, reservations and level of contempt are now clearer, Jonah was nevertheless wrong. It is this same sense of ideological arrogance that we today must guard against.

3

AWOL

"AWOL—this phrase is an acronym for
Absent WithOut Leave. In the military
a soldier needs to be in possession of a chit in order to have
an authorized leave of absence. A chit
is any small piece of paper
bearing [this] permission to do something
or requesting such permission."[104]

Jonah 1:3
But Jonah rose up to flee to Tarshish from being in the presence
of the Lord [as His prophet] and went down to Joppa and found
a ship going to Tarshish [the most remote of the Phoenician trading places then known]. So he paid the appointed fare and went
down into the ship to go with them to Tarshish from being in the
presence of the Lord [as His servant and minister]. (AMP)

THREE CITIES AND A TRADE ROUTE
GATH-HEPHER

Jonah was a Zebulunite from a small town called Gath-
Hepher (winepress of digging, winepress of the pit, winepress
of the well) that was located about three miles north of Nazareth.[105] [It is interesting to note that the treading of the winepress
has become synonymous with God's just judgment upon those
who refuse to obey Him, especially when we realize that this
was Jonah's birthplace and lifelong hometown.] Gath-Hepher

was located near the Zebulun/Naphtali border[106] approximately twenty kilometers northeast of the city of Megiddo and on the Northern edge of the Jezreel Valley (also referred to as Armageddon or the Valley of Megiddo, an area that has become known as a poetical expression for terrible and final conflict).[107] *(See Map 5: Trade Routes and Zebulun's Territory)* With nothing particular or special to offer, it was simply one of many inconsequential villages[108] located within the borders of Zebulun's well-positioned territory. This territory, however, was situated so that it exercised control over part of the upper portion of the Via Maris. Gath-Hepher then, though of no real consequence, was positioned near enough to this ancient trade route to be greatly influenced by those traversing the land of Israel. The book of Genesis describes that the allotment of Zebulun's land was to be toward the seashore, and that it was to be a haven and safe landing place for ships. (How ironic that Jonah, as a member and prophet of this tribe, would choose a ship as the means for his disobedient getaway.) In reference to the Jezreel Valley we know that,

> . . . *this valley was the breadbasket of ancient Israel. It was located by the most critical mountain pass on the Via Maris—Megiddo. Because of this pass, the city [Megiddo] and valley were probably the most strategic real estate in Israel. Battles fought in the Jezreel Valley were literally fought for control of the world: Whoever ruled the area could dominate world economics and culture. Some scholars believe more battles were [have been] fought here than in any other place in the world.*[109]

JOPPA

Joppa (meaning beauty), Jonah's escape hatch, was located approximately sixty-five kilometers southwest of Gath-Hepher on the coast of Israel. Research shows that Joppa was the only natural seaport from the Bay of Acco (just north of Mt. Carmel) to the Egyptian coast and naturally served as the port of

Jerusalem. As a major shipping port for Israel,[110] Joppa was utilized twice as the shipping destination for the cedars of Lebanon (II Chronicles 2:16; Ezra 3:7) that were later transported to Jerusalem and used in the building (and rebuilding) of the temple. Originally founded by the Phoenicians as one of their first colonies along the coast,[111] Joppa " . . . soon fell into Philistine hands; [and] it was rarely under Israelite control thereafter."[112]

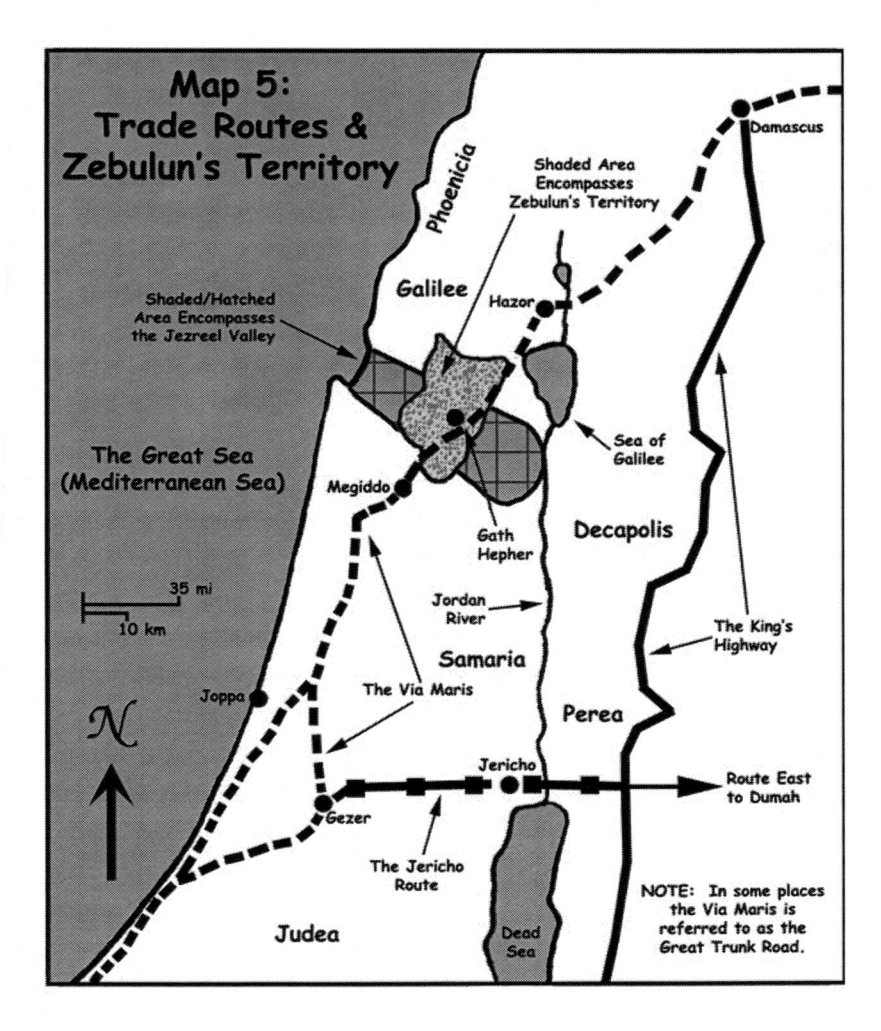

TARSHISH

Tarshish (meaning smelting plant or refinery) was Jonah's permanent vacation location and was located more than 3000 kilometers west of Israel in southwestern Spain (the exact location is currently unknown, but it was most likely near present day Seville. *(See Map 6: Jonah & the Phoenician Sailors' Voyage)*. In reference to Tarshish we learn that " . . . the Old Testament is replete with references to that old city. Take II Chronicles 9:21 as an example: 'For the kings ships went to Tarshish with the servants of Huram [King Hiram of Tyre]: every three years . . . came the ships of Tarshish bringing gold, and silver, ivory, apes and peacocks'."[113] This was a city of great wealth due to its impressive mining/smelting industry. As such, Tarshish was a city filled with wonders, riches, amazement and freedom. No wonder Jonah would want to flee to a place like this.

Tarshish, this city of great wealth, lured Jonah to its riches and splendor even before his conversation with God. For him to decide that quickly where it was he would be running away to, there must have been some previous thought given to this locale. It would be the same with us. If there is an emergency and we have to leave town quickly, most of us have already picked out our destination. Jonah was no fool, and I believe he felt that if he was going to run away, he might as well run to a place that promised prosperity and wealth, and possibly a place about which he had already done some research. He certainly was not going to run to a place of poverty where he would be forced to perform manual labor. Jonah was used to the prosperity abundant in Israel during this period, and he was probably used to a steady flow of cash from those to which he prophesied. It is clear when we read the fourth chapter of the book of Jonah that he was concerned about his personal comfort. I believe it would have been a deciding factor for him to run to a place where he could best hope to sustain that lifestyle.

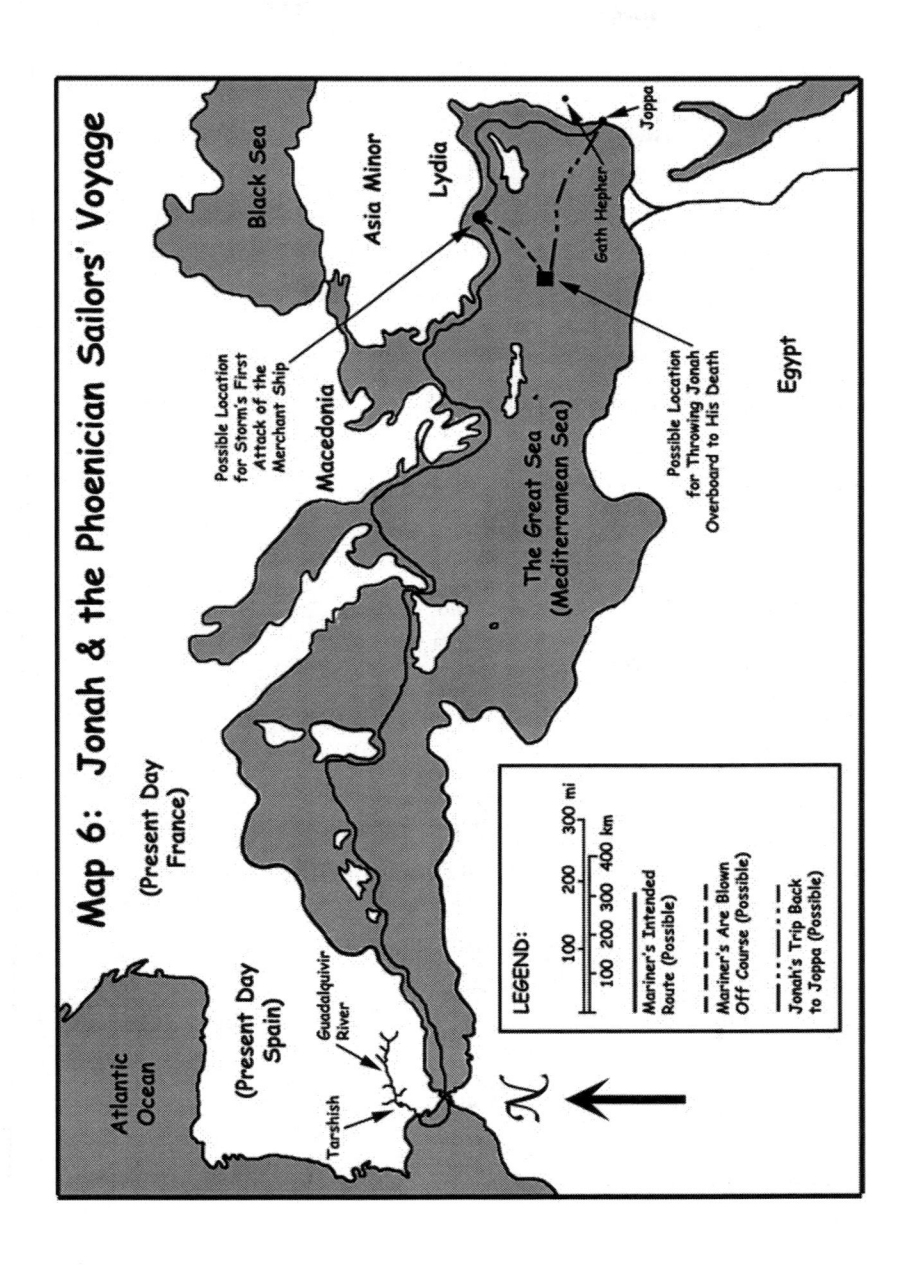

Map 6: Jonah & the Phoenician Sailors' Voyage

ANCIENT TRAVEL

In those ancient times, it was uncommon for most people to venture out over the open seas because " . . . ancient people had a great fear of the ocean . . ."[114] We also know that " . . . travel by sea in [the] early days was undertaken only when absolutely necessary."[115] What interests me is that Jonah, having these feelings of trepidation about sea travel, would still choose to flee and go to Tarshish. There were many other places to which he could have fled that would have been equally as far away from Nineveh and would not have required him to travel by ship. That is what leads me to believe that Tarshish must have held some other allure besides its distance and direction from Nineveh. This is why I believe that there must have been some fiscal considerations in his mind as well; if not then, it makes no sense why he did not choose to run to southern Egypt, western Africa or northern Europe. It makes the most sense when we look at it from this financial perspective. Jonah must have been thinking about his future comfort when he decided to run.

Since many Old Testament accounts depict the sufferings and privation of the prophets of God, we would naturally conclude that Jonah was poor as well; however, this does not appear to be the case. We can infer this from reading between some of the lines of this fascinating story. As we see, Jonah departed quickly from this hometown of the winepress on his way to the port of beauty in search of a ship bound for Tarshish. What makes this important is that normally, before an ancient traveler could set out on a journey of any distance, he would have to " . . . pay all debts, provide for dependents, give parting gifts, return all articles under trust, take money and good temper for the journey, then bid farewell to all, and be merciful to the animal he rides upon . . ."[116] In other words, a quick getaway for Jonah, as most believe it was, may not have been as quick a getaway as the language might suggest. It does appear that he had enough money to settle any outstanding debts he may have had, pay for food and transportation to Joppa, and easily pay the fare to Tarshish.

THE VIA MARIS

In journeying to Nineveh, Jonah could have taken one of two possible routes. He could have traveled north up the Via Maris, through Damascus, and then continued on in a northeastern tack until he reached the Euphrates River. At this juncture, he would have traveled downstream to Babylon, crossed the river and headed north up the Tigris River until he reached Assur (once the capital of Assyria) and then Nineveh. The second possibility for the trip would have been for Jonah to have traveled southeast from Gath-Hepher to Jericho, crossing the Jordan River and the King's Highway on the Jericho Route (due east), and then continuing on to Dumah (located in Arabia). *(See Map 5: Trade Routes and Zebulun's Territory)* Once he reached Dumah, he would have then traveled northeast until he reached Babylon. The rest of the trip (from Babylon to Nineveh) would have been the same no matter which initial route he took out of Israel. My opinion is that Jonah most likely traveled up the Via Maris on a route not all that dissimilar from Abram's when he traveled from the Ur to Canaan. The reason is that this route would have boasted the nicest scenery and the easiest trip. It would have been right through the heart of the Fertile Crescent, with not too many mountains to scale and no deserts to speak of to cross. The other route, however, would have demanded much more from Jonah, causing him to traverse mountains and cross the desert of Arabia. Knowing how much Jonah enjoyed his personal comfort, it is all but a forgone conclusion, then, that this alternate route would not have worked. Either way, the distance of the journey would have been about the same. *(See Map 7: Ancient Trade Routes to Nineveh)*

The Via Maris, the route that Jonah would have taken on his way to Joppa, is the Latin translation of the text in Isaiah 9:1 "the way of the sea."[117] Some believe that this road was the same as the Great Trunk Road that ran from Damascus through Megiddo and Hazor and then down to Egypt. Others believe this to be in error. Suffice it to say, though, that this was at least an important trade route and may have been, as some suggest, the greatest international trade route of the ancient world. Scholars at "That the World May Know Ministries" offer us the following insight into why the Via Maris was vital, and why Israel lost out on the tremendous strategic gift that God had placed in the midst of their nation and had desired for them to control.

WHY IT WAS VITAL

The rugged mountain ranges cutting through the middle of Israel made it incredibly difficult to travel east to west and transport goods. Civilizations such as Egypt, Babylon, and Assyria, however, depended on trade to exchange and acquire necessary goods. Whoever controlled the road between these empires dominated international trade and had a tremendous influence on other cultures.

WHY ISRAEL LOST OUT

Because they were so afraid of the Philistines and the Canaanites, the Israelites stayed mainly in the mountains or in the Shephelah (the foothills between the mountains and the coastal plain). The Israelites rarely controlled the key cities along the Via Maris, so they could not exert the degree of influence upon the world that God intended them to have.[118]

The reason that I mention the Via Maris is because Gath-Hepher, Jonah's hometown, was located near if not directly on this ancient trade route. This would have exposed Jonah, both as a child and as an adult, to many heathen cultures and ideas, including the Egyptians and the Assyrians. It probably also followed, just as it does today with major interstate highways, that the closer a town was to one of these major routes, the more crime and undesirable people it attracted to the community and the surrounding area. With Jonah's close proximity to the most strategic and important trade route of the day, he had ample opportunity for the fires of his ideological hatred of the heathen to be stoked and refueled. Someone who grew up a little farther off the beaten path may not have had the first hand experience with the vileness of the heathen as Jonah had, but that was not Jonah's case. This is, at least in part, what helped shape the angry prophet we see in the pages of this book.

Jonah was not as much rebellious when he ran (which is what most people label him as) as he was uninterested. Everything about his behavior screams this out loud. He was too idealistic in his theology and could not reconcile what God was asking him to do with his own belief system. Rebellion is defined as "a defiance of or opposition to *any* authority or control."[119] But this is clearly not who Jonah was. We see later that he did, indeed, submit to God's authority and control. The real problem was his theology. What God was asking Jonah to do could not fit within the confines of the neat little box that he had built to hold his religious beliefs. So we see that he was theologically unable to accept the command of God due to his preprogrammed set of life instructions. If this was how God was, then Jonah did not want anything to do with His command, due to the fact that his understanding of God could not be reconciled with that type of mercy being expressed towards the Assyrian nation. In many places, I have seen Jonah labeled as a reluctant prophet, and I would concur with reservations. In my mind, he is more of an idealistic bigot, a man who was blindly and arrogantly intolerant of anyone and any idea not fitting his conception of life as he wished it to be (and therefore, that was the root of his reluctance to obey God's command).

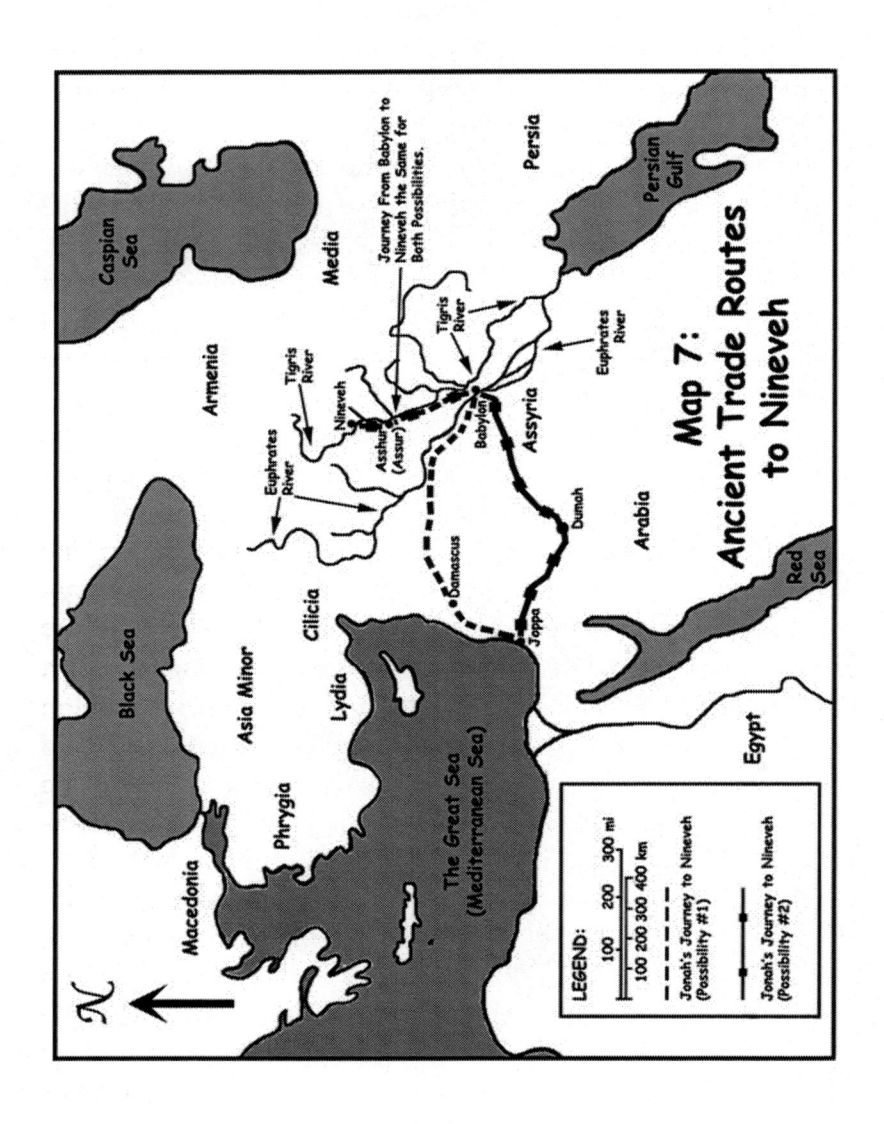

We are not as different from Jonah as we might expect. Where we grew up, how we grew up, the people that we were exposed to, the attitudes, behaviors, prejudices and preconceived ideas that we intertwined into the fabric of ourselves–these are what bind us irreconcilably. These generally make up the arsenal of equipment that we unconsciously revert to using during times of great stress. Most of these are the building blocks of our daily living, though we may not even realize it, and some of our more ominous prejudices only show their true colors when difficult embroilments ensue the storms of life. It was these inbred, inborn intricacies that were tightly knit into Jonah's conscience as well, and that were unyielding when faced with the command of God. The apple of his life truly had not fallen far from the tree of his upbringing. He hated the heathen so much that he wanted them all dead. Some may have considered his attitude noble or even righteous, but God abhorred it. Jonah could not see the forest of humanity for the trees of his bigotry.

In light of Jonah's twisted example, we must determine to change from our past and grow toward God, but this can only be accomplished with a herculean effort. Our lives can become beautiful apples that fall far from the trees of our upbringing, but not without God's help. In other words, we must fight within ourselves to change some of the very core beliefs that we hold dear because they are not part of God's psyche. Laying down the tightly held, ungodly beliefs that have kept us less vulnerable is part of the perceived unpleasantness of being a follower of God. Realizing that their belief system was entirely corrupt, the Ninevites immediately repented and embraced God's word. The Bible says the entire city of Nineveh turned from its evil ways, and so God commuted the death sentence; however, His prophet could not do the same in his own life. Even after all God had given him, Jonah did not and would not change. He held so tightly to his beliefs that God Himself could not talk Jonah out of them.

It is a precarious place to find ourselves in when we are unwilling to let go of our tired, old, ungodly doctrines, and that is why we must meticulously examine our attitudes and our lives. Once we have uncovered these ungodly strongholds, we must not rest until we have thrown out every evil, preconceived, selfish, bigoted attitude and desire within our life. What we must realize is that we are not correct in all of our views. Some of our opinions and attitudes may someday lead us down a road similar to the one Jonah traveled down if we are not quick to listen to God and to change. Jonah represents who we must not become. Eternity will list Jonah not as the greatest revivalist of all time (which he had every opportunity to become), but as the man who held too tightly to his religious beliefs and chose the sacrifice of his life, ministry and career over obedience to the Lord, a veritable loser in the high stakes game of life.

It may be that Jonah had grown up idolizing Samson or Elijah, prophets with a gift for the theatrical destruction of the enemies of God. Their legends rang through the halls of the school of the prophets where he was instructed in the law, poetry and sacred music, and in the traditions and beliefs of his people. Jonah may have dreamed of one day delivering hard messages to the heathen and then standing back to watch God destroy them in their sin. The stories of Samson and David, who both killed thousands of God's enemies, may have been those told to him as a child. His daydreams may even have been filled with stunning performances like Elijah when he commanded fire from heaven to consume not one, but two companies of men sent from King Ahaziah. Gazing into the evening sky, he may even have dreamt of being carried up to heaven in a chariot of fire as Elijah was. And as he came into his own, he might have had the idea that his ministry would be modeled after a hero like Elijah, a ministry whose mission was to accuse of sin and to command God's judgment upon those who refused to hear. What he never considered was that he would be used to spark repentance and revival in a ruthless, heathen nation. God's ways, ever merciful and kind though, upended Jonah's theology and sent him spiraling away from the very one he served. This is the danger we all face and must guard against becoming.

SO WHAT DID JONAH EXPECT?

The underlying reasoning for Jonah's flight from the command of God, although also bogged down in his ideology and financial success, stemmed from his intimate knowledge of scripture. He knew the penalty for disobedience was death, and this, ultimately, is why he ran. Three times in this short book Jonah speaks of it (Jonah 1:12; 4:3, 9), and thrice he requested his own elimination. It is undeniable that Jonah did not wish to live, believing within himself that he would be better off dead. Throughout the history of Israel, whoever disobeyed God received the ultimate punishment of excommunication or death (Genesis 4:8–16; 19:17–26; Exodus 12:29; 32:25–28; Numbers 15:30–36; Joshua 7—just to name a few examples). In Jonah's eyes, to die without having to carry the burden of obedience any longer would have been a fair trade for his disobedience, anything that would keep him from going to the Assyrians. That is why he remained calm and asleep during the storm when the others were losing control, because he was no longer interested in preserving his own life or ministry. Since his only desire was to die, why would the storm concern him? It was only after the raging sea had nearly consumed his life that he screamed out to God in his distress and seriously and earnestly remembered his Lord. However, this salty lesson would quickly be forgotten. His anger again flared against God and he begged for death (Jonah 4). He had no idea that God would rescue him with a fish and, furthermore, knew that he didn't deserve a second chance at life. But God had other plans for Jonah; God let him live.

THE PHOENICIAN CONNECTION AND JONAH'S DESCENT
ANCIENT SHIPS

Since ancient travelers did not have most of our modern modes of transportation, their choices of locomotion were confined to walking, riding on the back of an animal, or sailing. When travel over water was deemed necessary, anyone desiring to book passage was forced to procure a spot upon a freighter, merchantman or warship because there were no passenger ships in existence. In Jonah's case, he would be sailing and would need a Phoenician ship to carry him away. After arriving in Joppa, it is likely that he would have had to wait a considerable amount of time before finding or boarding a ship bound for Tarshish. In 2 Chronicles 9:21 we read, "For the king's ships went to Tarshish with Huram's servants; once every three years the ships of Tarshish came bringing gold, silver, ivory, apes, and peacocks." In other words, it took this fleet of ships three years to make the round-trip from Joppa to Tarshish and then back again (surmising, of course, that there were also other stops along the way as well). And since we also know that Solomon's wealth surpassed that of all the kings of the earth, it is safe to assume that no one else would have had the financial ability to send ships there as frequently as he did. It naturally follows then that, unless Jonah coincidentally found a ship leaving on the same day he arrived in Joppa, he would have had to wait until a ship was available and ready to set sail for Tarshish. Whatever the time frame involved in searching out and securing passage on this ship, we do know that Jonah eventually found such a ship, which he subsequently boarded.

In establishing the type and size of ship that Jonah traveled in, we must consult various historians and ancient texts. Since it is unlikely that a ship traveling to distant lands over the open and dangerous seas would have enjoyed much success (either economically or practically) without sails, especially given the diversity and intensity of the Mediterranean winds, it may be presumed that it was fitted with both sails and oars and only rowed when there was no wind or during severe weather.[120] One ancient picture depicts a Greek trader ship similar to this with its sail unfurled and ready to set sail. Although there is much speculation and debate by scholars over the size and type of ship Jonah set sail upon, the one item of which we can be sure is that it was a Phoenician vessel.[121]

The first characteristic we must examine when attempting to ascertain what this vessel may have looked like is the type of ship that it may have been. It is curious that there are only a few pictures in existence that portray trading vessels from circa 800 b.c., although there are hundreds portraying warships. One reason for this may be that it was popular during that era for merchant ships to be combination ships, both warships and trading vessels, and "it is possible, probable even, that when longer voyages were made where there was a risk for attack by pirates . . . [that] . . . such a combination of trader and warship was used . . . [which] . . . had a relatively large crew capable of [both] rowing and fighting."[122] With the threat of pirate attack real, especially given their valuable cargoes, this ship (which would have been similar to a Greek merchantman) would have been quick, maneuverable and heavily armed.

Size, being of particular importance on a long-distance trip, is the second characteristic that we will examine in reference to Jonah's ride. Most merchants in that era who were involved in local trade would have tramped up and down the Levantine Coast and along Asia Minor in small coasting vessels forced to hug the shoreline. And, although these smaller vessels were much more common in ancient times than large ships, we cannot discount the existence of larger vessels capable of carrying enormous cargoes over vast distances (for example, in Egypt 1500 years prior to this there were barges constructed capable of carrying loads in excess of 700 tons[123]). We can be confident, then, that this Phoenician ship was a large vessel with an upper deck as well as lower cargo holds and was staffed by many sailors and a chief pilot. The critical element that would have dictated the ultimate size of this long-distance trader was profitability. A ship (or fleet of ships in Solomon's case) that would have made the Joppa-Tarshish run only once every three years would have needed to carry enormous loads of goods and riches simply to remain profitable. After all, it would hardly be worth sending small vessels to fetch riches and exotic treasures for Solomon's kingdom if those boats were only capable of transporting small holds full of cargo. Further, it would have been of considerable risk to send small vessels out into the open seas against the Mediterranean's wicked winds and strong currents. And, not only would these vessels have needed enough room for these exotic riches, but they would have also needed enough reserve capacity in which to accommodate the crew and their personal effects, required sailing gear, spare sails and oars, fighting equipment, food, water, and the occasional passenger. It is not a large leap, then, to surmise that this Phoenician vessel may have been similar in size and composition to one recently discovered by a sponge diver and later brought up by researchers from the University of Pennsylvania. The fifteen-meter body of the ship was constructed of Jerusalem pine by its ancient architects and then covered with a protective film (presumably as a precaution against the Mediterranean shipworm).[124]

ANCIENT SHIPPING

There were two dangers inherent in ancient shipping. The first danger was pirates (which the ancient mariner could do little to prevent), and the second danger was storms. Neither could be predicted with any accuracy, and a trip without the occurrence of either would have been considered fortunate indeed. Since the ancient mariners feared both, they naturally attempted to follow routes that would afford them the most protection. In light of this we learn that,

In [the] early days of navigation, the skipper is forced to hug the shores, creeping round the coasts, often becalmed or driven back by contrary winds, and lying-to for the night. If he endeavours to cross the sea, he is compelled to follow fixed routes, by which alone he can keep in sight of land, threading his way between islands and following well-known channels.[125]

It is important to note that Jonah's trip would have been nothing like today's voyages through the open seas where no land need be in sight. Our modern method of sailing was simply not heard of in ancient times. The ancients followed the trade routes first laid out by the Minoans of Crete, and who are considered to have been the first great sea power of the Mediterranean. The trade routes the Minoans established were destined to last for millennia.[126] And so this Phoenician vessel would have wound in and out of coves, islands, outcroppings, peninsulas, and whatever else hugged the coasts as it ventured northward toward Asia Minor (present day Turkey) and then westward toward Greece, Italy, Sicily, Corsica, and eventually the Strait of Gibraltar (which would lead it to Tarshish).

JONAH'S DESCENT

We find Jonah, after paying the captain a tidy fare, safely aboard the ship and stowing his personal effects below deck. With the crew, captain and possibly the owner himself making last minute preparations to leave, it appears that no one objects to Jonah's arrival or to the news of his decampment. Maybe they had chuckled at his introduction. Imagine how the conversation might have unfolded. "Hi, my name is Jonah. Is this ship going west? It is. Great. I am running away from God and I want to get as far away from Nineveh as humanly possible. You say that you are going to Tarshish? Ha, that is even better than I had hoped. I have heard great things about that place. How much is the fare? That is fine. Money is no object; I just want to leave this place as quickly as I can." As unflattering as it must have been, his first conversation with these sailors certainly did not elevate their estimation of this man of God. As hypocrites themselves, I am sure that the crew could see right through him.

Given the distance they would be traveling, the considerable fare they would have required and the uncommon nature of Jonah's request, it appears odd that not one of them offered at least a word to the contrary. So why did they do it? Why would they take this man who was running from God and let him onto their ship? We are not sure. At first glance it seems like a reasonable decision, but upon further reflection it is ghastly preposterous. Given the history between their peoples, their clashing ideologies and the prevalence of superstitions among seafarers, who would do such a thing? In short, these Phoenicians did, and so have we. In fact, we will probably do it again. There is something within us that believes we can handle the disobedient runner, but we cannot and should not.

As we previously discussed concerning Jesus and His disciples, we must exercise extreme caution when allowing passengers aboard our boat. Further, if we do allow them on board, we should at least restrict their access to the different parts of our ship until we can establish that they are of no threat. The Phoenician sailors, though, were apparently unconcerned with Jonah in general and allowed him free access not only to board their ship but also to stow below deck. Why is this significant? It was generally understood, even in Paul's time, that the passengers aboard a ship were confined to the main deck; however, Jonah was allowed to go into the hold where the cargo, and possibly the crew's personal effects were stored. Were there no cargo, per se, on the first leg of the journey to Tarshish, there would have at least been money—coins or currency—with which they would buy the items they were seeking to transport back home. In short, whatever was valuable was certainly not going to be positioned on deck and in plain view, but was likely stowed below the deck and out of sight. Why then would they allow a running stranger to sleep amongst their valuables? It is a curious question to which I have no firm answer; however, I do have a warning: We should do all we can to avoid a repeat of the Phoenicians' disaster, and thus should keep tight reins upon all who have access to our boat.

JONAH'S IRONY

An ironic sidebar to this story is the fact that Jonah, an Israelite prophet, attempted to flee to Tarshish from a city founded and quite possibly still controlled by the Phoenicians in a boat built and piloted by Phoenician sailors. The reason for this is Israel conquered the Phoenicians (who were, of course, then known as the Canaanites).[127] Israel invaded the Phoenicians

> *. . . around 1380 b.c. [and] deprived them of most of Palestine and crowded them on[to] the narrow ribbon of coastland extending from Accho . . . to Ras . . . [and then] shortly thereafter the Aramaeans took the hinterland of Syria E of Mt. Lebanon. Thus hemmed in to the coast of northern Palestine and southern Syria, they took to the sea and became one of the most distinguished seafaring peoples of history.*[128]

It is also interesting to note that one of the Phoenician's most important deities was Baal, son of the supreme Canaanite deity El, who was the reigning king of their gods[129] and was an abhorrent offense to the Israelites and especially distasteful to a trained prophet of God. It was this false god Baal that was part of an ongoing argument between God and His people (over forty references through 2 Kings 14). Baal proved more interesting and less demanding than the one true God for many of the children of Israel, as is evidenced by their constant construction of temples and altars to honor it. It appears that the " . . . gaiety and licentious character of Baal worship . . . had a subtle attraction for the austere Hebrews bound to serve a holy God under a rigorous moral code."[130] These facts may seem insignificant or trivial at first, but let us consider the possible ramifications. The people of the East, like people throughout the world, hold grudges; only they seem to be more proficient at it than most. When we consider, for instance, that the constant upheaval in the Middle East today is based upon millennia of hatred, grudges and birthrights, then Jonah's convolution starts to make less sense. He was willing to risk his life at the hands of the very people his nation had driven from their homeland simply in order to ignore the command of God. In today's vernacular, one might ask Jonah, "What are you, crazy?" Is it not fair to assume that at least one of these Phoenician seamen had not given up his hatred of the nation who exiled his people and, so, might be a little prone to retribution? Yet here we find Jonah paying a considerable fare to a conquered people, who served an abhorred deity, to assist him in escaping from the command of the one true God whom he claimed to serve. It is now more clear to see just how far Jonah's disobedience had taken him from rational thought.

JONAH'S DISOBEDIENCE

It is clear that neither disobedience nor anger were new to Jonah. They came too quickly and without hesitation or remorse for either to have been a new experience. Disobedience is something that he had learned over many years. Though not recorded, there is little doubt that he had done something similar to this before. When more of the back-story is revealed in Jonah chapter four, we clearly see that his modus operandi was: argue first, run second, and then grudgingly obey as a final concession–all the while wishing for death rather than the willingness to obey. Maybe Jonah had watched his father disobey God like this and run or maybe even another fellow prophet. It is clear that he had watched the duplicity in the priesthood for years, and this could not have helped his frame of mind. The worst part isn't even so much that he disobeyed, for we all have done that. Jonah's larger degradation was that he disagreed with God's nature and vehemently objected to His display of mercy to the Assyrian nation. His flight had more to do with arrogant, religious pride than it did in not wanting to deliver a hard message. This situation reminds me of the pompous religious leaders who called for Christ's death and of the Sons of Thunder disciples who requested the delegation of His frightful judgment.

Jonah ran from God because he did not agree with God and could not stomach the reality of what God wanted to do. He embraced a part of his ancestry that dated back to the Exodus when the Israelites first cried out that God was sending them to the desert to die (Genesis 14:12). This complaining disagreement, this retardation at every suggestion of God's direction, is what slammed Jonah into the barbed wire of obedience versus sacrifice, an issue he never did satisfactorily resolve. There are many examples of these recalcitrant infractions in Israel's long line of ruling leadership and foolish tribe members as well that all point to the inheritability of lawlessness no matter who we may be. Men of God, even prophets like Jonah and Balaam, continually failed to live up to what God had asked them to do because they always seemed to know what was best (even if God did not agree). They worshipped their own ideas and creations, their Baal gods and masters. This was Jonah's sin. The predilection for his own superior opinions is what got Jonah into the biggest trouble of his life. It was a paradigm in his lineage that first taught him that it was commendable to disagree with God, and Jonah never defied this unholy dictator. He thought that he knew better than God did. Therefore, with his bags packed and his prophetic ministry left to rot, his insubordination drove him to Joppa. Jonah never realized what he had buried under the deck of his ship or had hidden within the secret compartments of his own life. Apparently even when he was finally faced with the storm, he was too far gone to actually come back to the place where God wanted him. Although he did deliver the message to the Ninevites, it was not what I would actually call obedience. Why did he do it? He did it for the same reasons we do, because it was easier to bury it than to confront it and throw it overboard, and this is what led to the most horrific storm of his life.

THE PHOENICIAN'S FOLLY

Earlier I posed the questions regarding the Phoenician mariners: So why did they do it? Why would they take this man who was running from God and let him onto their ship? Who would do something so foolhardy? It is true that I commented that we cannot be certain; however, when we couple their story with an understanding of human nature, we can draw some telling conclusions. Jesus once told the Pharisees and Sadducees that they knew how to interpret the appearance of the sky and its correlation to the weather, but that they did not know how to interpret the signs of the times (Matthew 16: 2–4). This is typical of these seamen as well. They understood the intricacies of their vessel and the complexities of ocean sailing, but they did not understand or comprehend the spiritual aspect of what Jonah had done to them, not until it was nearly too late. Their folly? They valued the fare Jonah paid them more than they believed the storm their superstition was predicting. We, too, fall into this same category. Possessing a vast understanding of computer code and complex mathematics, we can design and build skyscrapers that would make the men of old drool, but we still cannot interpret the signs of storms approaching our own lives. We have a blockage when it comes to discerning what is taking place around us. Even when we do hear the voice of God calling, we oftentimes ignore it and proceed with our own better judgment.

Like the Phoenician seamen, it is easier for us to take the promising chance that disobedience offers rather than to obey God. After all, we rationalize, we can always ask for forgiveness later (and still enjoy the benefits of our sin). Though the Bible says that His yoke and burden are easy and light, they are still, after all, encumbrances. Placing greater value on the fare that disobedience pays us, we ignore common sense and let rebellion aboard, and then help it to get comfortable below deck. High priced rebellion has a way of bending our ear and sweet-talking its way right onto our ship. These ancient seamen, with their wallets bulging from an unexpected donation, could now confidently advertise one more amenity to anyone passing by their ship, secret accommodations without prejudice or malice. Initially it may appear easier to do this than to obey, but this is a lie we should not believe. Sometimes it is easier to throw our possessions overboard if the need arises than it is to deny boarding privileges to the questionable and malfeasant. Our rationality, like the seamen's, is that we did nothing wrong. We were engaged in an honorable profession trying to make a decent living. Jonah is to blame for his disobedience, not us. Moreover, with these claims of inculpability, we masterfully turn a blind eye and attempt to distance ourselves from the violation. The truth is that the Phoenician sailors should have rejected Jonah's request no matter how much he paid them to acquiesce. And, although a cunning example of disobedience, we too must reject Jonah and his lawless request and learn the lesson these sailors nearly paid for with their lives. God will not hold us any less accountable for what we allow to reside on board our ship than He did the Phoenician sailors. It is imperative that we choose wisely and keep a critical eye upon all requesting passage aboard our vessel. The stakes are higher than we might dare to imagine, and our very lives and eternal home are on the line. Foolishness is not becoming for the people of God, so we should act more appropriately when the demands of the wayward begin to beckon us away from the truth of God's word.

Decks Awash

"Awash—Condition whereby the seas are flowing over the surface of an object; as in the decks."[131]

Jonah 1:4,5

But the Lord sent out a great wind upon the sea, and there was a violent tempest on the sea so that the ship was about to be broken. Then the mariners were afraid, and each man cried to his god; and they cast the goods that were in the ship into the sea to lighten it for them. But Jonah had gone down into the inner part of the ship and had lain down and was fast asleep. (AMP)

The Mariners, the Storm and Jonah's Weary Slumber
The Mariners

These men, these mariners, these Phoenicians were some of the greatest seafaring people of all time. As professional seafarers, they took pride in their work. Though life at sea was their glory and though it brought them great wealth, it was not without its pitfalls; storms, chiefly, were their nemesis. As men who made their living from the sea, they were cut from a different cloth than most. They lived by the rules of the ocean and operated within the envelope of the tides, all with a single-minded purpose that eluded outsiders. When the weather permitted, they were constrained to plow their furrows deep into the swirling blue fields, somehow hoping to ride on its froth-tipped wings to distant lands of treasure. With no guaranteed allotment of good weather, they would often travel during inclement conditions that would make flatlanders shudder in fear. This then, by necessity, caused most of these men to be rough, tough and determined. If these sailors did not sail, then they did not eat. So no matter what the risk, these men were going to ply the waters and broker their deals and deliver the goods.

By necessity, these ancient mariners were often out at sea for months (and possibly years) at a time, forced to live apart from family, friends and homeland. This separation from their roots and any meaningful relationships they may have sustained would have caused most of them to become emotionally closed. What emotions they would allow to surface while on board a ship with a group of roughnecks were probably not pretty. When their captain gave an order, they had to obey and pull their weight immediately and without questioning—for inaction could bring death or dismemberment. Anything less could spell disaster. If one was found to be a burden or a nuisance, then that sailor may have had to endure severe punishments designed to deter him from such future behaviors.

Second in concern only to storms were pirates. With an abundance of looters traversing the seas and hiding out in hidden coves ready to ambush unwary merchants, the wiser mariners always posted a man on the lookout. When we consider these ancient mariners, these qualities would define them. To endure the conditions by which they lived most would have adopted similar behaviors and attitudes, ones designed to keep them alive in the midst of turmoil and struggle and storms and attack. Realizing these traits, we can now better understand their decision to allow Jonah on the boat–but that decision was still wrong.

THE STORM

Similar in nature to a hurricane or typhoon, this storm was no normal meteorological event. High winds combined with a churning sea to bring about unbearable conditions on the ship, conditions that reduced hard seamen of great experience to whimpering children in fear for their lives. This storm scared the men so much that they perceived that it was more judgment than storm. It was wicked weather driven by an unseen force. Swirling gusts and heaving seas attacked the ship on every side, even from underneath. As the wind assaulted its gear, the rain blinded the sailors with piercing intensity. Enormous waves bombarded everything on deck, pummeling the planks toward the ocean floor. In the brief lull between crashing waves, unseen swells from the deep launched the vessel high upon its sickening summits as all of hell erupted from beneath. (For a map showing the intended voyage route and the subsequent encounter with the storm, refer to ***Map 6: Jonah & the Phoenician Sailors' Voyage***)

A storm for the ages was sent by God, intent upon returning His prophet to order. Jonah's willful act of treachery had invited this storm of life to attack. This horrific cataclysm had a purpose for its existence, a divine purpose, and that was to track down the man of God and deservedly consume him; the storm's intent was to devour him and any foolish enough to partner with him. It is one thing when we find ourselves the victim of an unexpected storm, but it is altogether a different story when we find ourselves being doggedly pursued by a possessed tempest that we have invited upon ourselves. Here was Jonah's predicament. God had granted this storm a mind of its own and a conscience that demanded retribution. Jonah could run from the presence of God, but he could not hide from the maelstrom his waywardness had created—no matter how hard he wished or tried. An unnatural event created by a compromising prophet, this storm was fury at its finest. Neither Jonah nor the mariners had ever stared into the bosom of such a beast.

JONAH'S WEARY SLUMBER

The prophet ran but could not escape. Jonah paid the fare but did not pay enough to escape. He hid himself but was not concealed. God's man slumbered but could not find rest.

How similar these are to our own displays of insubordination. A sleeping, rebellious prophet had fallen from a place of prominence, speaking to kings as the oracle of God, to a bed of sticks and debris, silenced by his folly and asleep on the dunnage (any loose wood, sticks or other material placed on the bottom of the hold and above the ballast upon which cargo was stowed).[132] While unspiritual, ungodly men cried out to their gods in terrified assaults, Jonah remained nearly unconscious in the bowels of the ship.

What a different picture Jonah is from that we saw earlier with Jesus asleep on a cushion in the stern of a boat. The differences are stark. Jesus slept out of peaceful obedience while Jonah slept out of haughty noncompliance. Christ epitomizes our example and His prophet Jonah defines the discordant. Despite all that would happen in the rest of the book, Jonah had already failed the basic test. The request from God had not been a difficult one. He had simply been asked to tell the Ninevites that their destruction was coming. Yet for all of his training and learning and history with God, and despite a promising prophetic ministry, he balked at following the elementary guidance of the One who knew far better than he did. Though Jonah's preaching would spare a nation, his personal life and ministry fell down around his ears in a heap of burning debris, and all he could do was sleep. Jonah played the game and lost. Instead of searching the deep recesses of his life for unhealthy attitudes, he slept with an indifferent heart of stone while a storm raged around his hired accomplices. With hearts devoid of remorse, how often are these actions descriptive of our own? Rather than taking the effort to root out our own sin, we bury it below the deck of our ship and let it fall into a deep slumber. The scary truth is that we allow this to take place more often than it should. So now tired of it all and uninterested in going back or in anything but escape, we sleep, as Jonah, while the rest we seek yet flitters away.

A HOLD FULL OF CARGO

With an impending sense of doom, the Phoenician mariners did what they deemed best when the storm refused to release its grip upon them; they threw out the entirety of the cargo of the ship. In their minds, this was the only way to survive against the storm. By lightening the load, they reasoned, they might just become buoyant enough to stay above the sea and not end up beneath it (this type of thinking and actions had no doubt saved them before). Any extra weight would drag them deep into the violent upheavals and would lessen their chances of survival. Jettisoning everything completely unnecessary to survival was the prudent course of action, and that included a cargo potentially worth a great deal of money. This cargo, though, was not anything that most would be prepared to let go of. Valuable treasures lined the hold of their ship; exotic riches that needed their brokerage and that would bring them wealth. Once we see what may have comprised this cargo, we will begin to understand the decisions these mariners made and the importance of their actions. If we can learn the lessons that these men did, then we may be able to avoid repeating their costly mistakes.

Though Israel did not dominate maritime trade, she certainly played an important role in its development and continuance. This fact lends credence to Israel's importance (along with the surrounding Canaanite territory) as a major stop along the ancient maritime trading routes. A ship bound for Tarshish that was stopping over in Joppa suggests that they were taking on cargo to be sold or traded along their journey, and that this cargo was very valuable. So what may have been transported in this ship, and why would anyone throw it all overboard? Since the sailors had certainly taken a great deal of time and expended more than a little money in obtaining their cargo only to later abandon it in the sea, I feel that it is important that we know a few details as to the ship's contents. Knowing the potential value of what filled the ship's hold will serve as an indicator of just how desperate things became aboard the ship, for only within the midst of hopeless despair would anyone in their right mind abandon the cargo these men carried. It will also serve as a reminder to us that we need not relinquish our valuable posses-sions–if we will obey.

Even from the mid fourteenth century b.c., there was a thriving maritime industry all along the Syro-Canaanite coast. The ships involved in this industry were known for their rich cargoes that often included cedar, gold, silver, lapis, lazuli, turquoise, incense, fat, honey and copper. These ships not only engaged in interstate trade along the coast, but some texts also indicate that they were reaching far into the Aegean Sea and beyond. [133] Some ships bound for Tarshish regularly carried iron ore as well for processing in that city's famous refineries. Other commodi-ties regularly transported would have originated in Israel and shipped from Joppa. Among them were olive oil, wine, salt-fish from the Sea of Galilee and garum.[134] Any of these liquid items were generally transported in clay containers called amphora, which were large, distinctive looking clay jars with one handle on either side of a narrow neck. A typical amphora was about three feet tall and weighed approximately fifty pounds empty and one hundred pounds full. Some ancient ships were large enough to carry over 3000 of these below the main deck. The stevedore, the ancient equivalent of our modern day longshoreman (dock worker), was employed to load and unloaded these ships. The process could take several days, depending upon the cargo and quantity of amphora to be loaded (i.e. depending upon the size of the ship), because it was only possible for a stevedore to carry one amphora at a time.[135] [For more information on amphorae and stevedores see the description of them in *Paul and the Alex-andrian Ship, Avast Ye Burdened Vessel, The Cargo*].

From the Institute of Nautical Archaeology's shipwreck excavation between 1984 and 1994 at Uluburun, near Kas in southern Turkey, we get a first hand look at actual items that went down with an ancient ship. This ship appears to have sunk in the Mediterranean sometime during the Late Bronze Age (gen-erally accepted as starting from around 3000 b.c. and extending to around 1200 b.c., although it varies slightly from region to region), and its cargo may not have been all that different from what was carried aboard the ship Jonah traveled in.

The ship's cargo, perhaps a royal one, comprised mostly raw materials, but manufactured goods were also present. The main cargo was approximately ten tons of what appears to be primarily Cypriot copper . . . [and] also . . . a ton . . . [of] tin ingots . . . [There was] approximately one ton of terebinth resin carried in most of the nearly 150 Canaanite jars . . . [as well as] ingots of glass [in a variety of shapes and shades] . . . Also carried on board as raw material were logs of Egyptian ebony . . . ostrich eggshells (probably intended for use as containers); elephant tusks, and more than a dozen hippopotamus teeth; opercula from murex seashells (a possible ingredient for incense); and modified tortoise carapaces (almost certainly sound-boxes for stringed musical instruments).

The largest group of manufactured goods on the ship consists of Cypriot fine- and coarseware ceramics. Nine large storage jars contained Cypriot finewares, pomegranates, and possibly olive oil. Four faience drinking cups were crafted as the heads of rams and, in one case, a woman. Poorly preserved bronze and copper caldrons and bowls suggest these must have also been a component of the manufactured part of the cargo.

Canaanite jewelry included bracelets and gold pendants. Scrap gold and silver was also found in some quantity, with Egyptian objects of gold, electrum, silver, and stone among them, including a unique scarab bearing the cartouche of queen Nefertiti. Thousands of beads are of glass, agate, carnelian, quartz, faience, ostrich eggshell, and amber. Other artifacts included two duck-shaped ivory cosmetics containers, a trumpet carved from a hippopotamus incisor into the shape of a ram's horn, and more tin vessels and jewelry than had previously been found throughout the Bronze Age Mediterranean. Bronze tools comprise awls, drills, chisels, axes, adzes, and a saw. Also found were bronze spearheads, arrowheads, daggers, swords, and stone maceheads. Lead net and line sinkers, netting needles for repairing nets, fishhooks, a harpoon, and a bronze trident are evidence of fishing from the ship. There were two wooden writing boards (diptychs), each consisting of a pair of leaves joined with an ivory hinge, and slightly recessed to receive wax writing surfaces . . . A bronze female figurine [was also found], partly clad in gold, [and] is similar to those of Syro-Palestinian origin and may have served as the ship's protective deity.

While the majority of personal possessions and shipboard items, such as tools, anchors, and oil lamps, indicate that the ship and its crew were Canaanite or Cypriot, the presence of at least two Mycenaeans on board is revealed by a pair of lentoid seals, a pair of swords, a pair of pectorals with glass relief beads, spearheads, curved knives, razors, chisels, amber beads of Mycenaean types, and more than two dozen pieces of fine- and coarseware pottery. A bronze pin, spearheads, and a stone ceremonial scepter/mace head, with its closest parallel (but of bronze) found in Rumania, suggest connections between the ship, or at least with some of those on board, and lands to the north of mainland Greece.[136]

In regards to this same wreck, K.C. Smith adds, " . . . the vessel probably began its voyage in Syria, Palestine, or Cyprus, but by the time it sank, it had acquired artifacts from eleven different cultures. This rich and diverse cargo proves that widespread trade existed and that seafarers from the eastern Mediterranean played a major role in the network."[137]

Upon realizing the type and quantity of cargo potentially aboard this Phoenician vessel, we realize that throwing it all overboard, except in the most extreme of circumstances, would have been a preposterous notion and a difficult task to physically accomplish. A cursory reading of the book of Jonah does not reveal this, but we can imagine the time involved in hauling a hold full of this type of cargo up from below the deck and throwing it into the sea—especially in the middle of a hurricane—not to mention the seeming lunacy of even mentioning its ejection. Not only did they discard all of the cargo, but they also jettisoned every piece of furniture and equipment and tackle and personal belongings that were not permanently mounted to the ship. It is likely that completely emptying the ship took several days of non-stop work to accomplish—enough time for Jonah to wake up, although he apparently did not? The question that begs asking is, "How could Jonah sleep through this and for this long?" With sailors tripping over him in order to empty the hold of the ship, how could his slumber continue—and for that much time? Why would these men, who could clearly see Jonah sleeping near the cargo, not slap him awake long before they did?

There are conflicting popular teachings today that make this story more difficult for some to dissect, creating a confusion that only adds to our misunderstanding of God's will and purpose for our lives. One group claims that God does not want His children to have material goods because they capture our hearts and drag us away from the purity He requires. The other group claims that God wants all of His children to be rich enough so that they have no material needs left unmet, somehow confusing Christ's atonement for our sin with a get-rich-quick scheme. This story, however, clearly speaks out against both of these trendy doctrines. Our story is one of riches gone to ruin, a man and crew lost in a tragic, but familiar, byline. What was at stake was this: For Jonah, a ministry of obvious influence that certainly paid him well, and for the Phoenician sailors, a ship and hold full of valuable cargo—not to mention all of their souls. One further lesson in this story is not that God wants us to be rich or poor, but that we do not have to sacrifice our possessions for obedience. Jonah's obedience would likely have only increased his fame and caused his ministry to become Fortune 500 worthy. The seamen's rejection of Jonah's request would have allowed them to keep this costly cargo and to prosper while in Tarshish. God did not want either of them to lose. He desired that Jonah keep his reputation and ministry pure, and that the sailors not involve themselves in the affairs of a wayward prophet. For us, our lesson is that God is more interested in our obedience than

He is in our financial status. It was not about riches, money, power or wealth for either Jonah or the Phoenician crew. None of these had anything to do with the crux of the story, because it all boiled down to obedience (even though the Phoenicians served idol gods). Yes, even the ungodly have to obey God.

Nowhere does God indicate that the crew must discard their valuable cargo or any of the equipment, containers or tackle and cast it into the deep. They do this of their own volition. The fact that the crew lost their possessions and cargo had nothing to do with God and everything to do with their choice to accept Jonah's companionship. Another point worth mentioning here that goes against the grain of trendy modern teachings is that neither God nor the Devil stole their belongings. Some teach that both God and Satan prowl around and continually steal from us, but this is not true. If all of our possessions are locked up inside our ship, and God has put His hedge of protection about us and we are obedient, then how can our stuff become stolen? These seamen willingly gave up the cargo and furnishings without so much as consulting God or his man on board the ship. I know that there will be those who jump up and down at these statements and shout, "But what about Job? Satan took all of his possessions." And to those I would answer, "Yes, but let us remember how incredibly rare an instance like Job's really is. Once we can say that we are the most righteous and upright person in all of the earth, then maybe we'll talk." Little is taken from us that we do not voluntarily give up either by poor choices or by disobedience. It is time that we stood up and took responsibility for our own actions, for or against God. We should not blame others for what we have willingly thrown away from the holds of our ships. Someone reading this might say, "Then does that mean that God wants us rich or poor?" The answer is neither. God wants us to be obedient to the path that He has chosen for us. Some are destined for riches and glory in this life and will be tremendously wealthy and influential. These have been given gifts of finance, business and leadership that most have not. Others in this life are destined to wade through the toil and reward of poverty, having neither the gifts to prosper nor the desire to become wealthy or influential. Following the path God has chosen for us, we must realize that we are not all destined for wealth or prestige or power; however, we are all destined for obedience—if we choose it.

God did not care about the cargo on board this ship. It was irrelevant to His requirements. He simply wanted Jonah to obey (and, obviously, for the men on the ship to serve Him instead of their dead and powerless gods). God did not mind if these mariners were wealthy, as long as they honored him with what they had. This is similar to Job's story. Job was very wealthy and that was all right with God. God does not mind us having a hold full of great riches and wealth (although most people will never be rich). What He does not want is for us to lose it or to throw it all away due to our disobedience or due to that of someone else. He urges us time and again that obedience is better than sacrifice. There are many who tout the glamour of sacrifice and of the widow with the two mites, and I am not discounting that; however, God would rather that we obey His commands than sacrifice our ship and that which it carries. We see nowhere here in this story where Jonah gives the mariners this good news; instead, he slumbers as they lose everything the ship contained. What a shame it is that Jonah was not a bigger man, and what a tragedy that these mariners lost all of this just because Jonah was too weak to be strong. It seems obvious, but if we allow ourselves to sleep while those around us are losing everything they own (due to our non-compliance), do we really believe that God will not require something of us due to this disobedience and sin?

On a final note, we will address one more issue commonly extricated from these proceedings. There is a common misconception that Jonah was spiritually asleep. This, however, cannot be true. Were Jonah to have been sleeping spiritually, he would not have had the capacity to hear God's voice or the ability to willingly disobey it. Clearly there was nothing wrong with his hearing but only with his obeying. Some other words that more accurately describe his deplorable condition are words such as ornery, disgusted, indifferent and apathetic. Jonah was not sleeping, he was ignoring. He knew exactly what God had commanded and precisely what he was doing. He was being willfully disobedient to a fault. His reasoning for going below the deck of the ship was probably so that he could avoid the crew, thus sidestepping any interaction where he would be challenged and required to explain again what he was doing and why. The plan was that he would stay out of their way and they would avoid him, and for both parties involved this was probably a good arrangement. After all, it was easier for Jonah to hide than to deal with the details of his sin. How easy have we made it for ourselves to hide away our disobedience? And how careless have we become when inspecting the passports of those wishing to hide something aboard our vessel?

JONAH'S LESSONS

There are many lessons that we can learn from examining Jonah below the deck of this ship, and there are some attitudes that we can uncover that are hiding in our own closets; however, in order for us to glean anything from this story, we must agree to bring it all out into the light. We must determine that we will root everything out from below the deck of our ship(s) so that we do not write a similar personal epitaph.

• Lesson: Govern the thought life. Jonah, having an unwillingness to govern his thoughts of superiority or deal with his bigotry and hatred, reasoned that his mindset was justified. This led him to the act of disobedience that in turn caused him to manifest a smug attitude. With his sin buried under the deck of the ship, Jonah appeared to be in control of the situation, when in reality his choices cost him any control he may have previously enjoyed over his life. The sense of calm that ensued is indicative of his lack of remorse for his actions. Growing increasingly calloused by his continual disobedience, he gained the ability to ignore what he had done in order to go below deck and sleep. Not once did he display any signs of repentance, tears, sorrow or remorse. Jonah had some serious unresolved (and possibly irresolvable) issues.

• Lesson: Beware of self-important doctrines. Jonah's self-centered attitude showed just where his priorities lie. His understanding of God told him that he and his people were most important, not the undeserving heathen. Here we see this prophet of God standing knee deep in his shame, disdaining both the Assyrians and the Phoenician seamen. He was a man whose profession it was to rightly know God's plans and judgments, and yet he easily rejected all God stood for based upon his errant doctrinal beliefs.

• Lesson: When off-track, somehow get back and do the last thing God said to do. Jonah's predicament could not get any worse while he was on the ship. Death was, in his mind, his last option and only hope, but it was not God's way out. What God needed him to do was the last thing He had commanded—to go to Nineveh. Without this nothing else would have ever worked out right for Jonah again (not that anything ever did again anyways).

• Lesson: Change and obey willingly, not grudgingly. Jonah eventually obeyed God, but only grudgingly. God was going to have Jonah deliver this message whether he liked it or not. Pushing God into an impossible corner was not going to get Jonah out of his duty. When he finally realized this and that God was not going to let him die, he did as God had commanded—although later he fell back into his habitual requests for death. There is no indication in the Bible that he ever reconsidered his position and changed. In fact, the feeling we get from God's last rebuke (Jonah 4:9–11) is that he would never change.

• Lesson: Geographic destiny has everything to do with personal destiny. Jonah had a geographic destiny that he did not understand. In order for him to fulfill the purpose of God for his life, he had to be in the right geographic region. If there was no Jonah in Nineveh, then they could not hear the message and repent, thereby thwarting God's plans. He had to get to the right location before God could move miraculously on either party's behalf.

• Lesson: Our disobedience affects those around us. The ramifications of Jonah's insurrection were not confined to his own life. His rebellion affected three different groups: himself, the Ninevites and the Phoenician sailors. First, it brought him to the edge of death's precipice, if only for a moment, and it surely cost him any future as a respected prophet of God. Second, it nearly cost the Ninevites immediate destruction. Though they would eventually revert to their prior ways, their repentance staved off their imminent destruction for at least a generation. Third, Jonah's rebellion cost the Phoenician seamen not only their gear and possessions but also an extremely valuable cargo and their reputations. No longer would they be remembered for never losing a shipment. Strapped with the impossible financial burden of coming good for all that had been lost may have even ended some of their careers.

More than anything else, we must not allow ourselves to be deceived into thinking that we can hide, bury, or otherwise get away with our disobedience. Not only must we guard against the act of disobedience itself, but we must also remain vigilant as we anticipate its predecessors. In these New Testament times, we often believe that, because God's judgment is not as swift as in the Old Testament, we can get away with more. This deception works wonders upon our psyche as we persuade ourselves into thinking that lack of immediate judgment equals acceptance by God. Sin in the camp in the Old Testament was taken care of immediately by stoning the offenders to death, while sin in these New Testament times does not come in quite the same fashion. Erroneously, we often convince ourselves that because of this New Testament lapse between sin and judgment, sin can be freely indulged in as long as we repent of it later. Somehow, we do not believe that God's judgment is as swift or as severe. This road, should we travel down it very far, will lead us to utter destruction. It is paramount that we obey God and that we obey God immediately and in the fashion He prescribes. God is not more lenient and understanding, and our superior doctrines and prophetic utterances do not give us licensure to abdicate our responsibilities. This all comes down to one thing: we must not fail in our first and only duty, which is to obey.

RHUBARB

"Rhubarb—(slang) an argument or disagreement."[138]

Jonah 1:6–13

So the captain came and said to him, What do you mean, you sleeper? Arise, call upon your God! Perhaps your God will give a thought to us so that we shall not perish. And they each said to one another, Come, let us cast lots, that we may know on whose account this evil has come upon us. So they cast lots and the lot fell on Jonah. Then they said to him, Tell us, we pray you, on whose account has this evil come upon us? What is your occupation? Where did you come from? And what is your country and nationality? And he said to them, I am a Hebrew, and I [reverently] fear and worship the Lord, the God of heaven, Who made the sea and the dry land. Then the men were exceedingly afraid and said to him, What is this that you have done? For the men knew that he fled from being in the presence of the Lord [as His prophet and servant], because he had told them. Then they said to him, What shall we do to you, that the sea may subside and be calm for us? For the sea became more and more [violently] tempestuous. And [Jonah] said to them, Take me up and cast me into the sea; so shall the sea become calm for you, for I know that it is because of me that this great tempest has come upon you. Nevertheless, the men rowed hard to bring the ship to the land, but they could not, for the sea became more and more violent against them. (AMP)

The captain of this Phoenician trading vessel, this rough and tough man of the sea, showed remarkable bravery and courage by his actions. But why did the captain wait until after they had dispossessed the ship of its cargo before searching for Jonah? Why did he leave his post to find Jonah and not send one of his senior officers? Did any of them actually forget that Jonah was aboard? Although being solely responsible should any disaster befall this ship and its cargo, the captain abandoned his post in order to find Jonah. He was supposed to be at the helm of his ship during a crisis and not below deck. Yet, in an act that can only speak to the depth of his fear and anger, he leaves that post and goes into the hold of the ship to find this wayward man of God.

What courage it takes to probe beneath the surface of our ship, to seek out the disobedience, to question it and then to hold it responsible. Can we embody the bravery it takes to leave our post, that place of assignment where we are expected to be in order to confront the host of our new disaster? We should take our hats off to this captain. He showed more character in this single act than Jonah does in the entire story. Oh how God applauds us when we dare look into the darkness of ourselves to find what may be frightening, to discover what holds us back and to uncover what lies beneath—the sin that does so easily beset us. This man set a timeless example for us all. Let us dare to be like this captain and not send someone else looking for the sin that we ourselves should be hunting down. Not becoming complacent at our post, let us have the determination, drive and conviction to find the underlying cause of our severe weather and to dust off and discard the skeletons that hang neatly in our closet. Shining the light of His word upon the dark evil that lurks in the shadowlands of our hearts will solve our most inexplicable riddles. Who dares to be like this captain? Only the ones who survive.

CASTING LOTS

There are over eighty occurrences in the Old Testament where the casting of the lot(s) is spoken about, but in spite of such numerous usages, nearly nothing is known about the actual lots themselves in any of the particular stories. What we do know is that casting lots was an ancient way of making decisions or ascertaining the will of a god (in Israel's case, the God). "The main and obvious reason for casting lots was the impartiality of a decision. No one could argue that the decision was the result of politics, nepotism, favoritism, etc."[139] Procedurally, casting the lots went something like this: "The lot, probably a stone, die, or other object, was cast upon the ground, the manner of its fall determining the question in doubt; in others cases, lots were cast into a receptacle and drawn from it."[140] These lots were typically stones, die, pieces of wood or sticks, or even coins. Thus, the outcome determined the answer to a question posed. The casting of lots brought a random intention of choice that bound no man with the conspiracy of the outcome.

Clearly what took place between Jonah and the crew and captain of the ship during this time was nothing less than an argument over who was to blame for their present situation. Finger pointing is not a modern art form. It has existed for millennia. Angered by what had befallen them, the sailors were ready to grasp for anything that would clue them in as to what was going on; even throwing a bunch of sticks or rocks on the deck of the ship was considered acceptable as long as it brought results. Therefore, they gathered and decided that casting lots would reveal the culprit. Ensuing the abrupt arrival of the storm, heated discussions led to verbal attacks and arguments over who was to blame. Finally, after building to a fevered crescendo, the call came forth for the casting of lots. With an uncontrollable situation facing them and no knowledge of who was to blame, the sailors decided to step back and let the gods point the finger. Whether the outcome was purely by chance or, as some insist, a direct revelation of the will of the gods, on this particular occasion the lot fell and correctly indicated who the guilty party was–Jonah.

Once the crew knew that it was Jonah's fault, they must have questioned him relentlessly. I can just see these rough seamen pointing their fingers and shoving each other out of the way just to fling a few choice words at him. With anger in their eyes and contorted looks upon their faces, they must have screamed these questions at him. Who are you? Where are you from? Just what did you do to make this evil storm come upon us? Why did you think you could outrun your almighty God? Are you crazy? How painful it must have been for Jonah to be singled out by this process since the casting of lots, as part of this idolatrous religion, was typically the work of a sorcerer and was, as such, distinctly forbidden by Jewish law (Deuteronomy 18:10–12). But pain to him was only another burden that he had to bear in his long line of heavily guarded secrets. What parallels we can draw from this situation as many of our recently fallen have been uncovered, naked in their wantonness, by the worldly media's blinding scrutiny.

If we could freeze this moment in time, we would see that these mariners were scared and afraid, more than they had ever been before. No doubt angry and desperately needing any lucid input, they mercilessly interrogated Jonah to see if he could reveal an immediate plan of action that would save them or offer up any insight as to why this storm had befallen their ship and what the outcome might be. But Jonah, now ashamed and overwhelmed with guilt, just wanted this ordeal to end. He had had enough. To be affronted by heathen questioning his country, his god and his religion, to be identified by bastardly lots and to be accused so correctly by men who did not even serve his Jehovah was more than he could bear. His world was crashing down squarely upon his own shoulders and he had no one else to blame but himself. Jonah knew now that he had no hope of ever making it to Tarshish. God had wanted his obedience instead of his sacrifice, and Jonah wanted nothing to do with either anymore.

For us the lesson is clear. When we eventually realize

that our rebellion will not work for us, that God will have His way no matter what, then we must go back and do the last thing that He told us to do. Driven by a raging tempest farther down our road of defiance than we have ever been, we sense that we cannot make it back on our own. Without divine intervention, our assessment may be correct; we may never get back. Being merciful to a fault, God knows that many times we need help getting back to where we last touched the shore. However, first we must give up and stop disobeying. The first step towards obedience is to renounce disobedience. It is all right if we cannot initially begin to do the thing that God told us to as long as we are willing to stop running. At this point in Jonah's story, he was no more able to go to Nineveh than any of us are able to swallow up the sun, but what he could do was to stop running away. What was within Jonah's power was to face the awfulness of his actions and give up his charade. This is our part as well, and it is our first step of faith back toward God. When we finally surrender our way to His, then He can prepare that fish for us that will transport us back to shore. Getting back by our own efforts will not work. Rowing to shore or walking back on water is not in the plan this time. The only way we can make it back to shore is by God's chosen vessel of repossession. In Jonah's case, it was a fish. In our case, who knows?

VAIN REPETITIONS

Jesus taught us that when we pray, we should not " . . . heap up phrases (multiply words, repeating the same ones over and over) as the Gentiles do, for they think they will be heard for their much speaking" (Matthew 6:7b AMP). Unfortunately, this is rarely taught today, and vain repetitions have become the norm. To most of us, prayer services consist of the same thing; we speak the same words repeatedly to God (while occasionally altering our inflection) and expect Him to answer lickety-split. Vainly we believe that somehow the very quantity of our words will move heaven. And if not simply by the sheer quantity of our words, then certainly by the vociferousness with which we utter them. What a preposterous thought. Instead of this, we should carry on intelligent, thoughtful conversations with God. Conversations filled with long periods of silence on our part so that He can speak to us without having to yell over our din. When the storms of life rage on around us, we need answers that we do not possess, not blather hurled at the sky.

As we drop in on our seamen again, we find them wailing and screaming, crying out to their gods in hopes that they had an answer. It is possible that they recited some incantations or chanted a particular phrase repeatedly. What they expected was that their forceful and repeated requests would be answered, that their vain repetitions would prove fruitful. In this they were wrong. Surely they reacted just as they had time and again, carrying out all of the tasks that we would expect a crew to perform in a storm situation. This seasoned crew made a concerted effort to get through the storm in the ways they were accustomed to and according to the way they had been trained. But it was of no avail. When in a fight for their lives and livelihood, they tossed everything overboard in order to lighten the ship, cried out to their dead, deaf gods with vain repetitions, and then tried to row out of the gale. Inappropriately we act the same way. Instead of discernment, we seem to choose what is familiar, ingrained and repeatable. We chose the path that will make us look like superstars if it works. Before considering what the mind and will of God is, we resolutely set our faith towards our desired outcome and overflow our prayer closets with cocky recitations. We become convinced that we can faith our way out of our storms.

Since Jonah knew that the only way out of this storm was for him to finally obey (or to at least to stop disobeying), he offered the mariners the only prescription that would work. His words struck even more fear into their hearts than the storm had already. "Cast me to my death within the open arms of the abyss and this bitter ocean's writhing will cease." This is the solution he offered, but initially there were no takers. Even though Jonah told them what to do, they still did not quite believe what he was saying could be true. Instead, they started rowing. I can hear Jonah now yelling at them as they resolutely pulled upon their oars in unison, "But you're not listening to me. Get it through your thick heads; this is not going to work. Here, let go of that oar. I don't care how ridiculous it sounds. No, I will not stop insisting. Get up off that rowing bench and throw me overboard. It is the only way out of this storm." Stubbornly they refused to accept his invitation to murder and only at the end, after they tried everything in their own power, did they listen to the wayward prophet. They finally acknowledged what was sinking their ship. Is it that not just like us? Sometimes it is hard to break the habits of the past and to learn how to start a new pattern of reactions. But in order to survive the storms of life, it is necessary to throw our sin into the mouth of the storm.

In wrapping up this part of our story, I have one more line of thought. If Jonah knew that his absence from the ship would calm the waters, if he knew that the storm was his fault in the first place, and if he was this brave man of God who was asking to be thrown overboard to save the crew and the ship, then why did he not throw himself overboard? Why did he have to be thrown off by the crew? Jonah had a responsibility toward these men to show them a godly example. Better yet, he never should have met them in the first place, especially not like this. He should never have run at all. But here we find him in a situation God never intended for him to be in embodying an example of ungodliness that was most unflattering. Even when he knew the solution, he had not the guts to carry it out himself. How often do we find ourselves in similar predicaments? Yet even when we find ourselves in these predicaments, we still have a responsibility to display godliness. This is yet one more thing that we can learn from Jonah. When we are on a ship and our rebellion has caused a storm to threaten the entire company on board, let us have the courage to get off the ship ourselves. Let us not place the burden upon the shoulders of others. When we do disembark, let us do so quietly and without complication. There are too many people leaving ships today either by forceful eviction or in a huff and with great theatrics, but we should be more mature than that. Finding the wherewithal to finally confront our own waywardness, let us take full control and cast ourselves aloft into the stormy wind's fury. Let us pray that God, too, will be as merciful to us as He was to Jonah and rescue us in the midst of our despair.

6

Oscar: Overboard and Negatively Buoyant

"Oscar - the dummy used for man overboard drills."
"Overboard - over the side [of the ship]." [141]
"Negative Buoyancy - A condition attained when
the submarine [or any object] weighs
more then the water it displaces,
thus causing it to submerge [sink]." [142]

Jonah 1:14–17

Therefore they cried to the Lord, We beseech You, O Lord, we beseech You, let us not perish for this man's life, and lay not upon us innocent blood; for You, O Lord, have done as it pleased You. So they took up Jonah and cast him into the sea, and the sea ceased from its raging. Then the men [reverently and worshipfully] feared the Lord exceedingly, and they offered a sacrifice to the Lord and made vows. Now the Lord had prepared and appointed a great fish to swallow up Jonah. And Jonah was in the belly of the fish three days and three nights. (AMP)

At this moment, everything became clear as to what had to be done. Jonah and the crew finally knew that, although decisive in some instances, no amount of confession and prayer, dancing and singing or shouting and marching would be enough to get them out of this mess. They now realized that it was Jonah's disobedience that had put them into this precarious situation and that his removal from the ship was the only hope for survival. It did not matter how much they attempted to abate the storm with their own efforts; it was all in vain. When in similar situations we practice our own brand of self-reliance, thinking that our performances will turn the hand of God's wrath away from us. As valid as speaking to the storms of life is and as important as positive confession, scripture recitation, prayer vigils and prayer chains are, none of these is the answer when our disobedience is the cause of these barbaric aggressions. In these circumstances, not one of them will do even one bit of good. Although these seamen did all that was within their power to bring this ship about and successfully rest her keel upon some shore of safety, none of their efforts proved fruitful, nor would they ever. When disobedience induces life's hellish marauding, then obedience is our only salvation, not sacrifice (1 Samuel 15:22).

It is too often that we react as the Phoenician mariners, tossing the wrong items overboard when we should simply obey. We cast aside what we should never discard including family, friends, spouses, children, jobs, hobbies, talents, and all manner of innocent belongings instead of discerning that we are to throw Jonah overboard instead. Our first reactions are rash and impulsive and do not resemble God in the least. Faltering badly, we put an end to what we term seasonal relationships and abandon anything we perceive might drag us further down; we abandon everything, that is, except our rebellion. An appallingly large mountain could be built out of the much valuable cargo that we have foolishly discarded during the disasters of life, and all because we do not take the time and effort to discern our situations. How many times do we have to rebuild broken and shattered lives because we dared not say no? Who could count the number of times that we have lost everything else but our sin? Is it too often and too many times? Are we too late? Never. We can always choose to change.

Before we jump too heavily upon these sailors, though, let us remember how hard it must have been to throw Jonah over the side of that ship. This was murder in anyone's book, but it was the right and proper thing to do. (Hold it. I am not advocating murder here. I am simply trying to make the point of how difficult it is to discard sin.) Imagine what must have been going through their minds. "This is not the way we were raised. Baal won't be happy. We cannot simply throw a man to his death based upon his request. What are we going to tell our families when we get back home, if we make it back? How will we ever convince anyone to sail with us again?" And while we imagine that, let us consider what the crew members could have said but did not say to Jonah upon learning of his folly, silly statements of counterfeit faith that we often pronounce such as, "Hey, Jonah, that's all right. Don't worry about it. We'll help you through this. We know you feel bad, but stick with us while we row out of this so you can be on your way again. Just go back below deck and ride out the storm. We are trained to handle this. Why don't you kneel down, pray to your God and ask forgiveness, and when we get to Tarshish you can hop on board another ship and head back to Joppa. Then once your feet hit the shore, you can head off to Nineveh. As long as you know you were wrong, that's all that really matters. I'm sure that you can get this straightened out once we get to Tarshish. We'll be fine. God won't let us drown or allow our boat to capsize." No, this is not how their conversations went. Finding themselves in the middle of an uncontrollable situation, they realized that to act now was to live and that postponing the inevitable any longer meant death. What a revelation for us. There does come a point, as we can see in the example with Saul, when it is too late to obey God. A point of no return will arrive when we can no longer choose to do right. This is why it is critical to discern the will of God and to act now while there is still time to quell the raging tempest that is attacking us.

THE CREW'S LESSONS

There are many further lessons that we can learn by examining the Phoenician crew and their reactions to what was taking place aboard their ship. When we dissect their story, we will unearth some amazing truths that will bring us freedom both now and in the future. We must determine that we will practice all of their good choices and guard against falling prey to their inconsistencies. Though they erred greatly, they at least, in the end, chose God over their own dead religion.

• Lesson: Ignorance of the law is no excuse. Just because these Phoenician sailors served other gods did not mean that they were given amnesty from sin's penalties. Allowing Jonah to book a fare on their boat brought them into partnership with him in God's eyes. They would suffer the brunt of the storm as much as he would. His folly would become their demise. They could not expect to escape the storm by ignoring the prophet's waywardness, especially when the only other thing it gained them was money.

• Lesson: Compassion is never wrong, but often wasted. In spite of the fact that the crew was at theological, philosophical and social odds with Jonah, and despite the fact that Jonah had caused this precarious situation, which cost them their valuable cargo and possessions, the mariners displayed incredible compassion towards the man of God. Not only did they initially resist his advice and again try to make it out of the storm by the force of their will, but they also showed visible signs of anguish before they threw Jonah to his death. These mariners cared for this stranger's life even more than he did himself; their compassion for Jonah may have been wasted, but it was not in vain.

• Lesson: Repentance means change. As the storm ceased beating, the crew, visibly humbled before the hand of an almighty God, repented. After having experienced both sides of His power, they were quick to make a change of heart and vowed vows to God and to His service. This is in stark contrast to Jonah's stiffnecked response to the power of God and His gracious kindness. In short, they changed, but Jonah did not.

• Lesson: Discernment first, action second. The crew had discernment, but later than they should have. First, they tried to escape this bitter fomentation in their own power and experience. Only after this did not work did they try discernment. As is obvious, discernment would have been their better first choice. Though God wants us to have discernment sooner, having it later is better than not having it at all.

CLOSING THOUGHTS

As this chapter closes, we see a group of exhausted mariners who have witnessed what no other person in recorded history ever has. Still shaking, afraid and glancing at each other and to the sky, they were not sure that what had just transpired had actually taken place. This may well have been the forming of a secret fraternity—one that would never divulge the defining event of its inception. But whatever their thoughts and reactions were to this miraculous event, they quickly made vows to God. The implication is that they performed an act of verbally consecrating themselves to God, devoting their lives to His service. Further, the connotation is that they would abstain from any acts or indulgences deemed unpleasant and unacceptable in the eyes of God and were to be bound by that promise of purity. A brief study of the context and original language indicates that they implied a promised gift for sacrifice and not merely a course of action. In other words, they promised to specifically do something for God and did not merely agree to watch out next time. There is no indication that this was considered either a rash or short-lived commitment, but was a genuine change of heart and a promise in which they pledged themselves to Him and renounced their former powerless gods. This was repentance.[143] Oh, how we should follow suit and renounce our powerless gods, ideas, formulas, agendas and policies, and make vows to God that we can and will keep. How much Jonah needed this to be true in his own life, and how much more we need it in our own. The sickening truth is that Jonah did not. My final question is, will we?

TRUE COURSE

*"A course steered by the compass
that has been corrected for variation and deviation."*[144]

Jonah 2:1–10

Then Jonah prayed to the Lord his God from the fish's belly,
And said, I cried out of my distress to the Lord, and He heard
me; out of the belly of Sheol cried I, and You heard my voice.
For You cast me into the deep, into the heart of the seas, and the
floods surrounded me; all Your waves and your billows passed
over me. Then I said, I have been cast out of Your presence and
Your sight; yet I will look again toward Your holy temple. The
waters compassed me about, even to [the extinction of] life; the
abyss surrounded me, the seaweed was wrapped about my head.
I went down to the bottoms and the very roots of the mountains;
the earth with its bars closed behind me forever. Yet You have
brought up my life from the pit and corruption, O Lord my God.
When my soul fainted upon me [crushing me], I earnestly and
seriously remembered the Lord; and my prayer came to You, into
Your holy temple. Those who pay regard to false, useless, and
worthless idols forsake their own [Source of] mercy and loving-
kindness. But as for me, I will sacrifice to You with the voice of
thanksgiving; I will pay that which I have vowed. Salvation and
deliverance belong to the Lord! And the Lord spoke to the fish,
and it vomited out Jonah upon the dry land. (AMP)

A PATHETIC PRAYER OF REPENTANCE

Here we find Jonah in the belly of a fish (read it, it is not a whale), a place where he does not want to be, and crying out to God. How comforting it is to know that in our darkest hour, when we are as far removed from God as we think we could ever be, God will still hear our cries for help, for mercy, for rescue, and will help us though we do not deserve it. As Jonah begins to pray, we have the feeling that he is going to repent, but the further we read into the prayer, the clearer it becomes that he has not. This prayer, though a shining example of thanksgiving for being delivered from death by drowning, is simply and always will be just that, a prayer of thanksgiving. It should not be confused with repentance, not even for a minute. For fine examples of repentant prayers we can look to David or Job, but not to Jonah. Jonah's prayer smacks of the "I got caught and am in big trouble, now how can I get out of this" sickening kind of attitude that too many shamelessly display. His heart had not turned to God, a reasonable supposition that is further supported by his ranting in chapter four. Having been measured and found wanting, he now only wanted to be free of the consequences of his sin. I can hear Jonah now. "Thanks, God, for saving me from drowning. Man, what a horrible experience that would have been. If you will just get me back to land, I will go to Nineveh now and deliver that message. We can pretend that this never happened, OK?"

It is critical that we are honest with our God and ourselves when we have sinned. Honesty is what will turn us around, and repentance is what will carry us home. If Jonah could not be honest with himself in the stomach of this fish, then when would he ever be honest again? How much lying does it take to convince ourselves that we are right, even over God? This pathetic prayer shows us just how far Jonah had fled in his heart from God. Jonah, while alone on the earth and stuck in the belly of a fish, could not even be honest with himself or God and admit that he was wrong. He did not admit to his sin and properly repent. God forbid that we repeat this.

When we compare Jonah's prayer with Job's, we see revealing differences. During his storm, Job replied to his friends' counsel that even if God killed him that he would still trust Him and defend his ways to God's face. He was convinced that this course of action would prove to be his deliverance (Job 13:15). Although God soundly rebuked him for some of his attitudes, he still displayed far more heart than Jonah did. How different his attitude is to Jonah's, who accused God of casting him down into the deep and into the heart of the seas (Jonah 2:3). God did not cast him down into the deep any more than I threw the moon into its orbit, but Jonah's judgment was hopelessly clouded with his own self-importance and theological disturbances.

In contrast, Job pleads with God saying, "How many wrongs and sins have I committed? Show me my offense and my sin . . . For you write down the bitter things against me and make me inherit the sins of my youth" (Job 13:23, 26 NIV). Also in contrast to Jonah's prayer is when David cried, "Have mercy on me, O God, according to your unfailing love; according to your great compassion blot out my transgressions. Wash away all my iniquity and cleanse me from my sin. For I know my transgressions, and my sin is always before me" (Psalm 51:1–3 NIV). Job was pleading with God to show him his sin, and David was begging God to forgive the sin that he already knew he had committed. But Jonah, on the other hand, offered no such repentance. What little Jonah could muster was this less than impressive prayer that feebly offered to sacrifice to God with the voice of thanksgiving, and further promised a vow that he would keep; that vow presumably that he would go to the filthy heathen in Nineveh and share God's message (Jonah 2:9). Here we find Jonah making a vow he never needed to make had he simply obeyed in the first place. Having found himself caught, Jonah's only attempt at a repentant tone was when he stated, "Those who cling to worthless idols forfeit the grace that could be theirs [probably a slur on the Phoenician sailors who just threw his to his death or in reference to the Ninevites or both]. But I, with a song of thanksgiving, will sacrifice to you. What I have vowed I will make good. Salvation comes from the Lord" (Jonah

2:8, 9 NIV). This prayer is markedly pitiful in comparison to the two heart-wrenching, repentant prayers of Job and David.

We see how Job was distressed and wanted God to reveal his sin. David was repentant and pleaded for God to blot out the sins that he knew he committed against the Lord. Jonah was selfish and did not even ask for forgiveness but, instead, prevailed upon God's mercy and grace to help him survive another terrible nightmare. Even the three Hebrew children, when they faced their own storm, said that they would never serve Nebuchadnezzar's gods or worship the image of gold that he had set up even if God did not deliver them from the fiery furnace (Daniel 3:16–18). True servants of God are willing to obey Him even to the death, but Jonah did not really want to obey Him, even if it meant death. Grudgingly he finally agreed to make good on his vow and take his message to the Ninevites, even though he would later get angry with God again and request death over whatever else God had in mind. In seeking to understand just how far Jonah had let himself slide down into the valley of pride, I have compared his attitudes with those of the three Hebrew children in *Chart 3: Attitudes of Pride, Attitudes of Humility: Jonah vs. The Three Hebrew Children*. Comparing their reactions side-by-side reveals a startling betrayal on Jonah's part. It may be that we have never peered at Jonah (or ourselves) under such a harsh light, but if we want to survive and be called heroes of God, then we had better learn from what his life reveals.

In closing this chapter, we see the dire necessity for honesty in our dealings in life and with God. It has never been promised that we will never face a storm, as we certainly will, but we will face enough of them in life without creating more of our own. When we are caught and God pulls the carpet out from under our feet, we should first consider repentance–true, honest confession to God with a subsequent change of direction. This is the only thing that will save us eternally. Not practicing repentance at every turn is true evidence of the wisdom that we lack. To survive the turbulence of life, we would do well to become students of history and the Bible rather than another disaster story on The Weather Channel.

CHART 3: ATTITUDES OF PRIDE, ATTITUDES OF HUMILITY: JONAH VS. THE THREE HEBREW CHILDREN

Attitudes of Pride: Jonah	Attitudes of Humility: The Three Hebrew Children
He chose death over serving God and repenting of his sin.	They chose death over serving Nebuchadnezzar and his idols.
He chose to run from his fears and abandon righteousness.	They chose to face their fears and stand up for righteousness.
He would not stand up and begged God not to spare him.	They would not bow down even if God did not spare them.
He chose to run away from his beliefs.	They chose to stand beside their beliefs.
He entered his storm by disobedience.	They entered their storm by obedience.
Jonah later got angry with God again and renewed his request for death.	They rejoiced at their rescue from death and then testified to the glory of God.
His clothing smelled like half-digested fish and seaweed and stomach acid after his storm.	Their clothing didn't even smell like smoke after their storm.
His clothing looked bleached and vomit drenched after his storm.	Their clothing looked just like it did before they went into their storm.
His reward was to go back and do what he had tried to run away from in the first place; he will forever be remembered for his selfish disobedience.	Their reward was being promoted to new positions of responsibility; they will forever be remembered for their act of righteous courage.
He stood up and ran and lost God in the middle of his storm, instead meeting with guilt and self-pity.	They fell down bound and met God in the middle of their storm.
He had to be both thrown overboard by other men and carried back to obedience by a great fish, not even able to walk on his own back to where he had gotten off track.	They walked out of the storm under their own power and were carried to places of prominence by their own feet.
Those physically closest to him during his storm repented and served God because of the intensity of the storm.	Those physically closest to them during their storm fell down dead because of the intensity of the fire.
He got angry with God.	They worshipped and glorified God.

FIVE BY FIVE

"Five by Five—Loud and clear."[145]

Jonah 3:1–10

And the word of the Lord came to Jonah the second time, saying, Arise, go to Nineveh, that great city, and preach and cry out to it the preaching that I tell you. So Jonah arose and went to Nineveh according to the word of the Lord. Now Nineveh was an exceedingly great city of three days' journey, and he cried, Yet forty days and Nineveh shall be overthrown! So the people of Nineveh believed in God and proclaimed a fast and put on sackcloth [in penitent mourning], from the greatest of them even to the least of them. For word came to the king of Nineveh [of all that had happened to Jonah, and his terrifying message from God], and he arose from his throne and he laid his robe aside, covered himself with sackcloth, and sat in ashes. And he made proclamation and published through Nineveh, By the decree of the king and his nobles: Let neither man nor beast, herd nor flock, taste anything; let them not feed nor drink water. But let man and beast be covered with sackcloth and let them cry mightily to god. Yes, let every one turn from his evil way and from the violence that is in his hands. Who can tell, God may turn and revoke His sentence against us [when we have met His terms], and turn away from His fierce anger so that we perish not. And God saw their works, that they turned from their evil way; and God revoked His [sentence of] evil that He had said that He would do to them and He did not do it [for He was comforted and eased concerning them]. (AMP)

THE PREPARATIONS

Now that God has had to speak a second time to his prophet, Jonah, he finally agreed to go to Nineveh (as if he was going to refuse after the ordeal he had just been through). In the middle of the first sentence of verse three, there is a considerable span of time left out of the story. To better understand what transpired between Jonah arising to go to Nineveh and his actual arrival, let us consider the following remarks.

In ancient times, travel was nothing like it is today. Traveling in the Orient was an uncomfortable, dangerous affair that came only at great expense to the traveler. It was not something that was undertaken lightly or quickly, especially given the distance Jonah was traveling, and therefore it was undertaken only when absolutely necessary.[146] The modes of ground transportation, as we discussed earlier, were limited to two choices, on foot or on the back of an animal. When traveling a great distance it was most likely done " . . . on the backs of horses, mules, or donkeys, and when traveling in the desert, camels . . . [and] In order to avoid the intense heat, and to escape detection by robber tribes, traveling is [was] often done by night."[147] Considering the route that Jonah traveled in order to get to Nineveh from Israel, and due to the many changes in terrain, Jonah may well have had to change his beast of burden a couple of times in order to match the animal to the area he was traveling through (Jonah traveled through rugged mountains, blistering deserts, across rivers and through lush, flat farmlands along the Via Maris and other interconnecting trade routes during his journey from Israel to Nineveh). Before departing for Nineveh, Jonah would have had to:

• Arrange for transportation (rental or purchase) on a donkey, camel or horse.

• "Gather food reserves including bread, parched grain, dried olives, dried figs and dates."[148]

• Map out his journey and possibly hire a guide or a helper.

• Purchase additional clothing, sandals, etc. and/or pack what he was going to bring with him.

• Eat, bathe and sleep at least a few hours (since he had just spent three stomach bile drenched days inside a fish).

• Gather or borrow enough money to sustain him on his journey.

THE TRIP

Nineveh was not just around the corner from anywhere in Israel. From Gath-Hepher (our assumed starting point of this journey), Nineveh was approximately 900 km (560 miles) as the crow flies; however, this is not likely the route that Jonah would have taken (mainly because there were no roads directly across to Nineveh from Israel). In attempting to ascertain the length of this journey, let us consider that "In the E [East], distances were commonly considered in terms of hours and days. Thus a day's journey might be reckoned as 7–8 hours (perhaps 30–50 km), but it was a somewhat indefinite expression appropriate to a country where roads and other factors vary greatly."[149] Jonah's probable route would have been along the Via Maris through present day Syria, and then East to Nineveh (roughly following a trail through the heart of the Fertile Crescent), the total distance of that trip being close to 1200 km (750 miles). Given our previous discussion of distances typically traveled in a day, and taking into account a few days for preparation, inclement weather, Sabbath days, the occasional day for restocking and replenishing supplies, and the difficulty factor, it is likely that this trip took Jonah somewhere around fifty days or nearly two months. Our supposition assumes that he neither traveled every single day (according to the law in Exodus 16:29, Jonah was prohibited from traveling on the Sabbath) nor did he cover the same distance every day due to varying conditions.

Imagine what Jonah was thinking about during that time! Fifty days of aloneness with God after a rebellious, near-death adventure. Likely with no one else to talk to (and possibly the need to remain quiet for fear of robbers), the trip to Nineveh would have been a long trip of reflection and soul-searching; or at least it should have been. What is more likely than intimate reflection upon the wrong that he had done is that Jonah was stewing over God's insane request of Him and the bizarre way in which he felt God was treating him. It must certainly have been filled with many conversations with God that were not recorded–one-sided conversations from an angry bigot. And what would be worse than what he had already been through? Having to remember it all over again for fifty straight days of nothingness, with only his grudging obedience to keep him company.

THE MESSAGE

The message God gave Jonah to preach to the Ninevites is of some speculation. Having no transcript of it, we are left to surmise as to the complete contents of his discourse. What is obvious after comparing the fourth and sixth verses of this chapter is that we are missing several key points. As is recorded in verse three, the message appears rather abrupt and biased. To deliver a rebuke containing only the words "Yet forty days and Nineveh shall be overthrown" seems a little unfair. It is a warning yet details no specific charges. It contains summary judgment but gives no room for change. A two-part question would immediately come to mind to any who would hear it: Overthrown by whom and for what reason? However, when we read verse six, which indicates that Jonah's story was lengthier than that, we can ascertain that the complete version of this message had more to it than what we immediately read. Although it would be disturbing to hear that destruction was to come upon us in forty days, it would leave us in a bit of a quandary as to how to proceed and as to why it was going to happen. The word used in verse six to describe Jonah's diatribe indicates that his message was terrifying. We can reasonably assume that his version of God's manifesto may well have been quite similar to the one delivered by Zephaniah to these same people some 125 years later.

> *And [the Lord] will stretch out His hand against the north and destroy Assyria and will make Nineveh a desolation, dry as the desert. Herds shall lie down in the midst of [Nineveh], all the [wild] beasts of the nations and of every kind; both the pelican and the hedgehog shall lodge on the upper part of her [fallen] pillars; the voice [of the nesting bird] shall sing in the windows; desolation and drought shall be on the thresholds, for her cedar paneling will He lay bare. This is the joyous and exultant city that dwelt carelessly [feeling so secure], that said in her heart, I am and there is none beside me. What a desolation she has become, a lair for [wild] beasts! Everyone who passes by her shall hiss and wave his hand [indicating his gratification]. (Zephaniah 2:13–15 AMP)*

9

A Bimini Gourd and Broaching God

"Bimini - A weather protection covering,
usually mounted on a frame over a portion of the cockpit."
"Broach - To go over violently toward
[the wind] and lose steering."[150]

Jonah 4:1–11

But it displeased Jonah exceedingly and he was very angry. And he prayed to the Lord and said, I pray You, O Lord, is not this just what I said when I was still in my country? That is why I fled to Tarshish, for I knew that You are a gracious God and merciful, slow to anger and of great kindness, and [when sinners turn to You and meet Your conditions] You revoke the [sentence of] evil against them. Therefore now, O Lord, I beseech You, take my life from me, for it is better for me to die than to live. Then said the Lord, Do you do well to be angry? So Jonah went out of the city and sat to the east of the city, and he made a booth there for himself. He sat there under it in the shade till he might see what would become of the city. And the Lord God prepared a gourd and made it to come up over Jonah, that it might be a shade over his head, to deliver him from his evil situation. So Jonah was exceedingly glad [to have the protection] of the gourd. But God prepared a cutworm when the morning dawned the next day, and it smote the gourd so that it withered. And when the sun arose, God prepared a sultry east wind, and the sun beat upon the head of Jonah so that he fainted and wished in himself to die and said, It is better for me to die than to live. And God said to Jonah, Do you do well to be angry for the loss of the gourd? And he said, I do well to be angry, angry enough to die! Then said the Lord, You have had pity on the gourd, for which you have not labored nor made it grow, which came up in a night and perished in a night. And should I not spare Nineveh, that great city, in which there are more than 120,000 persons not [yet old enough to] know their right hand from their left, and also many cattle [not accountable for sin]? (AMP)

BROACHING GOD

The very first verse of this chapter gives the major theme of Jonah's book away: Jonah was angry with God. He was not just angry with God in some nondescript and unimportant way; Jonah was displeased and angry at God's character. What arrogance it takes to become angry with God! Anger: "This word is related to a rare Aramaic root meaning 'to cause fire to burn' . . . the meaning . . . emphasizes the 'kindling' of anger, like the kindling of a fire, or the heat of the anger [fire], once started."[151] What this means in modern day English is this: Anger is a deep-seated feeling of revengeful displeasure and resentment resulting from the perception of an injury or offense, or from breaching a standard of behavior (however ambiguous or personal that standard may be). This is then expressed in a rage-like burning of intense emotion that often results in inappropriate actions labeled by normal, moral people as being incongruous with rational behavior. That sums Jonah up perfectly. God forbid that it is our epitaph as well.

Sometimes we naively believe that anger has only raised its ugly head in the past few decades, that it is a late twentieth-century disease due to the prevalence of violence on television, and that it is preeminently predominant in the "X and Y" generations; however, we see in this chapter that anger has a far more ancient history than that. Jonah's anger is referred to many times in this one chapter, and should raise a warning flag to all of us that we should beware of getting angry with God. Anger against

God can never lead us to do any good. Jonah was angry because God's intentions did not meet with his expectations. Having a preconceived idea in his head, Jonah based his perception of the way God should act upon his upbringing and faulty theology. Compared with Jonah's ideas of retribution, God had a completely different picture of justice and mercy. When these two ideas clashed inside Jonah's heart, he got angry. This was not a simple misunderstanding of purpose or direction either, but it was an awful tirade filled with resentment, disillusionment, and possibly even hatred. There are many who would defend Jonah's right to get angry, believing that his expressions of resentment were justified. Many state that it is acceptable because God can handle it. Nevertheless, we mistakenly buy into a lie when we nurture such thoughts. One grain of truth in this statement is that God can handle it, but the problem is that we cannot. The Bible says that we should be angry and sin not. I say that, if possible, that we should not get angry at all because it is nearly impossible to do it without sinning.

Jonah laments to God concerning His repealing of the sentence He had pronounced against the Assyrians (Jonah 4:2) and complains that he knew that God would do this before he ever left Gath-Hepher. In fact, that is the reason why he ran away. He knew that God would show them mercy if they repented of their wickedness and turned from their ways. On the one hand, Jonah wished them all dead, but when that did not happen, he wished himself dead. A powerful truth is uttered by Jonah concerning God when he confesses that he knew God would show the Assyrians *too much* kindness. Imagine that. One wonders how Jonah could honestly be angry with God about this when he had so recently been the beneficiary of that very thing, too much kindness. If any of us had been God at the time, we would have let him drown. Lawfully, God could have and probably should have smote him for his disobedience, but He did not.

We act a lot like Jonah when the "lesser ones" around us sin. To us Americans, this truth no longer smiles at us with gums, but it now has teeth that tear and rip and shred—oozing blood and tears. Often we look at the different creeds and cultures around us that do not serve our God and we wish them dead, especially when they hurt us or those of our country. Secretly, millions of Americans wish God (or man) would obliterate the terrorists who cowardly murdered our compatriots. Openly we dispute their holy books (which implore barbarity in the name of religion) and thumb our noses at their less-than-enlightened view of life. By this I am not advocating that we embrace their pagan gods and worship their dead idols nor am I defending their venomous acts of terror. What I am saying is that we are so intolerant and full of hatred toward those unlike us, and we are so eager to punish any who fail to match our more dignified sensibilities, that we miss the fact that God sent His Son to die for everyone so that all might come to know Him. That means that everyone is equally deserving of His mercy and too much kindness–even those we have determined should not be privy to it.

The attitudes that Jonah displayed suddenly make more sense when we see just how sharply they strike home. Would any of us be willing to go to a terrorist training camp as God's mouthpiece and declare that if they repent, then God will forgive them and show them too much mercy? Or is this "too much mercy" something we would like to hoard for ourselves? What if God sent us to the pusillanimous marauders roaming our cities and streets and asked us to pray with them so that He could forgive their evil deeds and make them our spiritual siblings? For most of us, these questions are too painful and sickening to even think about. But from God's perspective, He wants their souls the same way He wanted the Assyrians; He would that none should perish. God first wants to show them mercy. He wants to be too kind to them and let them live if they repent, but like Jonah, we have a problem with this. Jonah could not fathom God's thinking and he never sought to understand His ways. What he did seek, however, was that he be understood. Like Jonah, this is where we get off base as well. A simple phrase that we would do well to remember would help solve many of life's problems: Seek to understand and not to be understood.[152]

A BIMINI GOURD

Here we find Jonah still angry and sitting in a homemade booth. A silly looking and rather large gourd plant provides a lovely shade for his head. After at least three months of dealing with this Nineveh situation, he has not changed one bit.[153] Jonah sat in his grounded tree house, waiting on the outskirts of the city, in order to see what would happen to these wicked heathens. He acted just as we do when we come upon a car wreck. Jonah seems to have been the first rubber-necker in recorded history! He was sitting close enough to the city to see their destruction, but not close enough to get hurt. There was some amount of morbid curiosity in him that would not allow him to leave–not yet, anyhow. In this we see that Jonah's heart was like solid rock and was growing harder every day. Was he praying that they would choose righteousness and live? No. He was anxiously awaiting the judgment that he declared would come so that he could witness firsthand the destruction of the heathen (or more importantly to him, the fulfillment of his own prophecy).

The latter part of this chapter reveals something that most of us would like to ignore because it does not fit within the confines of our doctrinal framework. God Himself prepared two devastatingly painful object lessons specifically for Jonah: a cutworm (Jonah 4:7) and a sultry east wind (Jonah 4:8). God wanted Jonah's attention, so He blessed him with shade and rest. Soon after this He removed Jonah's shade, leaving him exposed to the harsh elements around him. He wanted to make an example for Jonah that would bring him pain and discomfort, and possibly help turn him around. It is not that God was trying to hurt Jonah, per se, but He needed to get through to him in order to help change his mind about this display of heroic mercy. As we can clearly see, though, this effort was wasted on Jonah because he remained stiff-necked and again wished he were dead.

Due to modern teachings of continual blessings from a good and loving God, the church has been bullied into thinking that the Lord can neither do what we perceive to be evil nor send a storm upon us. This then has caused most of us to reject some of the more pertinent lessons God wishes to teach us. When we do not understand and can find no place for this truth in our human understanding, we flatly reject and ignore it. However, God often abuses our sensitivities in order to get us out of our comfort zone. The problem we have with God doing something to hurt us is with our perception of evil. Like some fanatic animal rights or environmental organizations, we blithely misunderstand, misinterpret and misrepresent many of the truths around us. God can do anything, sometimes even that which we might perceive as evil. Now does this mean that it is evil or that God is sadistic? No. But that may be our perception from where we stand. In order to gain God's understanding of our situation, we must accept His perspective. Without this change in our vantage point, we will never see correctly. This is because we see through the lens of life dimly and misunderstand most of the lessons He desires that we learn. Our shortsightedness clashes with His vision because He has eternity in mind when He moves. We have our temporal, weak circumstances in front of us and can see nothing beyond.

Finally, we see that, though Jonah is angry through this entire book, God uses this bigot and rescues a great city of over half a million people, plus their animals, buildings and all of their belongings.[154] With his message of destruction delivered, and much to Jonah's dismay, this city took God's warning to heart, repented of their ungodly ways, and was spared. And for this, what do the members of our cast get? God gets the glory for saving this people and turning back His hand of judgment. The people of Nineveh get a ticker tape parade for their repentance and an extra 150 years of glorious splendor as being the cat's meow of ancient cities. Jonah forever gets to be remembered in the most negative of ways.

10

JONAH'S BITTER END

"Bitter End–the end of a line or last link of chain."[155]

A SCHIZOPHRENIC NATION

Here we find ourselves at the end of a wild ride of fantastic proportions. Following our discovery of a mixed cast of characters inextricably bound by one simple call, we have together journeyed from the obscurity of Gath-Hepher to the trauma of the sea and all the way to the fertility of the Mesopotamian marshlands. Along the way, we have encountered infantile treachery, uncommon valor, grudging obedience, unexpected transformation and morbid curiosity. Jonah's story, however previously misdiagnosed, is replete with lessons for the student who will honestly unearth them. As we look back at this intriguing history, we must reflect one last time and ask, "What final lessons can Jonah teach us?" As it turns out, there are quite a few. After examining the political climate during Jonah's lifetime (estimated to be from 800 b.c. to 740 b.c.), we will extrude this amalgamation of events into six reasons why Jonah hated the Assyrian nation and refused to go willingly to Nineveh. Let us now return for one more revealing look at this schizophrenic nation. To get a full sense of the following section, the reader should combine the information listed below with that found in ***Chart 2: Rulers and Prophets***.

Israel, under the reign of Jehoash, was locked in a civil dispute with Judah, under the reign of Amaziah. Unwilling to unite as one nation of great influence, the people of God were fighting against one another in a clash for power and possessions. Jehoash arrived by invitation on the battlefield to measure up swords with Amaziah and soundly defeated him. As the victor, he confiscated the gold, silver and vessels found in the Lord's house and in the treasuries of the king's house, as well as taking many hostages (including King Amaziah). All of this was claimed as the spoils of war and was transported back to Samaria (II Kings 14:8–14). It is also written that Jehoash did evil in the sight of the Lord (II Kings 13:11). Assuredly this is not how God had intended for His children to act.

After the death of Jehoash, the throne was assumed by his son Jeroboam II who " . . . did evil in the sight of the Lord; he did not depart from all the sins of Jeroboam [I] son of Nebat, with which he made Israel to sin" (II Kings 14:24 AMP). Instead of ruling in righteousness, he chose to continue in the idolatry of the golden calves at Dan and Bethel. And though spiritually he was a failure, militarily he was a powerful force. He was able to restore the north and east borders of Israel, which Jonah had prophesied of (II Kings 14:25), to where they had been during the days of Solomon (I Kings 8:65). In fact, Jereboam II was so powerful that he became the leader of all the kings along the Mediterranean coast,[156] and " . . . Israel became the largest and most influential country along the eastern Mediterranean."[157]

Under his reign, the nation enjoyed a period of great prosperity as well, with the Israelites finally in control of this critical area of the ancient world. Evidence of this prosperity is found in Amos' prophecy to Israel when he speaks of the people's lavish lifestyle: they had both summer and winter houses as well as those made of ivory (Amos 3:15). In addition to that they owned beds and couches of ivory and had wine to drink and the finest of oils with which to pamper themselves (Amos 6:4–6). A sad truth, though, is that this lavish lifestyle did not come by honest means. By God's own accusation, the Israelites were cheating the poor in the marketplace (Amos 5:11; 8:4) and practicing hellish deceit by falsifying the scales (Amos 8:5). Multiplying their apostasy, they abhorred those who spoke uprightly (Amos 5:10), took bribes openly (Amos 5:12) and worshipped false gods (Amos 5:26). At the height of their rebellion they even built an altar in Bethel (the house of God) of a golden calf that they worshipped unashamedly (Amos 3:14; 7:10). Clearly their unhealthy spiritual choices became a national condition, a sickness from which they would never recover. Jonah, though a prophet of God, was no different from any of them.

Though Jonah may not have worshipped the golden calves at Dan or Bethel or built physical shrines to Baal, it is obvious that he had erected some massive spiritual altars inside his own heart. The fact is that Jonah was suffering from the same condition of sin as the entire nation of Israel. Like Israel's rulers, he saw no incompatibility with leaving some of his idolatrous altars set up and in active condition, so long as he remained outwardly committed to God. Jonah loved his ideology and doctrine so much that even under the wrath of God he was not willing to give them up. He would rather be dead than change his mind. In his mind, there was no reason to destroy his idolatrous altars. In fact, to him they were not idolatrous at all. Instead of honestly worshipping and loving God, he showered his own ideas and doctrine with intense devotion and adoration. Being pliable in the hands of God did not matter. What mattered most to Jonah was his own way of thinking.

As we learned earlier, the Israelites rarely controlled the key cities along the Via Maris, even though they had expanded their borders to extents they had not been in decades. Even though they may have controlled the small, unimportant town of Gath-Hepher, this did not make Jonah immune to the effects of international influence. Molded and shaped by hatred passed down from generation to generation by parents and people of influence, Jonah's heart and mind eventually grew to resemble those of the evil rulers of Israel. Having never known anything other than superiority and spite toward the heathen nations, he continued this cycle of turmoil, causing it to rage inside his heart. He may not have even realized these emotions until he grew older, and he probably did his best to hide them even then; but the resentment towards the idolaters, some intermixed within his own society, ran too deep into his soul for him to remove it. After all, he was a trained prophet, and to be one he had to be an idealist; to him the heathen, ideally, deserved destruction.

WHY JONAH REFUSED TO GO TO NINEVEH

Why did Jonah hate Nineveh so much? His reasons, which are many, all stem from two basic trains of thought: First, what Assyria was, and second, what Israel was not. The peoples of the ancient orient lived sheltered but not cloistered lives, and the exploits of the Assyrians did not escape anyone's view. Intentionally, the Assyrians had spread their fear of domination throughout the entire region. Their brutality in battle has been well established, and this was part of Jonah's problem. His deep emotional opposition to their salvation is understandable, yet unacceptable. An incompatibility existed between his ideas and God's theology due to several political-religious factors that he could not forgive. It is this that leads us to his reasonings. With these thoughts in mind, let us examine each reason in depth.

REASON # 1:

Military Prowess: From the time Israel fist entered the wilderness, they struggled militarily. In one instance they would be valiant, effortlessly defeating their enemies and putting thousands of them to death; however, at other times when plagued by sin in their ranks, they floundered in battle and were embarrassingly whipped. Rarely able to keep lives in order for more than a few months, they repeatedly ran up against brick walls in battle. Finally, when given the command to take the Promised Land, many of them determined that peace treaties were a better choice than murder. Told by God to utterly destroy their enemies, including women, children and animals, the Israelites instead chose a less aggressive and more "sensible" solution to inhabiting the land. Directly opposed to this we have the Assyrians, who were ferocious in battle and merciless to their enemies. Having rulers who were driven to conquer, they seemed unstoppable. With annual military incursions, they continued to push out their borders and conquer new lands. In fact, the Assyrians are known to have totally eradicated entire civilizations. They were convinced that their "god Ashur had laid upon them the task of unifying the world under his aegis."[158] It was because of this that Jonah could not bear inviting God's "too much kindness" attitude to visit an Assyrian nation who more completely followed their gods' mandate than his own country followed the one true God's command.

REASON # 2:

Mongrel Breed: Being the chosen nation of the one true God caused Israel to look condescendingly upon those who racially bastardized themselves. From H.W.F. Saggs we learn that

The Israelites felt a national consciousness based on the concept of common descent from one man, with separation from breeds excluded from their traditions, their nation, and the protection of their laws. But the Assyrians were free of this kind of racialism . . . The Israelites' beliefs were linked to the tribal background of Israel. But the people of Assyria . . . were not basically tribal . . . [and] . . . the Assyrians never thought of themselves as self-sufficient or exclusive . . . and did not, like the Israelites, see any ill consequences as likely to arise from the mixing with other peoples.[159]

Ethnic purity was paramount to the Israelites, but to the Assyrians it was an irrelevance.[160] To the more elite in Israel it was all about where a person came from, but " . . . the test in the first-millennium Assyrian empire was not the line a man came from but how he behaved to the greater community."[161] As we can see from reading the books of Kings and Chronicles, it obviously didn't matter to the kings of Israel and Judah how pure they kept their lineage, so long as they did what they saw fit to do. However pure, though, that the Israelites were supposed to keep their lineage, many compromises were made in the taking of wives from their enemies. For a prophet of God trained to uphold and declare the commandments of God, this purity was a hill to die on—let no man or nation stand who would dare defile it, especially when his own slept with its hypocrisy.

REASON # 3:

Religious Counterfeit: Most would not surmise, given their predilection for violent barbarity, that religion would have been a high standard for the Assyrians, but it was. Even though most Assyrian rulers were known for their polytheistic tendencies, there are still examples of those who favored a type of monotheism.[162] In fact, in ancient Assyria,

The most potent unifying force was religion. All the peoples of the ancient near east believed in a multitude of gods, though accepting that in certain areas or social contexts a particular god or group of gods had a unique position. Ashur was such a god, believed to hold supremacy in a particular land, which was therefore called "the land of Ashur"–hence the name Assyria. The claim was made that Ashur's sway extended over the civilized world, and that it was the function of the king to assert and maintain Ashur's sovereignty.[163]

When comparing the Assyrian political-religious hierarchy to that of Israel's, we find that they bore striking similarities. Among these similarities were the following: The king was considered to be Ashur's chosen representative on the earth (similar to Israel's king). Each king had a staff of high priests and a royal priesthood (similar to the Tribe of Levi) with whom he would consult, as well as royal astrologers trained to predict the future (similar to the role of Israel's prophets). Temples (similar to Solomon's) were built by the Assyrians in which sacred rituals were continually practiced (similar to the daily functions both in the Tabernacle and Solomon's temple) and in which royal singers and musicians (similar to the members of the Tribe of Judah) worked. The Assyrian's believed that there were harmful (evil) spirits that existed all around them (similar to satanic/demonic spirits depicted in the Bible), which caused serious illnesses or even death. They also believed in benevolent spirits (similar to the angels of God) and often appealed to these kindhearted spirits to protect them from the mayhem and havoc created by the evil spirits.[164]

Jonah could not understand how God could ask him to go to a people who represented the very antithesis of what Israel was built upon. This is surely to have turned Jonah's ideological stomach into an ocean of unsettling waves of nauseous bile; the fact that God had every intention of showing mercy to this mockery of His own people was beyond Jonah's comprehension.

REASON # 4:

Political Stability: With the long line of political turmoil, treachery, coups and royal murders well substantiated, there is little doubt that Israel was politically unstable at best. Assyria, however, stands in stark contrast to that by displaying amazing royal continuity. H.W.F. Saggs informs us that

Politically, Assyria was remarkably stable over many centuries. There were occasional intrigues in the top level of society to replace the current king by someone from another branch of the royal family, but there are no known instances of popular rebellion or attempts to change social institutions. The political stability was both a reflection of, and a consequence of, the stability and unfragmented nature of Assyrian society.[165]

On the one hand, we have the Assyrians, ruled by a succession of kings from the royal family, encountering relatively little political upheaval for centuries, and remaining united in their efforts to conquer the world and revel in their own glory. While on the other hand we have the Israelites, who were in perpetual political upheaval; so much upheaval, in fact, that the tribes had split up into two nations because they simply could not get along. Jonah's ideological nature knew what this political instability meant to his nation. Somehow he knew that a house divided against itself could not stand (Matthew 12:25). What angered him the most, though, was the dichotomy between Israel's lack of political strength and this abhorrent, ungodly nation's ability to model that strength so perfectly.

REASON # 5:

Territorial Incompetence: God had given Israel the Promised Land, and they were content to occupy that corner of the world. However content they were to possess the land, they were incompetent in their control of it. In fact, there were large portions of the land and countless cities within Israel's borders that they exercised no control over. Not only that, some of the most important trade routes in the known world ran through the heart of Israel, giving them tremendous influence over a vast number of international travelers, and yet they could not testify to the world of the one true God. So after having made treaties with the inhabitants and alliances with their foreign neighbors, Israel's kings were now forced to pay tribute to surrounding nations or risk military reprisals. Israel was in control of the land, but they had not the integrity or moral uprightness with which to exercise the proper influence over the nations. The Assyrians, however, displayed an insatiable desire to expand their borders and to exercise their demoralizing influence over any who dared stand in their way. To perfect their assimilation of other nations and cultures and to display their complete dominance over them, they would deport the inhabitants of foreign lands and scatter them throughout Assyria's interior. For Jonah this would have been nearly impossible to ignore. Being sent to preach repentance to a nation that, again, so perfectly modeled what his people could not would have been unbearable.

REASON # 6:

Captive Audience: According to Hosea, the nation of Israel's punishment for forsaking its God and playing the harlot was that the people were to be carried off into captivity to Assyria (Hosea 9:3; 10:6). Since Jonah and Hosea were contemporaries, it is not hard to imagine that Jonah knew of his prophecy of Israel's captivity; if nothing less, he knew of the despicable spiritual condition of his own people. Israel may well have been the laughingstock of the nations around them due to their duplicity. On the one hand they condemned the idolatrous nations who whored themselves to false gods, while on the other hand they practiced the same hypocrisy. To all of this Jonah was witness, and it enraged him. When God called to Jonah to deliver a message to Nineveh, he could neither accept nor understand, since God had already condemned Israel to captivity. Not only were they to be carried away captive into a strange land, but that land was to be Assyria! Yet here God was telling Jonah to go prophesy to them so that He could ultimately show them too much kindness. God desired to show that kindness and mercy to the very nation that would soon lay Israel waste and deport her best and brightest into the heart of a mongrel nation. This did not compute with Jonah. He could not agree, and therefore he refused to be a willing participant.

CLOSING THOUGHTS ON THE BOOK OF JONAH

The most basic thing that the book of Jonah teaches us is that we must adopt God's view of sin and disobedience and of deceit and rebellion. He utterly abhors them all. Sin does more than turn His stomach; it repulses His very essence. Jonah's storm helps us understand that we must throw our own sin and failings out of our ship before they drag it to the bottom of the sea. If we choose not to learn from his tragic example, then we will be damned to repeat the painful and unfortunate mistakes of Jonah's life. We will be destined to relive the horrors of our own ancestors that were caused by rebellion and disobedience. Surely, during the storms of life that we create, it is time for us to listen and to change.

We have examined Jonah and the Phoenician sailors, as well as the Assyrian and Israelite nations, and have drawn some amazing conclusions. Considering their many failures and minor triumphs, it is fair to ask ourselves, "So, how do we compare?" The answer is something that we may not appreciate. Some of us still believe that sin, disobedience, and the atrocities evil men revel in will go away if we ignore them long enough, but this is a lie that we are supposed to be too smart to believe. To believe that the sin in our own lives will take care of itself and disappear on its own is foolhardy, a deception that will ultimately cost us our soul. This pacifism toward sin is the largest and heaviest blanket of deceit that the enemy has ever thrown over our eyes. It would seem that we have traveled no further down this road than the members of our cast did. In comparison to them, we have no excuse for our shortsightedness and unabashed embracing of sin and evil. Foolishly, we convince ourselves that God will ignore it, but He cannot.

Our attitudes toward sin and evil, disobedience and deceit have to change. The automated response of our soul has to become proactive and borderline militant. We must vigilantly seek out sin and disobedience, root it out from below the deck of our ships, and then drive it from our lives; however, we must also avoid calamitous witch-hunts that do not heal. Hunting down our dark skeletons is our mandate, but at the same time, we cannot turn simple mistakes into burgeoning conspiracies. Even as God demanded that all of Israel's enemies be utterly destroyed, we too must leave none of our sin alive. This type of war on sin, though, is not for the weak and faint of heart. It won't get rave reviews in the local newspapers, but this trait defines the unforgettable greats of Christian history. Simply put, this attitude of hating sin has to be part of our core existence.

Section Four

PAUL AND THE ALEXANDRIAN SHIP

1

THE STORY

"Since Paul demanded an appeal that would enable him to appear before Caesar (Roman Emperor Nero, who was adopted by Claudius as his heir), it was decided by King Herod Agrippa II and Governor Porcius Festus (the newly appointed procurator of Judea) that Paul, along with some other prisoners, was to set sail at once for Rome, Italy (where Caesar's throne and the seat of government were located). The prisoners were put under the charge of an officer of the Imperial regiment, the centurion Julius, who was a captain of the Augustan Guard (and part of the emperor's own regiment). Paul had claimed his rights as a Roman citizen for this appeal in order to avoid the assassination attempt that he knew the Jews would make on his life if he were to travel to Jerusalem to appear before the Sanhedrin. Now we, Luke and Aristarchus, voluntarily accompanied Paul on his journey (as his slaves or perhaps his physician and assistant) in order to be of help and a comfort to him.

We boarded a small coasting vessel in Caesarea of Palestine that was traveling to Adramyttium (an important seaport city on the Aegean Sea located in northwestern Asia Minor) along the difficult Palestinian coastal route and set sail. Though normally a person bound for Rome would travel to Alexandria, Egypt and board one of the grain ships there, the lateness of the season precluded us from taking that course of action as mariners were not typically heading to Rome during the late fall from Alexandria. The severe nature of the Mediterranean Sea winters prevented all but the most driven to even attempt the trip. The following day we docked at Sidon (about 130 kilometers North of Caesarea), where Julius allowed Paul to be cared for by his friends. Julius seemed to take a personal interest in Paul's welfare and, thus, gave him certain leeway and privileges that were not necessarily common for prisoners of the state. Paul's friends were able to manifest their affection and brotherly love to him as they refreshed him (and possibly gave him minor medical treatment due to his already long imprisonment). With much thoughtful and sympathetic regard that demonstrated their esteem for this man of God, they tenderly cared for his needs.

After pulling up anchor and putting out to sea from Sidon, we passed around the northeastern end of Cyprus for protection from the northwestern winds that were contrary to us. Sailing the entire length of sea, which lies off the coasts of Cilicia and Pamphylia, we finally and after much struggle reached Myra in Lycia. There the centurion found an Alexandrian grain ship (one racing against the odds in order to get a last trip in to Rome before the end of the normal shipping season) bound for Italy, and he transferred us to it. For several days we made slow progress, literally sailing slowly and tacking before the wind as we had been since leaving Sidon—tacking is a zigzag course that is used when sailing against the wind. After much difficulty and toil (due to the constant activity on deck of shifting the rigging and swinging the sails from side to side on the masts), we arrived off the coast of Asia Minor near the city of Cnidus. But now that the land that had been sheltering us from the wind was past us, and the strong northwest wind did not permit us to proceed any farther west along the straight and normal route, we turned and sailed southwest towards, and finally under, the lee (shelter) of Crete off Salmone (located on the northeastern tip of the island).

During these many days, our forward progress was not without much difficulty. The only way we could make any headway was by hugging the coast and keeping the ship in as close to the shore as we could without running her aground. Finally, we arrived at a place called Fair Havens (Snug Harbors), a town located about halfway along the southern Cretan coast, near which is located the town of Lasea. Our major problem, however, was that the season was well advanced (it was nearly winter). A lot of time had already been lost due to the buffeting of the wind and navigating these now frigid and dangerous waters of the Mediterranean. The time for the Fast, the Day of Atonement, which occurred on October 5 of this particular year—a.d. 59–had already gone by.

Paul, their prisoner, now stepped to the forefront and offered his unsolicited advice in a manner most remarkable and unheard of for a man in chains. He had clearly won the respect of the centurion, and now used that favor as the leverage with which to launch into his warning. Paul offered his strong opinion and urged them saying, "Sirs, I have observed our situation more or less as a spectator since we left Myra. I have concluded that, due to the time of year and the difficulties that we have encountered thus far and after careful observation and much prior experience with shipwrecks, this voyage will not end well if we continue on from here. I can say to you with a great degree of certainty that if we continue on, our journey will be escorted by disaster and encumbered with much heavy loss; loss not only limited to that of the cargo, financial gain and profit, but also a complete loss of the ship and most likely of all of our lives as well." However, even though the centurion ranked above all others on the ship and had the authority to halt their progress, he did not do so. Instead, he paid greater attention to and allowed himself to be persuaded by the experience of the pilot (steersman) and the self-motivated arguments of the owner of the ship rather than adhering to the truth and reality of what Paul said. It was obvious that Paul's arguments did not carry enough weight—yet. What may be more accurate is that the centurion simply trusted the opinions of salty seamen over the words of a religious zealot. He feared the criticism he would face in Rome if he acted timidly, thereby delaying the arrival of this critical shipment of wheat to her citizens. Another probability is that the owner of the ship was grievously conscious of *the economic impact of missing his delivery to Rome. He was fully aware that if he, his ship and crew were to winter over there, then the expenses and overhead charges would become crippling, and that his cargo of wheat would likely be no good to sell by the spring. The potential for a large financial burden was something he did not wish to bear, so, instead, he took the calculated risk of going in exchange for the promise of another hefty payday back in Rome. The other problem with staying anchored in Fair Havens for the winter was the harbor's location and lack of protection. It was too open to provide favorable shelter from the winter winds. In reality, it was more of an inconvenient, but not impossible, place to winter in. The difficulties of adapting to this problem would soon seem more palatable than dealing with the impending doom and total loss of the ship and cargo.*

The majority, therefore, after having convened a council of the officers and passengers of the ship, favored attempting the captain's plan of putting to sea again from Fair Havens. They naively believed that somehow, against the already impossible wind, we would reach Phoenice (Phoenix), a harbor of Crete facing southeast and northeast, and spend the winter there. On the surface, this seemed like the smartest idea given the fact that Phoenice was the only town on the southern Cretan coast that had a harbor that was properly fit and situated to winter in. It was also probably the only town that had the equipment and facilities to dismast a ship of this size and store them for the winter. However, we would soon learn that it was not worth the risk that we took in trying to reach her harbor. Though some may have had reservations unbeknownst to us as to the soundness of their decision to leave this port, a gentle southerly breeze began to blow softly and all but convinced the majority of their brave decision making (after all, the intended port was a scant forty miles up the coast—a half-a-day's journey under normal conditions). This favorable wind so convinced them that they were right that we immediately weighed anchor and left Fair Havens without even securing the small dinghy on deck. Again, we crept along hugging the coast.

It was not long after we first imbibed the redolent breeze that a violent northeaster with gale force winds (of the character of a typhoon or hurricane) unleashed its torrent upon us. The squall seemed to detonate in the mountainous highland slopes just west of Fair Havens at the same instant that it rushed us like a charging bull. Our ship was thus caught off-guard by the storm's blindsided charge and mercilessly crushed in its unflinching grip (not that there would have been anything we could have done to prepare for or avoid this tempest—except staying put in Fair Havens). We were unable to turn into the wind in order to maneuver or hold our ground. It was at that point that we gave up the fight with this monster and let the ship be driven by the beast's ferocity (since we had not had time to furl the mainsail and were catching more of the beast's icy breath in our sails than we cared to). This possessed wind nearly tore the sails free of the masts and rigging as it continually pummeled our ship toward the southwest.

We scudded across twenty-three miles of turbulent seas until we reached the small offshore island of Cauda, which we were able to run under the shelter of (under the southern coast). In a similar fashion to the way that Crete had protected us from the northwest winds for a while, so did Cauda protect us from this gale-force, northeast wind just long enough for us to wrestle our waterlogged dinghy aboard and secure it to the deck. The providence of being sheltered by Cauda from the violence of the storm also provided us with enough time to undergird and brace the ship with frapping cables (ropes). This was done in order to hold together the nearly shattered and straining timbers of the ship, which were barely resisting the stress of the violent sea and the leverage of the masts under full sail. (Frapping a ship is a process whereby cables, chains and/or ropes are passed under the hull of the ship, either from side-to-side or from front-to-back, and secured on the deck. The purpose of this is to hold together a badly damaged ship and to keep it from literally bursting at the seams and tearing apart.)

Not that there wasn't already enough to think about, the

crew also informed us of another deadly danger that could befall us–running aground on the sandbanks of Syrtis, the notorious graveyard of many ancient ships. They were so afraid that with the sails fully furled the ship would be driven into the quicksand of Syrtis Major (off the northern coast of Africa between Carthage and Cyrenaica), that they found a way in this impossible weather to lower the gear (slacken or reduce sail and then lowered the ropes). In doing this, we were able to slow our forward momentum considerably and to fix the ship into the wind while being driven along. With this accomplished, we were able to travel in a more westerly direction and avoid being run aground off the coast of Egypt.

However, it was also during this time that we were being so violently attacked by the wind in sudden and furious waves that we were nearly overcome. On the very next, day we began to lighten the ship by carrying the cargo up from the ship's holds and throwing it overboard. This continued almost non-stop until, by the third day, we had thrown with our own hands nearly everything overboard that was not bolted down, including all of the ship's dispensable tackling, gear and furniture and our personal belongings. All was discarded except for the precious shipment of grain. After many days of this tumultuous raging within the ever tightening grasp of this relentless storm, and without even being able to believe that the sun and stars were still overhead, we had all but given up any hope of making it through this ordeal alive. The storm methodically stripped our hope away day after day and layer-by-layer until we were impossibly doomed and in deep despair; with all hope of our being saved lost, we finally and grudgingly abandoned it.

It was during these many days when we were so distraught and had not eaten anything for a long time (due to seasickness and the inability to build a cooking fire) that Paul, their prisoner, again stepped forward with God's boldness and exhorted the entire company of people on board the ship. He admonished those who had not listened to him, saying, "Gentlemen, you should have listened to me and put more weight to my words of warning. When I told you in Fair Havens that we should not sail further on this winter, that we should stay the winter there, you should have listened. The economic impact of delaying this trip should not have swayed you, nor should the great need for this shipment in Rome have persuaded you to proceed against my advice. Though it may not have been the ideal harbor to winter in, it would have been a far easier and less costly moratorium than that into which you have led us. But, instead of heeding my advice, you listened to those driven by profit and ego and greed and convenience, and have now put us all into a situation fraught with disaster and harm and misery and loss. I now remind you of my unheeded earlier wisdom so that you will listen more attentively to me this time, and so that we may avoid even further loss. Even now, I beg you to believe me and to heed my words. Let us each reach inside and grasp that last shred of hopefulness and courage that we have left, and let ourselves experience a joyous change in our attitudes. We can all take heart and be joyous for, though the fate of this ship is sealed and the final resting place of its stalwart wooden members marked, not one of us is going to die because of or during this storm. I know this because only a few minutes ago, an angel of God, to Whom I wholly belong and Whom I completely serve and worship, stood by my side and substantiated my undying faith in God when he said 'Paul, stop losing your hope and do not be afraid of this storm any longer, for it is essential and mandatory (it has actually been ordained) for you to stand before Caesar and to bear witness in Rome of all that Christ has done. What that means is that you will make it through this storm as well. And be assured that because of this unbreakable appointment in Rome, God has graciously done you a favor (and presented you with a gift) by giving you the lives of all those who are sailing with you.' So keep up your courage and take heart, men, for I have not irreplaceably lost my faith (complete confidence) in God. His word is enough to keep my heart from faltering any longer. I know everything that happens next will be exactly as it was told to me; however, it is a necessity in this case that we, finally, are to be driven aground and wrecked and stranded on some island."

As midnight of the fourteenth night of our ordeal had come and we were being driven along the lower Mediterranean Sea (at the rate of about 70 kilometers per day), the sailors heard the sound of breakers and surf and grew uneasy. They suspected that our ship was quickly drawing upon some land and would be dashed into the rocks. With this concern now a potential reality, they hove the sounding lead down into the sea for the purpose of finding out the depth of the water we were in (called taking the soundings) and found the depth to be twenty fathoms (thirty-seven meters). A short distance farther on, they took another sounding and found that the depth had decreased to fifteen fathoms (twenty-eight meters). This rapid change in soundings unnerved the crew, as they feared that we might fall off our course and be accidentally driven onto the rocks. So, as we kept praying that daybreak would somehow come sooner that it should, they dropped four large anchors from the rear of the ship in hopes of bringing the ship up short. They felt that if they were able to stop our forward momentum, there was a good chance that the anchors would dig in and not break under the strain of the storm and thus keep us from smashing into the rocks. (If the ship had been anchored from the front, then the real possibility existed that the rear of the ship would swing around on the anchors—either snapping them off or at the very least leaving the ship facing the wrong direction with its stern toward the rocks and with no way to maneuver away from them.)

Now shortly after this, the sailors, on a fairly transparent pretext, were caught lowering the dinghy into the sea (apparently they were trying to secretly escape). When Paul caught them, they used the excuse that they were putting the dinghy out in order to lay out the lines and anchors from the bow (possibly even landing them on shore) in order to secure the ship more properly; however, he did not believe their feeble story. Paul again took this opportunity to make himself heard. He warned Julius and his soldiers that if they allowed the crewmen to escape that all hands would be lost. He knew that these crewmembers, men familiar with every facet and nuance of the ship and its rigging and tackle, were necessary if they were to land this ship or at least run it aground and be saved. Paul had no intention of lying down and letting God do all the work in their rescue. This was not a spiritual decision to make, nor was it a difficult one. It was absolutely practical and critical. Unless these men remained with the ship, there would be a frightful loss of life because there would be no one left on board who could sail her. Then Julius, now willing to take Paul's sound advice, commanded his soldiers to cut away the ropes that held the small boat. They cut them and let it fall off and drift away.

Paul, clearly now in moral control of the situation, kept on exhorting them until dawn began to break, for he was concerned with their health and strength for what would be the final day of this ordeal. While we waited, Paul urged us all to eat a meal saying, "This is now the fourteenth day that you have been continually in suspense and uninterruptedly on the alert without taking any regular meals but only bits of food now and then. I beg and advise you now to eat something for your personal safety and strength, for not one hair from the head of any one of you will be lost or destroyed." With these words he took some bread, after giving thanks to God in front of us all, and broke it into pieces and began to eat. Paul's courage was contagious. It lifted our spirits to hear him speak such words of faith and caused us all to take heart and eat. We all began to believe in a good outcome again. All told there were 276 people on board the ship (presumably a roll call or muster was taken for two possible reasons: one, to verify that none had been lost during the fortnight, and two, to get an accurate headcount for the meal that they were about to partake of).

Now after we had all eaten as much as we wanted, we again and for the last time proceeded to lighten the ship by hauling the sacks of wheat up on deck and throwing the entire shipment of wheat into the sea (these sacks of Egyptian wheat would most likely have made up the bulk of the cargo). When morning came, the storm began to weaken enough so that we were gradu-

ally able to see some land, although no one recognized what land it was. What we did notice, however, was an inlet with a sloping sandy beach on which the crew thought we could run aground. They conferred with one another to ascertain whether it was possible to beach this ship there, and finally decided that it was at least a chance worth taking. Upon reaching this conclusion, they cut the ropes, thereby severing the four stern anchors, and abandoned the anchors in the sea, while at the same time unlashing the ropes that tied the paddle rudders and hoisting the mainsail to the wind. It is as such that they steered our badly damaged ship for the beach. But with a probable draft (the amount of the ship's hull beneath the surface of the water) of at least eighteen feet, we did not make it to shore. Unfortunately, on the way into the inlet, we ran aground on a sandbar that was the result of two converging crosscurrents (a place open to two seas).

With our ship's prow stuck fast and immovable, and with the stern perilously exposed to two strong ocean currents, we were again at the mercy of the sea and still quite a distance from shore. Though an expensive and stalwart ship, the stern could not withstand the pounding surf for long before it began to break up under the violent, hammering force of the waves. It was at this critical moment that the soldiers recommended that all of the prisoners be killed. They were fearful that if any of the prisoners were to swim ashore and escape that they would be held responsible (and possibly even put to death) because of it. In their minds, the unsanctioned murder of the prisoners (even uncharged ones) would carry with it a much more palatable reprimand than letting even one of them escape from their custody.

But Julius, the centurion, who alone among the soldiers and crew realized just how much we all owed to Paul and his wise words of exhortation, thwarted their plans and prevented them from carrying out their dastardly purpose. He ordered all of those who could swim to throw themselves overboard first and to make for the shore. For those that remained and could not swim, he urged them to find anything that would float and thus ride it to shore. Of all that were on the ship, some swam to safety on their own strength, some floated ashore on pieces of the ship, and some (who were not able to make it alone) were ferried across on pieces of plank and wreckage by passengers and crew who could swim. In the end, we all escaped safely to land (which we soon found out was the Island of Malta, our place of refuge) because of Paul's dynamic personality and his faith in the promise that God had made to him [Adaptation of Acts 27:1–28:1].[166]

TACKING

*"Tacking—(Nautical) a course against
the wind whereby a vessel
advances toward its intended destination by performing
a series of zigzag maneuvers, which require
a repeated shifting of the sails
from one side of the ship to the other."*

Acts 27:1–5

Now when it was determined that we [including Luke] should sail for Italy, they turned Paul and some other prisoners over to a centurion of the imperial regiment named Julius. And going aboard a ship from Adramyttium, which was about to sail for the ports along the coast of [the province of] Asia, we put out to sea; and Aristarchus, a Macedonian from Thessalonica, accompanied us. The following day we landed at Sidon, and Julius treated Paul in a loving way, with much consideration (kindness and care), permitting him to go to his friends [there] and be refreshed and be cared for. After putting to sea from there we passed to the leeward (south side) of Cyprus [for protection], for the winds were contrary to us. And when we had sailed over [the whole length] of sea which lies off Cilicia and Pamphylia, we reached Myra in Lycia. (AMP)

LAYING SOME GROUNDWORK

Paul's storm, unfortunately, is not uncommon either in the natural sense of the actual meteorological event or in the symbolic sense in reference to the storms of life. If there were a listing of storms arranged by frequency of occurrence, Paul's type would rank second only to Jonah's. It is quite often that we, like Paul, find ourselves in some menacing maelstroms of life due to those around us who are not listening to wise advice or who want to hurt and take advantage of us. One thing we must realize is that, though Jonah felt it was necessary, jumping ship in a Pauline-type storm is both unacceptable and deadly. These types of storms must be walked through completely and cannot be prayed away. With a lot of ground to cover and many lessons to learn, we will begin our examination of Paul's storm by looking into the events that took place just prior to his imprisonment. As we proceed from there, we will uncover the true breadth of his storm and what lessons Paul's situation can teach us. (For a detailed timeline of the breadth of Paul's storm refer to *Chart 4: A Timeline of Paul's Last Voyage*)

Paul (Saul), although of pure Jewish descent (of the Tribe of Benjamin—Philippians 3:5), was born a Roman citizen (inherited from his father) and had been marked for religious service even from his youth. As a boy in Tarsus, he received a classical Greek education, and as a young man had been instructed in Judaism by Gamaliel, a doctor of law and member of the Sanhedrin[167], in Jerusalem. No doubt impressed by what they saw in him, the high priest and entire council of elders (Sanhedrin) gave him letters of official authority permitting him to direct the campaign of persecution against the Christians.[168] Having already become a Pharisee, it was not long before he was made a member of the Sanhedrin[169] and was given a vote in sentencing Christians to death (Acts 26:10). So completely was he part of this religious cleansing that he was even found standing nearby at the stoning of Stephen with haughty, hating approval (Acts 8:1). Born on the right side of the tracks and having always been a religious zealot, Paul was convinced that it was his duty to eradicate the followers of Christ and to exterminate this uprising. With this fervor, he relentlessly pursued and imprisoned those following this wayward sect of Jesus of Nazareth.

However, one day on the road to Damascus he was apprehended by God and was converted. He no longer persecuted the Disciples of Christ but became a member of their sect instead. After this, Paul's world started to turn against him. Though the Christians were a recognized religious sect by this time, albeit a young one, " . . . the Jews were faithful to a cult of the greatest antiquity and, moreover, had long made their peace with Caesar, Augustus . . . [however] . . . It was a peace that could not extend to people who had (it would be alleged) apostasized from their own Judaism."[170] The Sanhedrin could not stand by and let one of its former members openly betray the council and attack their religious traditions, so they secretly determined that he had to be stopped at any cost. With a bitterness against him that was almost palatable, they gathered a group together and conspired to ambush and kill him.

Although Paul had repeatedly been warned about going to Jerusalem, and even though the Holy Spirit affirmed his impending imprisonment to him on numerous occasions, he was compelled by the convictions in his own heart to go anyways. In spite of warnings and prophesies and even the urgings of good friends, he would not let himself be talked out of arriving there in time for the Day of Pentecost. Shortly after his arrival in Jerusalem, he was attacked by an angry mob of Jews and then arrested by the Roman commandant—the latter event was supposedly done to protect him. However, once the commandant learned of the trouble Paul could cause him (due to the religious embroilments and his dual citizenship), he had him secretly escorted to Caesarea and handed over to Felix. (For a detailed map showing important locations as they relate to Paul's imprisonment and subsequent final voyage refer to *Map 8: Mediterranean Locations*)

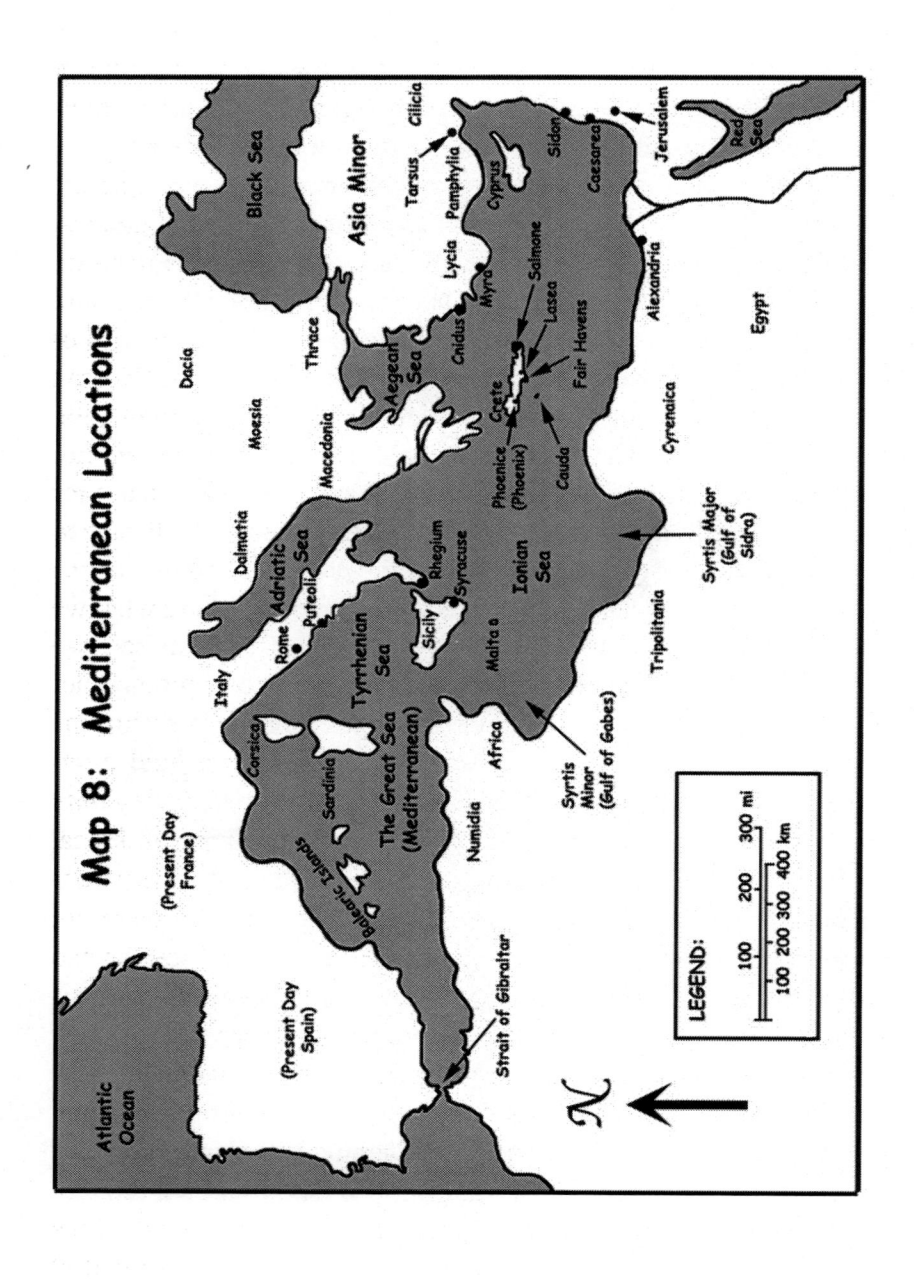

Map 8: Mediterranean Locations

We now fast-forward ahead two years and find Paul still in prison in Caesarea. Felix, his original captor in Caesarea, had been succeeded by a new procurator named Festus; this, then, effectively made Paul a pawn in a second regime wishing to ingratiate itself with the Jews. (Felix had left Paul in prison hoping to both appease his Jewish constituency and to extort money from him.) Festus, ultimately proving equally as weak as his predecessor was, made Paul's case one of his first official acts, not wishing to lose his appointment due to a religious uprising over a zealot. Keeping his subjects happy with his leadership was paramount, and doing the right thing regarding Paul was of no real concern to him. When Paul claimed his rights as a Roman citizen, it gave Festus the out that he needed. Paul's relocation to Rome could be blamed upon Paul himself, and the governor would not look any worse in the eyes of the Jews than he did for holding him in the Roman barracks. The appeal helped Festus to save face; after all, he was only doing what the law demanded.

When Paul appealed to Caesar, he was claiming what we would today term his civil rights, those rights due him because of his birth as a Roman citizen. His rights included, among other things, the freedom from scourging and arrest, except in extreme cases, and the right to appeal to the emperor for a final judgment on the crime of which he was accused. Festus, having only recently obtained his appointment as the procurator of Judea, was already in the hot seat on a number of fronts. One potentially dangerous situation existed with the Jews, who were not happy with him for holding Paul in the first place, feeling he had no authority over these religious matters. The second was his hasty decision to scourge Paul before he had clearly established his citizenship. Deftly, though, he dodged both bullets.

After hearing Paul's defense and learning of his appeal to Caesar, King Agrippa and Governor Festus determined that they, Paul and some other prisoners, should set sail at once (since it was already fall) for Rome. Paul was then bound with a chain (a fetter or manacle similar to our modern day handcuffs) to his guard and loaded aboard the ship. The chain was a device used to confine a prisoner and to make escape impossible. It was typically made with a short length of chain attached to a cuff of some sort on either end. In other words, the prisoner was kept nearby by the use of a pair of handcuffs—one around the prisoner's wrist, and the other around his guard's wrist. In this way the prisoner could not escape; but neither could the guard. He would spend a lot of time with Paul as he spoke of God's grace and mercy and of the plan of salvation. The chains that bound the man of God and brought him to Rome could also be the chains that freed the heart of the Roman soldier, if he listened. When Paul later arrived in Rome in Acts 28:16, he would be handed over by Julius to the "captain of the guard," who was the Prefect (commanding officer) of the Praetorian Guard (in this case it was Sextus Afranius Burrus). Amazingly, Sextus would also show Paul uncanny kindness by letting him live alone with only the soldier who guarded him (rather than in a prison cell where most prisoners would be fettered). This would be in stark contrast to his treatment by his former captors (Felix and Festus), who did not treat him with much kindness. The fact that their minds were clouded by haughty political ambitions precluded them taking any personal interest in a potentially career-ending situation such as showing mercy to Paul.

Therefore, with Julius in charge, Governor Festus was free of any more responsibility to Paul and would immediately be on better terms with the Jewish constituency of his great city. It is obvious that though he was new, he had the political shrewdness of an elder statesman. He knew what he needed to do in order to get his term off to the best start. He remained cold and calculated, and operated strictly by the letter-of-the-law with Paul's case. He may have alienated a small but growing part of his constituency (the Jesus Freaks), but he was not about to commit political suicide by letting Paul go free and thus enrage the powerful, ruthless members of the Sanhedrin. Whatever his actual motivations were, the ship was now loaded and the prisoners were in charge of another and headed for Sidon—the next port of call. (For a map of Paul's voyage see *Map 9: Paul's Journey*)

CHART 4: A TIMELINE OF PAUL'S LAST VOYAGE

Stops Along the Route to Rome	Approx. Distance (in km.)	Approx. Days There or in Route	Running Total Days of Paul's Storm
Paul's arrest and subsequent imprisonment under Felix in Jerusalem (57 A.D.)	N/A	730	730days
In the company of Porcius Festus and King Herod Agrippa II	N/A	30	760 days
Caesarea to Sidon (Late fall of 59 A.D.)	130	1	761 days
Sidon to Myra	770	6	767 days
Myra to Cnidus	250	6	773 days
Cnidus to Fair Havens/Lasea	400	4	777 days
Fair Havens/Lasea to Malta	900+	14	791 days
Malta (Winter of 60 A.D.)	N/A	92	883 days
Malta to Syracuse	150	1	884 days
Syracuse	N/A	3	887 days

Syracuse to Rhegium	130	1	888 days
Rhegium to Puteoli	330	2	890 days
Puteoli	N/A	7	897 days
Puteoli to Rome	130	1	898 days
In Rome and under house arrest	N/A	733+	1631 days
N/A (62 A.D.)	N/A	N/A	Total Length of Paul's Storm: 1631 days (4 _ years) ±

NOTE: I have used 130 km (Acts 27:2-3) as a general approximation of the distance traveled in a day, although considering the conditions they were sailing under, the distance may have realistically been only half of that or 65 km per day. The exceptions being from Myra to Cnidus, where it is indicated to have taken considerable days (which I have estimated as 6), and any place where there is an actual reference given as to the exact number of days. This delineation of cumulative days in this storm is for illustrative purposes only and is not meant to be an exact accounting of the total number of days Paul had suffered through this storm, nor a perfect historical record of the actual years in which it took place (although both are relatively close to reality).

AN OFFICER AND A CITY

Before we dive headlong into Paul's storm, we will first examine some background information. First, we will look at the life of a centurion and what typified his position. Through this we will gain an important perspective into why Julius may have acted as he did on the ship with Paul. It will also show us just how instrumental he was in getting Paul to Rome. We will see that, had he not turned from the norms of a soldier, all hands may have been lost at sea, Paul's body among them. Second, we will examine the impressive city of Caesarea and what she would have been like in those ancient times, thus giving us a clearer picture of what was involved with Paul's initial imprisonment and the struggles his captors battled in keeping him in chains. These details concerning Caesarea will give us insight into why Paul was taken there and why neither Felix nor Festus had the guts to do the right thing and release him.

THE CENTURION AND HIS INCENTIVES

As a Roman centurion, Julius would have held a prestigious position in the Roman Army. As such, he was a principle officer—a career man by definition, and among the most experienced of all the soldiers in the ranks. Due to his elevated position of commanding a centuria (centuries of 100 men were the smallest unit inside the legion of 6000 men), his pay scale was much higher than a regular soldier's and included a generous bonus, which would be granted upon discharge. The centurion, in exchange for this rate of pay and prestige, was required to give twenty years of service to the great Roman army. However, it is believed that Julius was part of an imperial cohort dispatched by the emperor and stationed in Caesarea,[171] a cohort known as either the Praetorian Guard or the Augustan Guard. It was an elite corps of soldiers originally established by Augustus in 27 b.c. in order to protect the emperor. As a member of this elite guard, a centurion's daily duties . . . were varied. First, he was responsible for discipline; hence, his vine-staff emblem [he carried a staff of vinewood as his badge of office], which he knew how to use on the backs of his men. This would include supervision of scourging and the execution of capital penalties . . . Then there was the responsibility for drill, inspection of arms, quartermaster's duties, and command in camp and field. He assigned detail to his men and might be bribed to the point of exacting tribute, thus greatly augmenting his already considerable pay. He himself might [also] be detailed for command of the auxiliaries, or for a variety of special tasks.[172]

It is one of these special tasks that Julius was chosen for when he was assigned to escort Paul to Rome. When it came to special assignments, the Roman centurion was not the low man on the totem pole. In fact, in Paul's particular situation, "The . . . centurion ranked above the captain and [the] owner [of the ship]. As a military officer the centurion was responsible for the soldiers, the prisoners, and the cargo of wheat."[173]

CAESAREA'S ENTICEMENT

Now let us examine the city of Caesarea (a.k.a. Caesarea Palaestinae or Caesarea Maritima—Caesarea by the sea) and what she represented to the Governor of Judea. Caesarea was originally an ancient Phoenician settlement and first appeared as Straton or Strato's Tower. Building upon these ruins, the city was rebuilt and enlarged by Herod the Great and renamed in honor of the Roman emperor Caesar Augustus. The city itself occupied a space approximately half the size of Manhattan Island and boasted a population of nearly 250,000. Though already the administrative city of Palestine for some time, Caesarea went on to became the military capital of the Roman province of Judea in 6 a.d. In addition to serving as a navy base, it also boasted many modern buildings similar to those found in Rome including an enormous amphitheater with a seating capacity of 3500, temples, baths, a marketplace, several palaces, a temple, Herod's own palace of limestone and marble, a court, public buildings, a shrine and two aqueducts. Built by the sheer force of Herod's own will, this city arose from the ruins of Strato's Tower almost overnight.

Sebastos, the deep-water seaport at Caesarea, was no small feat of ancient ingenuity. Having to overcome nature itself, Herod built an all-weather, artificial harbor on a shoreline that didn't boast of even one good reason for constructing it there. As part of a building project that was the biggest in the ancient Near East, this seaport was the only open side of a walled and fortified city. Small coves were enlarged to create a deep, large protected ship anchorage that allowed even huge ocean-going freighters to unload their cargoes at dockside. The harbor area itself, covering an area of over forty acres in size, was larger than that at Athens and included many storage warehouses, markets, public buildings and a lighthouse. Herod turned a little strip of sandy coastline into the largest harbor on the eastern Mediterranean coast. While unimpressive compared with modern standards, the construction of the harbor itself was a technological marvel in ancient times, as it was accomplished by submerging huge stones of concrete into the sea. "Two immense breakwaters . . . [were] . . . constructed to frame outer and inner basins . . . [in which] Hydraulic concrete was used in a sophisticated way, and sluice gates and [the] subsidiary breakwater [which] provided protection against siltation."[174] These artificial breakwaters (moles) were over 200 feet wide and extended 500 feet out into the sea to provide a haven from foul weather for any ships that docked there.

Boasting of many modern amenities for a city of this era, Caesarea maintained a progressive sense of style while maintaining an air of stately beauty and influence. Caesarea became the city of choice for the rulers of Judea, and "It was the Roman metropolis . . . and the official residence both of the Herodian kings and the Roman procurators."[175] Although it was largely a Roman city filled with foreigners from abroad, Caesarea was an inter-racial city that boasted a large Jewish constituency, a mix that would soon cause great turmoil. Coupled with its political presence and modern amenities, this celebrated maritime complex was a bustling center of activity along the Israeli coast and a proud Jewel along the Via Maris—that most important of all ancient trade routes. It is now easy to understand why neither Felix nor Festus dared upset the delicate balance of their varied constituency for fear of losing their appointment and plush residency in a city with the allure of Caesarea.

AVAST YE BURDENED VESSEL

"Avast—a nautical command to stop or cease." [176]
"Burdened Vessel—the vessel without right-of-way
that must keep clear of a vessel that does
have the right-of-way." [177]

Acts 27:6–13

There the centurion found an Alexandrian ship bound for Italy, and he transferred us to it. For a number of days we made slow progress and arrived with difficulty off Cnidus; then, as the wind did not permit us to proceed, we went under the lee (shelter) of Crete off Salmone, And coasting along it with difficulty, we arrived at a place called Fair Havens, near which is located the town of Lasea. But as [the season was well advanced, for] much time had been lost and navigation was already dangerous, for the time for the Fast [the Day of Atonement, about the beginning of October] had already gone by, Paul warned and advised them, Saying, Sirs, I perceive [after careful observation] that this voyage will be attended with disaster and much heavy loss, not only of the cargo and the ship but of our lives also. However, the centurion paid greater attention to the pilot and to the owner of the ship than to what Paul said. And as the harbor was not well situated *and* so unsuitable to winter in, the majority favored the plan of putting to sea again from there, hoping somehow to reach Phoenice, a harbor of Crete facing southwest and northwest, and winter there. So when the south wind blew softly, supposing they were gaining their object, they weighed anchor and sailed along Crete, hugging the coast. (AMP)

THE ALEXANDRIAN SHIP

Upon landing in Myra, one of the chief cities in Lycia in Asia Minor, Julius immediately set himself to the task of finding a ship that could transport the prisoners, soldiers and himself to Rome. It is uncertain whether he would have actually traveled into the city itself, which was located about two miles up the river from the harbor and boasted many amenities similar to those in Caesarea (including a Roman bath, a theater and a fortress), or if he would simply have poked around the docks until he found what he needed. There may have been many boats to examine and many captains to question before he found the ship he was looking for; however, it is more than likely that this Alexandrian freighter was the only ship sailing to Rome at that late date and that had enough room for them all to book passage. Once again we see that these ancient vessels, " . . . like practically all other merchantman, were owned, commanded, and manned by Greek or Phoenician or Syrian or other maritime-minded subjects of the empire."[178] This put a personal weight of responsibility upon the owner to make sure that the boat paid for itself, covered all of the expenses of the voyage, rewarded the crew with their share of the take, turned a tidy profit and always returned home safely.

The Alexandrian fleet, of which this ship was a part, was over eighty vessels strong and showcased an impressive display of shipbuilding both in terms of size and construction. As for the sheer mass of these ships, Casson informs us that "The shipwrights of antiquity built vessels as strong as those of later ages and bigger than those of most; the aggregation of oversize freighters that carried grain from Alexandria to Rome, for example, was not to be matched until the eighteenth century."[179] Lucian, the essayist, once witnessed one of these great ships when it got off course and landed in Athens. The ship, as he recounts, was 180 feet long, its beam (width at the widest point) was nearly fifty feet, and the deck to bottom height was forty-four feet. This ship that Julius found " . . . was indeed a mighty vessel, able to carry, to judge from its dimensions, between 1200 and 1300 tons . . ."[180] of cargo, equipment and crew. If he was to be forced to sail to Rome in the winter, Julius was going to take no chances on a smaller vessel. Choosing this behemoth assured him a large margin of safety and boasted a main deck large enough for the entire complement of 276 souls to be camped out on it.[181]

In reference to the construction of these ships, Casson also informs us that these ships were built from a shell of planking that was held tightly together with mortise and tenon joints and which were then transfixed by dowels. With each seam thus locked into place, the resultant ship boasted a hull that was so strong and watertight that it needed no caulking.[182] Although the hull constructions were similar, and with each ship sporting an upswept bow and a raised stern, it was natural to exploit these similarities in order to give each ship its own unique identity. Traditionally the bow was carved or painted with a figure, which represented the ship's name, and a statue of the home port's patron deity mounted on the stern. In addition to that, each ship was outfitted with rudders operated by ropes attached to a tiller arm, a central mast, a foremast, a galley, several large anchors (six or eight—each in excess of 4000 pounds), windlasses and capstans (both referring to a mechanical winch or spool-shaped cylinder used to pull in or let out the anchors), cargo holds, the captain's deckhouse, and a large main deck.

Since these oversized freighters made such frequent trips to and from Rome, and given the fact that passenger ships did not exist in ancient times, it was natural for people to catch a ride on one of them as needed. In order for us to understand that these passengers were not necessarily of low estate and thus not able to afford their own private charter, it should be remembered that even the Roman emperors frequented the Alexandrian grain ships in making their trips across the seas.[183] There was no telling who might come by the docks and request passage aboard one of these workhorses. But since passenger transportation and passage fares were only of incidental importance to ancient merchantman and would have paled in comparison to the money to be made in transporting goods, these ships provided only the minimum in facilities for those unlucky enough to be on board. About all these merchantmen did furnish for the passengers was water and deck space.[184] Therefore, a typical journey like this would have seen the ship setting sail with hundreds of passengers scattered across the deck scurrying to set up their tent-like sleeping structures before they hit the open seas.

What is particularly frightening is what would have taken place during stormy weather. "When a ship ran into danger, the passengers' only hope of survival was to cling to it [the ship], for there were no life boats; ubiquitous today, these were unknown in ancient times. Ships had merely a single small boat to serve as jolly boat, which normally was not kept on deck but towed astern."[185] It would have been quite a sight on board this ship during their storm with people clinging to anything and everything that would not move. It may have been that some of the passengers fought over the most secure spots while others tried to wedge themselves between the cargoes below deck. Still others may have even attempted to lash themselves to the masts or wrap themselves within the netting. What is certain is that under these gale-force conditions, the ship was an amalgamation of frenzied activity. Minor injuries such as bumps and bruises, cuts and scrapes would have been common, but major injuries such as broken bones or partially severed limbs would also have been real possibilities. With yardarms swinging wildly and debris flying everywhere, this would definitely not have been the place to be.

THE CARGO

It is sure that "There was a fortune to be made in maritime commerce in Roman times. Staples and luxuries, from as near as France and as far as China, poured into the capital . . ."[186] of Rome. It was all carried on the backs of the great shipping fleets of the Roman Empire. And with a " . . . sprawling metropolis of more than million people . . ."[187] to feed, this fleet of ships was constantly on the move. Although certainly varied, the majority of each ship's cargo was "Rome's second great line of trade [which] involved a bulky and cheap commodity essential for the daily existence of a million people—grain."[188] However, as much as the Roman people valued their foreign grain imports, they prized their exotic luxuries from India and the Far East much more. Many ancient Romans intended to live as rich and lavish a lifestyle as they could afford, and do as little work as possible as is evidenced by their exorbitant quantity of official holidays—for " . . . there were no less than 159 holidays in the year."[189] What this means to our story is that, along with the grain, the ship was carrying at least some of the other popular commodities of the day (garum—a fish sauce, wine or olive oil[190]), as well as a certain quantity of luxury and other goods. The quantity of supplementary cargo on this ship was so large, in fact, that it took the crew three full days just to throw it off the ship.

Cargo in ancient times was stowed within the holds of the ship below deck and, since there were no metal drums, food-grade plastic barrels or cardboard boxes with which to store their goods, the ancients typically used a clay pot called an amphora. Stevedores carefully carried these pots one by one from the dock, up the gangplank and down into the cargo holds in a slow dance that could take days to complete. [For more information on amphorae and stevedores see the description of them in *Jonah and the Phoenician Crew, a Hold Full of Cargo*]. It was the stevedore's job to pack the cargo as tightly as it could be while at the same time filling the hold with as many amphorae or sacks of grain as possible. This, of course, would make the trip as profitable as it could be. We can get an idea of the incredible amount of work involved in filling the ship's holds (and thus how much harder it would have been to unload it while sailing under gale force winds and turbulent seas) and the delicateness of that job by realizing that

> . . . in order to avoid breakage ancient stevedores stowed the amphoras in the hold with extreme care. The jars were set

upright in superimposed tiers, each jar being so placed that its pointed bottom would fit into the open space around the necks of those in the tier below; on big merchantmen carrying thousands of jars there could be as many as five tiers. Dunnage of twigs and branches cushioned the jars against each other and the lowest tier against the bottom of the hold.[191]

THE TYPICAL TRIP

A typical summer for these Alexandrian freighters was something of a race. It was a matter of who could make the most round-trip excursions while raking in the most money, a story that is typical even with today's merchantmen. With the variety of the Mediterranean winds, however, this task took a lot of guts and luck to pull off twice in one year. Casson aptly describes the situation facing the skippers of these ships.

The winds that prevail over the waters between [Egypt and Rome], during the summer months when the ancient mariners sailed, are northwesterly. This meant that freighters raced downhill from Ostia or Pozzuoli to Alexandria with the wind on their heels in ten days to two weeks. Everything added up to a quick voyage: the direction of the wind made possible a voyage straight to the destination [and across the open sea], the wind itself was strong and steady, and the vessels most often traveled in ballast since the city [Rome] had a lopsided balance of trade, taking in far more than it shipped out. But the skippers paid heavily for this on the return: it was uphill work against foul winds all the way. The northwesterlies dictated a course that was a third again as long as the voyage out. Following the preferred route, the ships, now fully laden, headed for the southern coast of Asia Minor on a port tack, there turned west and, on a starboard tack, coasted along to Rhodes. From here they worked south of Crete and then, tacking continuously, beat their way to Syracuse in Sicily, with perhaps a stop at Malta en route. Here they could wait, if they had the time, for a southerly to carry them through the Strait of Messina and north; otherwise they headed into the northwesterlies once again and slogged it out the rest of the way. The voyage took at least a month and on occasion two or more. A vessel could count on only a single round trip or, at most, a trip and a half during the sailing season.[192]

So why would a ship carrying a desperately needed staple, many commonly traded commodities and lavish luxury items (not to mention a complement of 276 people including passengers and crew) take this chance of sailing back to Rome so late in the year? Why would a lucid, sane businessman be willing to take the risk of cramming in a second round trip to Rome when the odds were stacked so unfavorably against him? The reason was money. Although it was not typical to attempt two round trips in one year, it was sometimes attempted and even encouraged. There is even evidence of Roman Emperor Claudius offering special rewards to skippers who were willing to sail during the winter and complete the improbable double-round-tripper.[193] Whether the owner was trying to recoup expenses caused by deadheading, cash in on the lucrative international trade in luxury goods, or collect on a government contract, the bottom line was purely financial. Now that we know that, the reasons are completely understandable why they would choose to set sail for Rome so late in the season, even though to some these reasons may still be unacceptable.

MOVING ON AGAINST BETTER JUDGMENT

Although Paul's journey had been tough thus far, it had not been anything out of the ordinary for that time of year. Upon arriving in Fair Havens, this may have played against Paul's warning since the captain and owner had most likely encountered similar weather and successfully moved on as their schedule dictated. Their stop in Fair Havens was typical because it was the last place where a ship could enjoy any protection from the northwest winter wind before rounding the promontory on the way to Phoenice.

Due to an ill-situated harbor, any ship wintering in Fair Havens would be less protected than in a properly oriented harbor like that in Phoenice. Though it would have been possible to winter there, it was by no means ideal. However inconvenient it may have been, though, it would not have been impossible to spend the winter there but simply incovenient. What is also possible, although not known, is that the harbor at Fair Havens may have lacked key facilities and may not have been capable of dismasting this large ship or restocking its supplies adequately.

Often, like Paul, we find ourselves in situations that are not ideal. We may have stopped our ship at some inconvenient harbor where there may be a lack of facilities, our ready cash may be short, or the allure of a better place is too much to resist. Desperate for a better location and for greener grass and larger pastures, we often fall into the same trap as the majority on this infamous cruise. Choosing against better judgment, we set our sights on Phoenice (a palm tree) instead of staying put in an ill-situated place even though it is the right thing to do. Never content with good enough, we typically are always on the lookout for a more ideal situation than the one that we are in. In real estate, this is translated as a starter home, and in employment situations, we refer to it as a stepping stone. God refers to it as unsatisfied and covetous—in other words, sin. Nevertheless, we must consider that in the grand scheme of things Fair Havens, though providing only a modicum of protection from the cold blasts of winter, was at least a moderately adequate place to winter a ship. Surely, throughout the centuries, at least one ship had successfully wintered over in that harbor. Though it may not have been optimal, it would have certainly been an easier situation to deal with in comparison to dealing with the disaster that awaited those aboard this Alexandrian freighter further on.

When faced with the choice of where to anchor their ship for the winter, the majority decided that it would be best to advance to a more ideal location like Phoenice rather than dealing with the uncertainties and inconveniences of wintering at this locale. What followed their fateful decision was a lesson that will continue to teach for eternity. Sometimes "not ideal" should be translated as "good enough" (this is known by some as the Good Enough Rule). Though Phoenice was the best harbor to spend the winter in due to its strategic location and protection from the winter winds, they never got the chance to find that out firsthand. Instead of listening to Paul's common sense logic, the owner of the vessel risked a very expensive boat with an expensive and a critical cargo, not to mention nearly 300 lives, for a paycheck. What Julius risked was a possible smear to his reputation (or possible disciplinary action or the loss of rank and benefits) if he was not able to deliver the prisoners in a timely fashion. Both men made poor decisions based on less important concerns. It is alarming to admit the regularity of these same thought processes in our own daily lives.

So how do we know where to remain and when to stay put? What we must learn is to listen to the voice of God through whatever orifice it is coming to us—whether that voice is coming through an angel, a best friend and confidant, or from the mouth of a donkey. His voice will guide us through. He will not stop speaking words of wisdom to us if we will continue to hear and listen. Comfort and convenience should not come into our decision making process at this point. Considerations about the success of our endeavor do not matter. We cannot suppose the will of God by what we think it will gain us—even if that is security and ideal conditions. Our job at this point is to choose with the wisdom of God despite what the current conditions are or what the future conditions threaten. As the old saying goes, the end does not justify the means. In fact, the end is irrelevant. It is difficult to stay put when life is inconvenient and does not appear to be going our way. This is the challenge today, especially given our penchant for success, fame, fortune and the earthly glories with which charismatic ministers enchant us. Courage is what it takes to stick it out and not take the chance against God's better judgment. However, like the majority aboard this Alexandrian freighter, we are usually unwilling to stay put. We strike out for a better place and wind up running headlong into aggressive, butchering cataclysms that we could have easily avoided if we had only obeyed God.

Two remarkable situations took place aboard the Alexandrian ship that would not have been normal. First were Paul's freedoms. Not only was Paul given uncommon considerations for a passenger and a prisoner when he was allowed to disembark at Sidon, but he was also allowed to address the company of the ship and offer his advice. What warden in any penitentiary would allow an inmate to voice his opinions as to the direction of the prison? Who would let a prisoner leave their custody to intermingle with his like-minded zealot friends—even for a little while? The amazing part in all of this is Paul's reputation. Can we imagine any man putting that much faith and trust in us if we were in a similar situation? A reputation beyond reproach (one that cannot be even accused of or blamed for any fault or wayward thinking) is what the Bible instructs us to have. That reputation is what Paul exhibited, and the trust he engendered is overwhelming. It should be the same with us.

The second remarkable situation was Paul's behavior following his advisory speech and the rest of the trip. After making his impassioned appeal of staying put clear to those on board the ship, he shut up and said no more until he encouraged their desperate morale later in the storm. It is unfathomable in today's world of riots, uprisings and public mutinies for us to witness such an occurrence, but this is exactly what Paul did—he kept his tongue within his control. Paul spoke his peace, but once his voice was overruled, he shut up. He did not attempt to get Luke and Aristarchus in on a scheme to win more votes, nor did he try to use his influence with the centurion to make his suggestion become the law that overruled the owner of the ship. Paul said not one word to attempt a coup, nor did he continue to make his appeal louder and more obnoxious than it was the first time just so that they would follow his advice. Neither threatening nor grandstanding nor posturing nor berating was found to be part of his arsenal; in fact, he did not have an arsenal or agenda. With his mind spoken, he let the decision of how to proceed fall to the rightful people and to the will of God.

Once Paul made his suggestion known, he had fulfilled

his duty because he realized that it was not his decision to make. Today we seem to have trouble with the deciding part. We feel that we have the right to have our way–even in church. After all, this country was founded by people who were fed up with the poor decisions of those above them, and those wishing to experience the freedom that comes from having a voice that can be heard have continually repopulated it ever since. Now do not get me wrong; I am not knocking freedom or our country, but I am pointing out one of our more destructive habits. It is common today that if our elected leaders do not carry out what we suggested, then their tenure will be cut short or that person will not be reelected. What has happened is that we have become too familiar with our leaders and in having our own way, and we have unfortunately lost a lot of the respect once given to officials and presidents, popes and dictators. In today's society, with some of our more interesting spiritual leaders, this territory is pillaged repeatedly. They have not learned Paul's quiet lesson and neither have we. When something goes awry today, or when one of our spiritual leaders disagrees with the president or congress, the issue never seems to get resolved because these men cannot control their own tongues. Crying out in the streets, they make their voices heard, but if circumstances do not change, they then attempt to negatively influence public opinion (sometimes secretly but usually right out in the open) and try to garner support for their side. Arranging political mutinies, they care not what their actions are really saying because the only voice they hear is their own. Mutiny originally carried with it the penalty of death, but nowadays it is just another way to establish a person's own cult or clan or movement. However, Paul would have no part of such shenanigans.

An even sadder development is that these attitudes are not only found in our national religious leaders but have become the norm in most of our churches as well. Parishioners feel that they have the right to have their opinions become the direction of the church. The deacons feel that they are more informed than the pastor, and the staff members become more than disgruntled at the leadership in general. However, speaking our mind in a kind, courteous manner is not within our vocabulary. Not having our way will cause us to take the next step and begin to spread our dissension. Attempting to swing as many votes our way as possible, we make no effort in taming our tongue because we cannot accept the fact that our way is not always the way it will work out. Are we spoiled? I think not. We are undisciplined. If our child was mistreated, then a lawsuit is the only recourse that will satisfy our thirst for vindication. For the sexually abused, prison bars are the only barriers that will make us stop our holy march against the violator. Am I advocating that we sit down and give up when the world around us goes haywire? Am I suggesting that we can never take it to the next level when we have been wronged? No.

What I am saying is that our first reaction is usually to take it to the limit every time. We have never learned to sit down and shut up. Our military was built around a hierarchy of command that is never questioned, like it or not. But in today's non-military constituency we have somehow forgotten Paul's lesson. We get confused between giving our opinion and becoming policymakers. The thoughts we have, although they may be valid, are our opinion, but if we are not the decision makers then we have no right to go any further. Instead of mounting mutinies, we should concentrate more on living within the parameters of the decisions that are made above us. But some will still stammer out protests against this, insisting that they are the watchmen upon our walls crying out of the intruders about to pillage our land. If this is true, as it sometimes is, then it is our individual responsibility to act upon the warning. It is not the watchman's responsibility to get the people of his city to change or fight or do what he thinks they should. His job is to cry out the warning and then shut up. After that, it is our job as the citizens of our community to wake up and to fight; but then again, maybe this watchman is the one who is always crying wolf or maybe his monocular is dirty. We must learn self-control and patience. After all, that is the lesson of this storm—to walk through what is someone else's fault because God wants to help us to grow. Tough lessons to learn, I know, but vital nonetheless.

ADRIFT AND SCUDDING BEFORE THE WIND

"Adrift—not moored, at the will of the wind and tide." [194]
"Scud—to run before a gale with little or no sail set." [195]
*"Before the wind—going the same direction
as the wind is blowing."* [196]

Acts 27:14–26

But soon afterward a violent wind [of the character of a typhoon], called a northeaster, came bursting down from the island. And when the ship was caught and was unable to head against the wind, we gave up and, letting her drift, were borne along. We ran under the shelter of a small island called Cauda, where we managed with [much] difficulty to draw the [ship's small] boat on deck *and* secure it. After hoisting it on board, they used supports with ropes to undergird *and* brace the ship; then afraid that they would be driven into the Syrtis [quicksands off the north coast of Africa], they lowered the gear (sails and ropes) and so were driven along. As we were being dangerously tossed about by the violence of the storm, the next day they began to throw the freight overboard; And the third day they threw out with their own hands the ship's equipment (the tackle and the furniture). And when neither sun nor stars were visible for many days and no small tempest kept raging about us, all hope of our being saved was finally abandoned. Then as they had eaten nothing for a long time, Paul came forward into their midst and said, Men, you should have listened to me, and should not have put to sea from Crete and brought on this disaster and harm *and* misery *and* loss. But [even] now I beg you to be in good spirits *and* take heart, for there will be no loss of life among you but only of the ship. For this [very] night there stood by my side an angel of the God to Whom I belong and Whom I serve *and* worship, And he said, Do not be frightened, Paul! It is necessary for you to stand before Caesar; and behold, God has given you all those who are sailing with you. So keep up your courage, men, for I have faith (complete confidence) in God that it will be exactly as it was told me; But we shall have to be stranded on some island. (AMP)

GALE FORCE WINDS AND SWIRLING CURRENTS

As this chapter opens, we find that the Alexandrian ship has been attacked by a brutal tempest that threatens to destroy it and everyone on board. Though this ship was no stranger to stormy weather, this tempest was more than it had possibly ever encountered. The situation in the Mediterranean Sea during winter was less than ideal because storms were quite common, as were strong and violent winds. So frequent are these winds that pummel the area from nearly every compass direction that even today, most of them bear names that indicate their region of origin and the regularity of their arrival. In order to get some idea of what was involved for these ancient mariners in navigating a ship in the Mediterranean Sea during the winter months, we will first look at some of the air movements (winds) that affect the area. Let us keep in mind that though these winds may bear some modern names, they were no less physically present during the first century a.d. (For a map showing these storm/wind directions and locations see ***Map 10: Mediterranean Winds and Storms***)

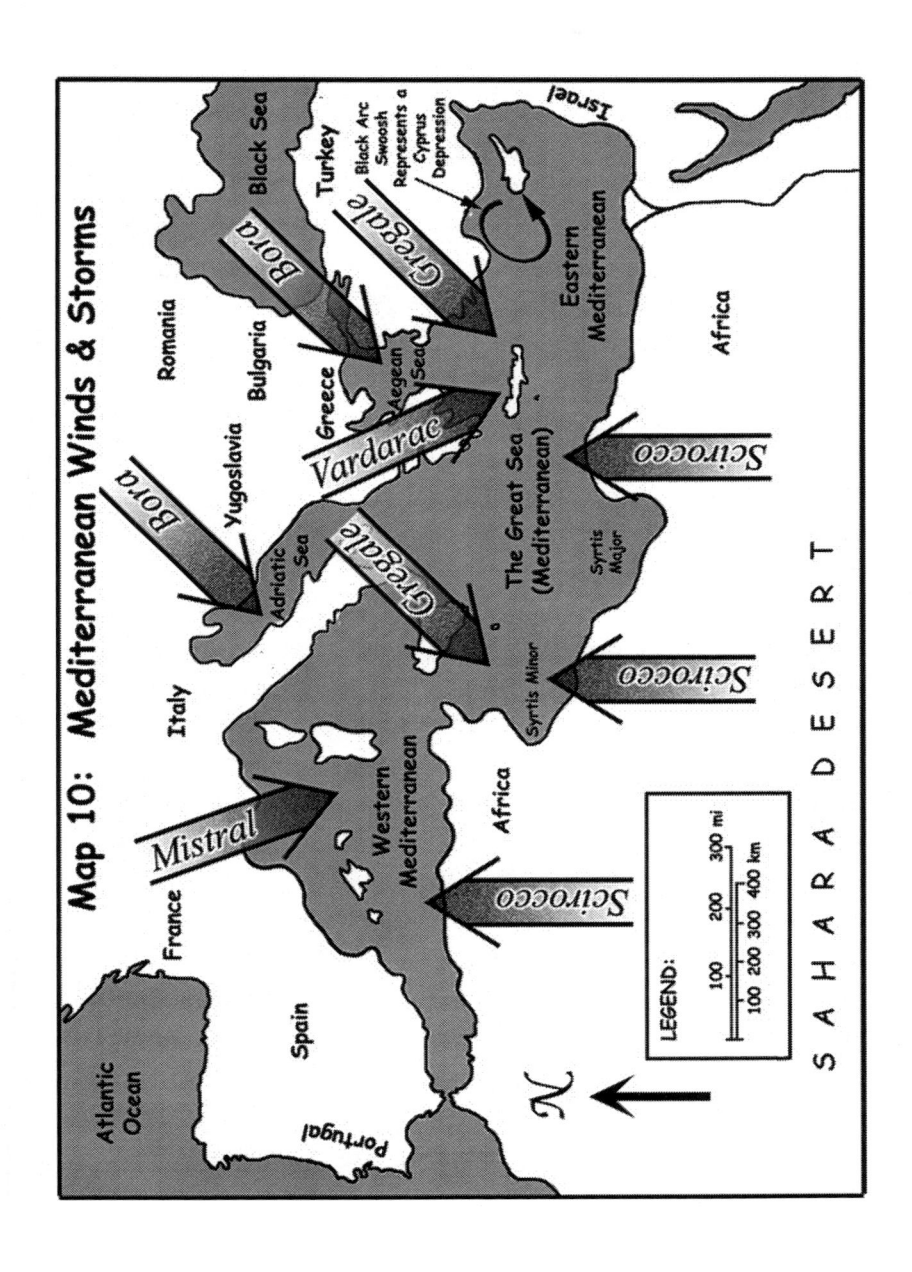

• The Bora is a dry, cold, northeasterly wind that is in full swing from November to April that mostly affects the Adriatic Sea.

• The Gregale is a strong, gale-force, northeasterly wind that mainly occurs in the wintertime over the central Mediterranean Sea. This wind is also referred to as Euroclydon or Euraquilo.

• The Mistral is a strong, cold, north or northwesterly wind that mainly affects the southern French coastal areas north of Sardinia and the Balearic Islands, although its influence can be felt further south at times.

• The Scirocco (Sirocco) are violent southerly winds that bring masses of hot air and dust from the Sahara Desert and across the North African coast into the southern Mediterranean Sea as far north as Malta, Sicily and the southern parts of Italy.

• The Vardarac is a strong, cold, northwesterly wind that blows down through the Greek valleys into Macedonia in the winter months and can reach gale force winds for days on end.[197]

Next, we will look at some of the other systems and movements that would have affected how any ancient mariner sailed the Mediterranean. Some of these other factors involved had to deal with navigation in the midst of the living, breathing cycles of the sea, conditions that further complicated traversing her waters. Unlike most seas, this large body of water whirls in a strange dance with the elements that causes it to act alive. The many currents, systems and other events that seasonally affect the Mediterranean Sea added to the difficulty of sea crossings, and this was especially true during the treacherous winter months. (For a map showing the current directions and flows see *Map 11: Mediterranean Flows and Currents*)

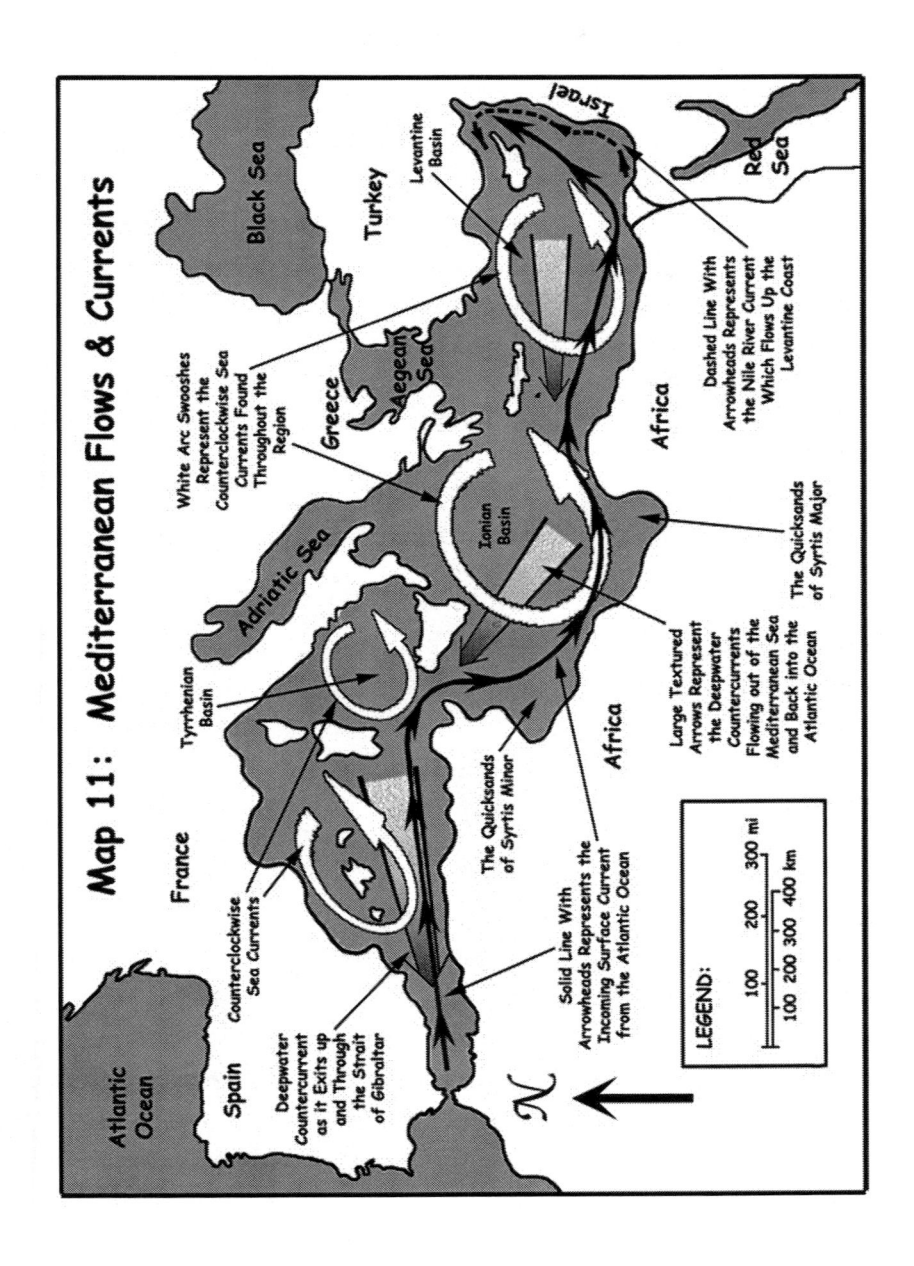

Map 11: Mediterranean Flows & Currents

• Surface currents—the water in the Mediterranean evaporates so quickly that its freshwater supply sources cannot replenish it quickly enough; therefore, there is a continuous inflow of surface water from the Atlantic Ocean. This current (main body of surface water) flows in through the Strait of Gibraltar and hugs the northern African coast as it flows eastward and creates eddy pockets whenever it flows past islands.

• Subsurface currents—due to the intense surface evaporation (especially during the summer months) there is an increased salinity in the water, which makes it sink to the bottom of the sea. It only reemerges as it travels westward beneath the surface current and slips back out of the Strait of Gibraltar and into the Atlantic Ocean.

• There are distinct and separate counterclockwise surface currents in both the Levantine and Ionian Basins.

• The Nile flows northward from Egypt up the Eastern Mediterranean Coast toward modern day Turkey.

• The Mediterranean has been metaphorically referred to in the past as something almost human, as it inhales huge amounts of surface water from the Atlantic Ocean and then exhales a deepwater countercurrent of highly saline water back through the Strait of Gibraltar into the Atlantic. This intake/outtake of large volumes of water causes the entire sea to churn and pump, thus adding to its imbalance.

• There are a number of low pressure systems that cross the Mediterranean every year during the winter and early spring months. Some of these cyclonic depressions arise in the area between the Gulf of Antalya and the island of Cyprus. *(See Map 10: Mediterranean Winds and Storms)*

• This region of the world is tectonically active, geologically unstable and has frequent earthquakes—some even underwater, which could then cause tsunamis to form.

• The geological formation known as the Hellenic Trough (a.k.a. the Hellenic Trough Complex or the Hellenic Trench) extends from the western edge of the Levantine Basin far into the northeastern corner of the Ionian Basin. It is comprised of a number of deep-water depressions that reach depths of approximately 3 miles, and it is parallel to both the Hellenic Arc (a volcanic arc that includes several volcanic islands) and the Mediterranean Ridge (a submarine crustal swell that extends from the Ionian Sea to Cyprus). This further creates swells and chaos as the waters move over varying underwater terrain. (These are not shown on any of the maps)

• The airflow into the Mediterranean Sea is mostly through gaps in the mountain ranges surrounding her shores that cause violent local disturbances that sideswipe anything crossing their path.

It is easy to see that any captain that sailed in the Mediterranean Sea, even an experienced one, would have had his hands full in simply trying to stay on course during a winter trip. Without radar and marine weather forecasts, it would have been a guessing game as to which of these winds or currents was going to be their next beastly hurdle. The proclivity of the Mediterranean Sea to display the dramatic is indicative of the general tendency to not sail during these winter months due to the confusing and dangerous movements of the air combined with the pumping and swirling currents of the sea that plague the entire area. Is it any wonder why this ship had such troubles right from the start? At one point their ship was pummeled by northwesterly winds, and at the next by northeasterly gales, all the while both riding on and fighting against the steady counter-clockwise ocean currents. What a confusing mess in which to navigate and what a hellish hole to have to be dug out of. Indeed the Mediterranean Sea was no place to be in the winter, especially when the ship's only means of propulsion was the wind—which is as fickle as a giggling teenager.

THE GREGALE

Though we have discussed many varying winds and storm systems that affect the Mediterranean Sea region in general, and given the fact that any or all of these were opposed to this ship's progress at various points along their journey, there is but one type that commands the latter part of the book. The air movement that was most likely the cause of this typhoon is the gregale. This cold and strong northeasterly wind blows through the western and central Mediterranean mainly during the winter months and is likely what they encountered.[198] Gregales are known to have their most pronounced effects around the island of Malta, though these effects are still noticed farther east. Any particular gregale has the potential to grow in strength to hurricane force winds (winds in excess of 73 mph). The gregale occurs most often as a result of a strong flow of air from central or southern Europe, and may indeed be borne out of some combination of the Bora, Mistral, Vardarac and Scirocco winds (as well as many other regional air patterns not mentioned here). Whatever the origins of a gregale are, though, the outcome is often a storm of horrifying force that dominates everything within its reach.

In today's weather terminology the storm that Paul and the passengers aboard the Alexandrian ship encountered would be called a tropical cyclone. (A hurricane, cyclone and typhoon are all synonymous and the differing nametags are assigned by region depending on the geographic location of the storm system.) The life span of these storms can vary from a few hours to nearly three weeks. Although they all begin their life as only a slight circulation of air moving around an area of low pressure called a tropical disturbance, at any time these storms may progress from there to a tropical depression, then to a tropical storm and finally into a hurricane. During this progression, the sustained wind speeds steadily increase (those in excess of 120 miles per hour are not uncommon) and a pronounced rotation develops around the storm's central core as spiral rain bands rotate around the eye of the storm. These winds whip the sea's surface into a foaming froth and magnify the undulating subsurface activities. When these powerful forces conspire together to devastate an area, there is little man can do to stop their cruel march. With their voices in unison, these unseen forces combine their brutal strengths as they orchestrate a deadly dance with waves of enormous size.

While we cannot know the exact conditions aboard this Alexandrian ship during this storm, we can come close by examining the details of meteorology and other eyewitness accounts of similar events. With a thorough investigation completed, we can piece together a fair idea of just what they may have been experiencing. As we put this storm's many facets together, we see that, first, this storm was either very much like, or in fact, a hurricane. What this means is that the general wind direction would have been further complicated by the spin of the storm, thus causing the wind to come at the ship from many different directions. Earl Hinz describes it this way:

> *As the wind speed increases in strength, wave confusion grows until it becomes the maelstrom of hurricane-driven waves. The reason for this pattern of confusion is that the wind is not steady in direction and each wind direction creates its own waves. When waves from more than one direction intersect, a mixed pattern of waves ensues, yielding pyramidal breakers of extreme height. Add to the wind waves the swells arriving from afar and you have chaotic wave patterns that defy description. When multiple trains of breaking waves intersect, it creates a scene of total confusion, one that is most difficult, if not impossible, to navigate.*[199]

Second, we know that the surface current in the Ionian Sea (where they encountered most of the wrath of the storm) is counterclockwise. What this indicates to us is that they were fighting against the current from the time the ship was exposed in Cnidus until they reached Malta. Third, we know that the wind was pummeling the ship from out of the northeast, thus making the general wind direction opposed to the sea's natural current direction. Again, the insight provided by Earl Hinz is most illuminating:

> *Finally, [add to the confusing, uproarious conditions caused by the hurricane's spinning winds] the unreal seas that develop when the wind blows against the current [which] . . . causes a compression of the waves reducing their wave length, making them steeper, and causing increased breaking [and we have an unimaginable situation at hand].*[200]

This is what those aboard the Alexandrian ship were facing. Sea conditions such as this have been encountered by many a mariner, but not by many flatlanders. This was an occasion that would have caused the initiated to shudder and the uninitiated to panic. Similar conditions were recorded after the disaster at sea during the 1998 Sydney-Hobart race where one survivor described it this way: "It looked like the 'gates of hell' and building the greatest b---- of a sea you could ever design."[201] What desperation is heard in this man's words. Is it any wonder why those on board the Alexandrian ship did not eat for weeks? How they even managed to stay on deck is a mystery and no small miracle. It is no wonder why they eventually capitulated and let the storm take complete control. With what strength could they fight so ferocious and terrible a beast? Where did their endurance come from in order for them to withstand weeks of being caught in the middle of this storm? Why did none on board give up and jump to their death in the sea? Could it be because of God and His voice of steadiness through the apostle Paul? Is the basic reason because God needed His man in Rome? Can we now begin to realize the power that our witness reveals? Let this be a lesson to us that we must, even in the most dire of situations, remain under control, steadfast and listening to the voice of God.

THE UNDERPINNINGS OF DISASTER

Now when we are faced with a similar critical situation (as those aboard the Alexandrian freighter were), it is clear what we should do; we should stop and go no further. Disaster awaits us if we go on so we should stop now, but why are those in charge not listening? A deep-seated urge within us wants so much to grab the tiller, jamb it to one side and turn this boat back toward home. With a fury rising up within us, we contemplate pushing the crewmen aside and stepping into the owner's compartment and demanding that he do as we say. Desperate to stop this fated progression, we even devise a scheme by which we could quickly cut the lines that hold the anchors fast and drop them all to the ocean floor. But we cannot and we must not even try, for it is not our place or our ship. It is not our responsibility to decide but simply to abide. God did not put us in charge of this ship, so we cannot force decisions to be made as we perceive that they should. Wishing intently that we had never boarded this floating disaster, we are struck by the realization that we are committed to this ship and must stay on board.

We have every right to express our opinion, but once we have aired our views, our hands are tied. Others nearly convince us that jumping ship is our only way of looking out for ourselves, but then we remember that God said to stay aboard. Jumping ship now would only worsen our situation and jeopardize our already slim chances of survival. God never told us to get off the ship nor did He ever give us any legitimate way out. We are stuck. He did tell us that if we continued to do as He directed that we, as well as all on board the ship, would make it; however, He also indicated that the ship was doomed and that all except our lives would be lost. The promise was that the ship, cargo, furnishings, tackle, grain, personal belongings and reputations of the crew, captain and owner would all be lost, but no one would die.

Imagine just how hellish this storm must have been. Today, if we have to endure an overcast weekend we nearly fall apart, but can we even imagine the fear we would experience after two to three weeks of living within the perimeter of a lunging, screaming hurricane? Many times in the midst of trouble, we become fearful. The fear I am exposing here, though, is not the normal fear of dying in the storm (for we all face that fear), but the fear of ending up like someone else. Like those aboard the Alexandrian freighter, we fear being driven into the banks of Syrtis as well. Syrtis Major and Minor are both areas off the northern shores of Africa where many ships have run aground and have been destroyed by the surf when venturing too close to their treacherous quicksands. For us the quicksands of Syrtis represent a graveyard of sorts. What we fear is that during this storm we may be driven into that same graveyard where so many others have been shipwrecked. Feeling helpless as our ship is driven closer to this treachery, we allow fear to grip our hearts and nearly destroy us. In our situations, the quicksands may represent marital unfaithfulness and other sexual indiscretions, questionable financial practices, or a return to some illicit practices of our kin. To others these quicksands may represent ego, pride, dishonesty or shady dealing. Whatever the quicksands that we fear, we must act quickly in order to avoid the wreckage there. With little control over the wind and waves, we can at least muster the courage and strength to trim the mainsail, so that it does not catch so much wind, and we can fight the rudder in order to point our ship away from where we do not want to end up. During this crisis, it is within our realm of control to not be driven by this fear, but, instead, to use our fear to help us make intelligent decisions and brave choices. No one wants to shipwreck, but if we must and can have a choice, then we should shipwreck in the most manageable place we can find. Landing in quicksand would never be a wise choice.

Surely, during this ordeal, many of the passengers were questioning the competence of the crew, the motives of the captain and the sanity of owner of the ship. With Paul's warnings and his centurion guard, most would have been even further confused as to what was going on. The crewmembers were tired and hungry, frustrated that their training was to no avail, questioning the captain's ability to command, doubting the supposed good intentions of the owner and secretly wishing they had never signed on for this voyage. Passengers, who made up the bulk of the people on board, were griping at the crew of the ship, fighting with each other for prime deck locations and casting condescending looks toward any in command. The captain, mad at himself for letting the owner talk him into piloting this voyage, knew that this spelled the end of his career, and he cursed the day he ever met the man. The owner, now humiliated by the unheeded warnings of a religious zealot, was now the woeful proprietor of a ship with no cargo and a badly damaged vessel that would not see the sunshine of another day. In stark contrast to all of this we see Paul, not partaking in any of the wicked undercurrents of the ship, remaining focused on Rome and listening for the voice of God.

TWISTED ADVICE

One of the most unhelpful and frustrating annoyances that we must deal with during the storms of life is the unsolicited advice we will be given. It seems as though everyone becomes an expert when we are being ruthlessly attacked (but they somehow fall far short when it is their turn at the helm). In our desperate hours, free advice is more plentiful than dirt as we are left reeling from limp suggestions and loose tales. "Why not try the state," they offer, "my uncle's brother got a job there when he was . . ." or "We think you should go to this agency and ask them for financial assistance. You have to look out for yourself and forget about the others. They all chose to get on this ship just as you did. What do you owe them anyway; you don't even like any of them." "When it rains, it pours," they reiterate, shaking their forlorn mops. "Yeah, we know," we growl with both hands balled into fists, "we are soaked to the bone." This is not the comfort or advice that we need to hear during the storm, but it is seemingly all that most can muster.

The voices bearing this advice are increasingly vocal

at the beginning of our severities and especially hard to ignore when coming from well-intentioned family members. But as the storm progresses, a curious thing happens; by the time the squall has been raging around us for days, the voices from the mist taper off until we are left with silence. Having dispensed with their nickel's worth of wisdom and with nothing left to say, their voices have grown weak, hoarse and silent—compelling evidence that they have given up on us altogether. Now, as we are resigned to sit and watch helplessly as the storm drags us under, the only communication we receive is their idle conversation and small talk. Phone calls turn into minutes of dead air time, and all other forms of communication virtually cease. Even our closest friends and family members, at times, will be content to sit idly by and admire our drowning.

What we need most during the showdowns of life is someone in our corner who can offer us some useful assistance; however, too often those who could help us (and probably should) try to do so in futile ways, not having the wisdom to know what they should and should not do. Naively believing they are helping us out, they further compound the hopelessness of our dire situation by throwing out lifelines tied to stones at the bottom of the sea. Or we find that the anchors that we sunk deep into their lives now prove weightless and attached to nothing more than bags of water. Never having dealt with reality themselves or having gone through it with blinders on, they have no practical, helpful advice for us. What they do offer us are half-hearted by-lines of Christian-ese and thoughtless babblings that tear us down instead of building us up. When they have the power to rescue us, to do the good that God requires of them, they hold back and lavish more upon themselves—and, thus, to them it is sin and a millstone around their own sagging necks.

Our self-proclaimed benefactors continue with words of abuse, not content with damning us alone. "How could anyone trust that captain or the owner of that ship again?" they cry. "He led his passengers and crew into a storm that nearly took 300 lives." They second-guess our rationale and foolishly believe that they would have known better than to board a doomed vessel. The list of their utter failure toward us is staggering. Do they offer us any comfort, peace, safety or security? Or do they throw us a satisfying crust of bread or cup of water, a familiar wink or happy smile, a word in season or a thoughtful gesture? Even though God requires them to help those of us in need from the abundant store of their barns (willingly and without strings attached giving to a brother in need), they continue to make us fake offers that lead us deeper into despair. Though the following few paragraphs may seem brutal, I am simply regurgitating the weakness I have seen portrayed repeatedly by those who should know better. This is the truth of what takes place during our worst nightmares, but it should not. Behaviors such as the ones I have described have no place in humanity, much less within the walls of our sanctuaries, and God forbid in our families.

There is one good thing, however, that can arise from the ashes of arson's inferno. In seeing how others treat us during the vulgarities of our own lives, we can learn one of the most valuable lessons in all of Christianity—how not to treat others. From most of those around us, family and friends topping the list, these situations are, unfortunately, the norm for most. On the other hand, gushing from a few selfless individuals deeply concerned about our welfare and courage and faith, we can glean the priceless jewels of real Christian love and respect. This love extends from our immediate family to our friends and neighbors, and even reaches out to our enemies. It is this selfless love that Christ came to model but that most are simply content to hear about. To take from our storms life lessons that we willingly pass on to those around us is critical. God desires that we get our hands dirty in the lives of other people by helping them clean up after the excrements of life have defiled their ships.

VITAL DEPORTMENTS

There are many important lessons that we can learn from this Pauline situation that can become life-changing monuments for us. The only drawback is that we must choose to listen, learn and then put these lessons into practice. Knowledge is only good if it becomes understanding, and it is only useful if it then becomes applied wisdom. With these thoughts in mind, let us observe some of the following thoughts.

FRAPPING

With their freighter in desperate condition, literally falling apart at every seam and joint due to the stresses of the storm, the crew frapped the ship. Many might question what this is and if it was really of any use. The answer to both parts of that question is yes. Frapping a ship is the " . . . passing [of] ropes under the ship, [and] from side to side, [in order] to hold its timbers firm."[202] A storm imposes incredible stresses upon every part of a ship, starting with the masts and sails and ending with the hull itself. When it detects even the slightest weakness, it viciously attacks and exposes it— attempting to capitalize upon the stress and destroy the ship. And so it is during our times of trial that the marauder discovers our weaknesses and attempts to dismantle our lives. Under the strain of our weakening attachments, we often give up, let her drift and do nothing more to save ourselves. But we should not allow ourselves to do this. We must use the cords of faith in God, of friendship, of the Word of God, of past prophecies we have received, of honesty with ourselves and the situation we are embroiled in, of our faith past (those times when we have successfully endured the storms of life), of family and of the knowledge of our destiny in order to undergird our ship. These ropes and many more can bind the failing members of our ship together. Allowing ourselves to fall apart is unacceptable; once we have allowed this there will never be a complete reassembling—we will always bear some scar. Though God can repair any fissure, it is less painful not to have to go through that healing process. The most prudent course of action during our difficulties is to strengthen and encourage ourselves in the Lord. As David found out, this course of action will prove more beneficial than succumbing to the ravaging effects of the storm.

LISTENING EARLY

There came a point in this storm when the entire complement aboard the ship realized that Paul had been right all along, but at the point of that revelation, it was too late to avoid the shipwreck. The only course of action left to the owner was to follow normal operating procedures during times of extreme marine distress and to offload everything except the people. What is important to note here is that everything on board the ship was lost (and this time the ship as well), but that if the owner had simply listened to Paul earlier he could have avoided this entire disaster. Such is the tragic end of those who refuse to listen to wisdom; they end up losing what they did not have to lose. The lesson for us is clear. Listen to God and we may not have to lose anything; however, there are times when we are doomed and the only correct course of action is to lighten the ship so that it can stay afloat.

While those in charge of this vessel initially chose not to heed Paul's advice, they eventually changed through the storm and finally became remarkably receptive to anything he had to say. Often the storms of life have a way of silencing even the most arrogant among us, causing us to come crawling back to God with our proverbial tail between our legs. Though they rejected his first advice of not leaving Fair Havens, when the sailors attempted to escape they listened to his wisdom and cut away the dinghy (lifeboat). As I stated earlier, if they had listened the first time then the ship, its furnishings and the cargo could have been saved. Nevertheless, they were given a second, more costly chance to listen this time. Witnessing the horror the entire company on the ship had to endure tends to clear up our vision. What God wants is for us to listen before it is too late. Moreover, let us not forget the reason why any of those on board escaped with their lives; the Bible clearly indicates that it was because God granted Paul a favor. God would rather that we listen and obey rather than to sacrifice what we have, but if we will only listen after tragedy has struck, then He will take that as well. The key to God is that we will finally listen.

NO PRAYER OF DELIVERANCE

It is interesting to realize that Paul never once prayed for deliverance from this storm, even after realizing that the shipwreck was inevitable. For four and a half years he was in prison, chained to a guard and shipwrecked, and not once did he utter one complaint. All too often, when life gets difficult, the people of God reach for the prayer of deliverance instead of the prayer of perseverance. How much more we could learn if we would honestly study Paul's life. Before most even pray for discernment or think about their situation at all, they start binding and loosing and praying that God would take them out of their bad circumstances. True to our cowardly nature, most opt for the way of escape. When escape does not come, though, their faith in God is crushed, all for the mere misunderstanding of the purpose and nature of the different storms of life. What is truly amazing is that we continue to miss this spiritual lesson, though it has been in print for nearly two thousand years.

I have touched on the fact earlier that some people in religious circles persist even to this day in teaching that we need not go through the storms of life. Their teachings spill over with man's vanity in thinking that life is all about us. Our problem, they insist, is that we do not have enough faith or that we do not understand our covenantal rights with God. For the more enlightened, they claim, there are ways out of trouble that we simply reject by our willful blindness. The problem with this pie-in-the-sky mentality is that it is clearly unbiblical. What ultimately takes place is that confusion swirls around our heads as we partake of these half-truths, threatening to disillusion us irreparably. I quote, on God's authority, that "Yes, though I walk *through* the [deep, sunless] valley of the shadow of death, I will fear or dread no evil, for You are with me; Your rod [to protect] and Your staff [to guide], they comfort me" (Psalm 23:4 (AMP)–italics mine). Sometimes faith, or the lack thereof, is not the problem. Sometimes obedience and perseverance are our more pressing issues. Not even Paul the Apostle was exempt from walking through some difficult times in his life (some being an incredible under-statement as it relates to the sufferings Paul endured). In addition, Jesus, the Son of God, had troubles that we dare not honestly consider. The more enjoyable topics seem to surround irrelevant details such as the color of Christ's tunic and what that means for us or the number of wealthy people with whom He rubbed shoulders and how encouraging that should be to us. Answering these questions, many believe, will clue us in to His considerable financial portfolio. We always, as a dear friend and former pastor used to tell me, appear to put the emphasis on the wrong syllable. The harsh truth is that we all have our burdens to bear and mine-fields that we must walk through. Key factors in God's eyes are how we walk through the turbulence that surrounds us and what our reactions are to the venomous bites we bear. Too often, we pray for God to rescue us *from* our malignities when typically, God wants to take us *through* our severities.

Paul's admonition in Second Corinthians states, "But He said to me, My grace (My favor and loving-kindness and mercy) is enough for you [sufficient against any danger and enables you to bear the trouble manfully]; for *My* strength *and* power are made perfect (fulfilled and completed) *and show themselves most effective* in [your] weakness" (2 Corinthians 12:9a AMP). Isaiah revealed that, "When you pass through the waters, I will be with you, and through the rivers, they will not overwhelm you. When you walk through the fire, you will not be burned *or* scorched, nor will the flame kindle upon you" (Isaiah 43:2 AMP). Contrary to what some are teaching today, the Old Testament is still a valid scriptural resource and has life lessons and truths that are just as valid today as they were the day they were written. What God has continually promised through His mouthpieces for thousands of years is that He will take us through the dark times in our lives. So get ready, it will sometimes be a wild ride!

Brought up Short

*"A sailing ship underway could only be
brought to an emergency standstill
by dropping the anchors. Not a pleasant experience."* [203]

Acts 27:27–28:1

The fourteenth night had come and we were drifting *and* being driven about in the Adriatic Sea, when about midnight the sailors began to suspect that they were drawing near to some land. So they took sounding and found twenty fathoms, and a little farther on they sounded again and found fifteen fathoms. Then fearing that we might fall off [our course] onto rocks, they dropped four anchors from the stern and kept wishing for daybreak to come. And as the sailors were trying to escape [secretly] from the ship and were lowering the small boat into the sea, pretending that they were going to lay out anchors from the bow, Paul said to the centurion and the soldiers, Unless these men remain in the ship, you cannot be saved. Then the soldiers cut away the ropes that held the small boat, and let it fall *and* drift away. While they waited until it should become day, Paul entreated them all to take some food, saying, This is the fourteenth day that you have been continually in suspense *and* on the alert without food, having eaten nothing. So I urge (warn, exhort, encourage, advise) you to take some food [for your safety]—it will give you strength; for not a hair is to perish from the head of any one of you. Having said these words, he took bread and, giving thanks to God before them all, he broke it and began to eat. Then they all became more cheerful *and* were encouraged and took food themselves. All told, there were 276 souls in the ship. And after they had eaten sufficiently, [they proceeded] to lighten the ship, throwing out the wheat into the sea. Now when it was day [and they saw the land], they did not recognize it, but they noticed a bay with a beach on which they [taking counsel] purposed to run the ship ashore if they possibly could. So they cut the cables *and* severed the anchors and left them in the sea; at the same time unlashing the ropes that held the rudders and hosting the foresail to the wind, they headed for the beach. But striking a crosscurrent (a place open to two seas) they ran the ship aground. The prow stuck fast and remained immovable, and the stern began to break up under the violent force of the waves. It was the counsel of the soldiers to kill the prisoners, lest any of them should swim to land and escape; But the centurion, wishing to save Paul, prevented their carrying out their purpose. He commanded those who could swim to throw themselves overboard first and make for the shore, And the rest on heavy boards or pieces of the vessel. And so it was that all escaped safely to land. After we were safe on the island, we knew *and* recognized that it was called Malta. (AMP)

SCUTTLE

As we rejoin the effort aboard this Alexandrian freighter, we find that we are in the middle of an intense argument. Crewmembers, sailors who have nothing to lose except a paycheck, are attempting to jump ship and abandon the passengers, captain and owner. Probably fed up with dirty looks and with any payday in serious jeopardy, they had endured enough. What did it matter to them about the passengers or ship? Their only concern was for their personal safety. Once caught, however, the men were sheepish and apologetic (and possibly a little angry at their foiled attempt of escaping undetected). Again, Paul steps up and speaks his mind. The only difference being that this time they listen to him. Here we find that Paul has convinced Julius to have his soldiers hack away at the rope until the rowboat disappears within the hungry gape of the surf. Wow! Julius, having full authority on this ship, could have seized it for his own use, but he proved the wisdom of his assignment and did what the man of God recommended. Of one thing we can be sure, in this situation, what Julius did was unthinkable and courageous to say the least.

Ships in the ancient world were not like ours are today. That one little rowboat was all they had with which to get off that ship and to the shore. In our modern world, commercial ships and recreational boats have safety standards that must be adhered to that define the particular number of lifebuoys, lifeboats, self-igniting lights, self-activating smoke signals and buoyant life-lines that each type and size of vessel is required to carry.[204] These standards have developed over a few hundred years due to the meaningless loss of life by disasters at sea. Ships today are required by law to have at least enough lifeboats aboard to accommodate every person on the ship in the event that an emergency evacuation of the ship is necessary. Now imagine being in this gregale with nearly 300 people on board and cutting away the only practical means of escape–that and the fact that only a handful of people could have fit in the dinghy at any one time. With the spiritual imperative aside and in a purely practical vein, since this Alexandrian freighter had only this one small dinghy in tow with which to reach shore, it made no sense whatsoever to cut it away at any point during this storm, let alone when they were finally so close to shore. So what does this matter? It matters because most of us would never dare to cut it away. When we are in the middle of a storm that is hell-bent on destroying us we will do anything to save ourselves, but we generally will not cut off any chance we have at escape.

Too often, when trouble comes our way, we try to escape by any means available; sneaking away, running away, lying, cheating, or anything that gets us out of our mess and promises a lesser commitment than the storm. That is not always what God has in mind for us, though. The embarrassing reality is that we nearly always have an escape plan in mind. Not only that, we also have the items necessary for escape lined up and ready to go at a moment's notice. If financial difficulties should arise, we will not go through them. We will just sell the house, boat, or third vehicle and use the money to pay our creditors back. If it gets unbearable, we will simply declare bankruptcy. If our marriage gets too rocky and it does not look promising, we already have the divorce lawyer's phone number on our speed dial and an alternate location picked out in which to live. On and on the list goes; we can call it quits or relocate or burn bridges or sever relationships. We will do whatever promises to temporarily evacuate us from our storm.

Obey That Strange Urging

In situations where the worst is taking place all around us, the critical key is that we do what God is telling us to do, no matter how shortsighted, arrogant or disastrous it may seem—and we must do it sooner rather than later. It is at these times that we should not allow the turbulence or even common sense to dictate to us the proper course of action. In all seriousness, and in light of practical and common sense procedures, the entire complement of people on board this ship should have at that point jumped overboard and made for the shore. It was foolish of them to stay and even more foolish to cut away the lifeboat; however, when we have a word from God, it makes all else fade in importance. Sometimes we must suffer through the heartache and hardship of financial ruin and the loss of possessions, but it is not the end of the world. Yes, God wants to prosper His people, but not all people will experience financial prosperity to the same degree or at all. Moreover, some good, Godly Christians may never be able to climb over the cliffs of poverty and up the mountains of prosperity. Most times the financial ruin that we must suffer through is due to our poor choices and bad decisions, and no amount of faith will reverse the course of ruin. Many times our physical struggles are due to the overwhelming abuse that we have heaped upon ourselves with decades of gluttony and improper diet literally tucked under our belts. In these times, the disease or sickness that results is justified by our own neglect and abuse and may not be rectified by God in some shining, glorious moment. When life gets this tough and rough, it is often too hard for us to get a word from God and stick to it. It is much easier just to abandon the ship and skulk away. During these moments, however, it is critical that we obey that strange urge, cut away all means of escape, and let them go. Not doing so will deny us the joy of knowing the freedom, victory, and peace that comes from staying on board and sticking this storm out as God has commanded—even if it means that we float to safety on the tattered pieces that remain of our broken down lives.

COURAGE

Paul displayed a critical quality of character that we must possess–courage. Courage is what will enable us to choose what is right and not what is popular or recommended, or even what looks to be the smart choice. Without it, we will never dare to perform the sometimes-bizarre gyrations that God requires. With it, we will be driven by what is beyond us and our understanding to attempt what may appear impossible, and then see God come through for us like never before. So, just what is this courage, and how can we define it so that it makes sense?

Courage is that quality and firmness of spirit that enables us to face fear and difficult situations with full possession of our own powers, with full assurance and firm determination that the reward kept continually in view shall be obtained, and with an unbroken spirit which is unshaken in purpose and belief.

So what does this mean to us today during our circumstances of doom? Simply put it means this: That we will have the wherewithal to chose the right and difficult road, if need be, in order to make it out of the storms of life alive and well, even if that means that others oppose us or that the road we chose to travel down does not appear to lead anywhere. We all desperately need this simple yet elusive trait that we cannot seem to embody. It is this tour de force from which we shy away. We need courage to make it through the storm God's way and to retain our sanity and purpose. Not many people choose courage. Most choose to lose during the storms of life by their inability to make the tough, gritty decisions, but God wants more out of us than losing. God is encouraging us to be more like Paul.

In my definition of courage, I indicated part of the trait was that we are to have full assurance and firm determination that the reward kept continually in view shall be obtained. What exactly does that mean? For Paul it meant that he must go to Rome because God told him so. In our particular circumstance, we must find out from Him what our "Rome" is. Despite all that was taking place around him, Paul hung on firmly to his destination like nothing else. He could not become frustrated with how long it was taking or how sidetracked he had become, because it was up to God to get him there. The situation was out of Paul's control. This is why we must know what destiny awaits us. When we do, we can have something to hold on to during our life's most tragic upheavals. Yes, we must hold on to God's unchanging hand, but just how do we go about doing that? It is simple. We must hold on to that which He has confided to us, and we must become assured that what He has said will actually come true—whether that be good or bad in our eyes. Many of the early Christians knew that they were to be martyred. How did they face it? Because they knew that this was their ultimate destination, and the freedom and peace that came from knowing that gave them the strength to face the music. Most of us will never be required to make that life's blood commitment, but we are given what I believe is sometimes a more difficult task. We are assigned the task of living for Him. The fact remains that we must go on; we must reach our "Rome" no matter what storm stands in our way.

WHY CHALLENGE AUTHORITY?

Though Paul had a lot to say during this cursed voyage, there is one word that we do not see escaping his lips–why. He did not ask God why because he already knew and understood (and penned) the words that answer this question. "We are assured and know that [God being a partner in their labor] all things work together and are [fitting into a plan] for good to and for those who love God and are called according to [His] design and purpose" (Romans 8:28 AMP). Having experienced both good and bad times, Paul understood that "To everything there is a season, and a time for every matter *or* purpose under heaven" (Ecclesiastes 3:1 AMP). His vision was more distant than ours tends to be, less focused on the temporal, and keenly searching the eternal realm. He had no reason to question God, so why do we find it so necessary?

Storms come up. That is it. We must deal with it. But questioning authority has taken on a life of its own in recent decades to the point where it now parades around as verbal murder. Today's culture is in your face and believes that anyone can confront anyone else on any matter deemed undesirable. In the situation where we experience a relentless tempest and don't think we should, we simply fall back onto this behavior and whack away at God. Forgetting Solomon's wisdom, we shout at the heavens as if its occupants were common fools. We would do well to heed the voices of reason that warn us against such suicidal tendencies. Solomon said, "For the word of a king is authority *and* power, and who can say to him, 'What are you doing?'" (Ecclesiastes 8:4 AMP). And let us not forget the words of God when He rebuked Job saying, "Then the Lord answered Job out of the whirlwind and said, Who is this that darkens counsel by words without knowledge? Gird up now your loins like a man, and I will demand of you, and you declare to Me. Where were you when I laid the foundation of the earth? Declare to Me, if you have *and* know understanding" (Job 38:1–4 AMP).

By God's design, His church is supposed to be a model

for the world—a picture of the way life should be lived. But most of the time our churches end up mirroring society, only we dress up our arrogance in finer clothes. With a mindset that believes we have a God-given right to challenge authority, we cannot seem to get out of our own way long enough to realize that it is reckless to challenge God. Our misunderstanding of God's ways leads us to nurture the questioning urge and to rebuke His perceived shortcomings. With that said, I will tread lightly here and say that sometimes it is right, acceptable and necessary to question authority, but this should only be done with the humble, meek spirit that Christ embodied—never in a challenging manner. However, with that situation aside, it is never acceptable to question God's veracity or integrity. We must not lean to our own understanding and should never forget that God is still sovereign and omniscient; we are not. Attitudes like those that Paul displayed in not questioning God are those that we should embody lest we be overtaken and condemned.

SIGNS OF THE STORM

At times in life, we become confused with what is going on around us. Unsure of whether our recent attack is an isolated incursion or if the current weather conditions are indicative of something more sinister, we are often in need of a guide by which we can objectively judge our circumstances. We need a spiritual forecaster who can interpret the weather patterns and give us well-advanced warnings of things to come. Unfortunately there is no such person upon whom we can rely except Christ and what He has given us in His word. What follows is a basic guide that will, when examined, lead us to the correct and obvious conclusions. The items on this list, when added together, mark the various blows of a storm. When planning a family vacation, even though we have the routes and stops mapped out, we must still rely on the billboards and signs along our highways in order to pinpoint our location successfully. Therefore, it is with our spiritual lives as well. We must use the signposts of severe weather as indicators that can help us mark out where we are in our storm. One could already be barreling toward us, or we could be in the eye of the worst hurricane imaginable and not realize it (although we would have to be nearly comatose not to realize that). What we cannot allow ourselves to believe is that the foul weather is simply going to pass over our lives and leave us untouched while simultaneously devastating the rest of the neighborhood. We must face the reality of the storm and realize where we are in it. Although no commentary accompanies each blow, they should be self-explanatory to anyone experiencing the hell brought about by a marauding tempest. If any of these resemble our current circumstances, then we would be foolish not to take another reading and get ourselves in under cover. (All are taken from Acts 27.)

- v.4 "the winds were contrary to us."

- v.7 "we made slow progress and arrived with difficulty."

- v.7 "the wind did not permit us to proceed."

- v.9 "the season was well advanced."

- v.13 "when the south wind blew softly."

- v.14 "but soon afterward a violent wind . . . came bursting down."

- v.15 "and when the ship was caught and was unable to head against the wind."

- v.17 "and so were driven along."

- v.18 "As we were being dangerously tossed about by the violence of the storm."

- v.20 "and when neither sun nor stars were visible for many days."

- v.20 "and no small tempest kept raging about us."

- v.27 "And we were drifting and being driven."

- v.41 "But striking a crosscurrent."

- v.41 "and the stern began to break up under the violent force of the waves."

NOTE: This list is not all-inclusive and should be only considered as a basic guide in reading the signposts along our route. Please refer to the entire testimony of the Holy Bible for a complete list of all storm related billboards and warnings.

CROSSCURRENTS

Finding ourselves at the mercy of the harrowing atrocities of life, we have set our anchors deep as a last ditch effort to avoid the shattering effects of running against the rocks of destruction. As we have made our last stand, however, we often briefly catch a glimpse of solid ground through the mist—a shoreline that beckons gleefully—and we determine to run our ship aground. Upon reaching this conclusion, we are confronted with a critical decision and a disturbing choice. In order to go for the shore while in the midst of this wild northeaster, we really cannot expend the time and effort necessary in hauling the anchors back up on deck and securing them to the ship. Moreover, even if we wanted to, we could not while fighting the violent winds and massive swells. The only choice left is to cut the cables, thereby severing the anchors from the ship, and leave them behind in the sea. This is precisely the situation that faced the mariners as they contemplated their excursion toward the shore. Unsure as to whether it would actually work and concerned that if it did not they would be missing four critical anchors, they bravely decided to go for it.

Unceremoniously they cut the ropes away and abandoned the anchors that earlier had been their safety net. These anchors represented the faith and hope that setting them out would keep their ship from danger; they were the security resident within a proven methodology. In addition, they also unlashed the rudder (the steering mechanism), hoisted the foresail (their means of propulsion), and carried out the duties that they had not performed in over two weeks. The foresail and rudder represented their way of rescue seated within their own natural, common sense thinking. Like those aboard the Alexandrian freighter, we cut all ties, burn any bridges connecting us with our past situation, and display an impressive flash of courage as we lumber towards the shore.

The only problem with our approach is that the sandbar that lies hidden from our view, scarcely submerged beneath this wicked water, is awaiting our ill-advised proposition. Though a slender piece of sandy beach now epitomizes our hope and destiny, we have failed to consider one last, critical element. Was this the way of God's choosing? Minutely pleased to be back underway, we briefly enjoy a moment of self-assurance before the unthinkable happens again. We run into one last problem, a sandbar of which we were not aware and crosscurrents that will tear us apart. Often when striking out in a last, desperate effort to reach a place of refuge, we strike a situation that exposes us to vicious crosscurrents—a place open to two seas. Had God instructed these mariners to run the ship aground? No, the Bible says that they took counsel and purposed amongst themselves to do it. Falling back to their carnal ways of making decisions, they began backtracking down a road destined to failure. In our lives, we must remain empty of ourselves and open only to God's voice. It will do us no good to chart our own course and to then rationalize those decisions when God is speaking something entirely different. The main problem with the mariners' decision and God's direction was that they were from two opposing schools of thought—a crosscurrent, if you will. Whenever we are open to opposing schools of thought, we have the potential for a dangerous and unpredictable crosscurrent that neither our ship nor we may be able to handle. It may have been in the back of their minds to run the ship aground and then haul it back off the beach after the storm had passed, but it was in God's mind that this ship was marked for destruction.

In speaking of the crosscurrents they encountered, we must keep in mind this idea of opposing schools of thought. Any time that we allow differing viewpoints within our realm of consideration, we are exposing ourselves to danger–crosscurrents. This is not to say that we should never allow this situation to occur, but it is to say that when it does we must be careful to choose on the side of God. Let us look at what crosscurrents the passengers aboard this Alexandrian ship were exposed to:

• The crosscurrent between the storm and their ultimate destination, Rome.

• The crosscurrent between the faith of God and the fear of the men.

• The crosscurrent between the crew and the other passengers on the ship.

• The crosscurrent between Julius and the soldiers.

• The crosscurrent between their desires and those of God.

The situation that we must avoid is to have come so far down the road of our aggression, weathering countless days of wind and rain, only to find ourselves stuck at this last, resolute place. Having held on to a word from God and having valiantly fought to retain our hope, we now find ourselves mired down within a few yards of refuge and with no means of getting there. We find ourselves stranded on the verge of a miracle. Many people, they say, give up just moments before their dreams begin to come true, unable to believe any longer (some even take their own lives in a moment of extreme and selfish weakness). This is exactly the situation that was taking place aboard this ship. With the boat irreversibly stuck and with the addition of the two currents now hammering against the hull, the soldiers implode as they suggest that every prisoner be executed. How many times have we done this very thing? On the verge of our rescue and moments before our escape, we send out the dogs with the command to kill every dream we have ever held dear. Giving up, we finally acquiesce and believe that it was all an elaborate fantasy after all; however, we should pause just one more time and inquire of the Lord. Maturity must take over as we enter this final stretch of our journey, and we must not kill (figuratively) those who are legitimately on board our ship. Salvaging what we can from the wreckage of our lives, we must now jump ship and swim or float to shore. This is that dogged, determined faith that says, "I am going to make it to shore (my refuge) and then on to my destiny (my Rome) no matter how I have to get there (on pieces of wreckage) and no matter how much salt water and seaweed I have to swallow (the storm). What God is looking for is this type of person; one who can hold on even after broken dreams and incredible loss and again strike out towards destiny's island of refuge.

A FINAL ROLL CALL

As we end this journey, we find nearly 300 people staggering to shore. Some have made it to land under their own power, while others were transported upon wooden barrels and chunks of the ship's hull. As we take one final look out to the sandbar, we faintly hear the whoosh as the remains of the huge freighter repose beneath the sea. Turning our eyes back to the sandy beach, we take in a compelling scene. Hundreds of people are scattered about, some vomiting up seawater and blood, while others lay collapsed upon heaps of debris and wreckage. The captain is sobbing over his failure and drowned career while the owner stares blankly out to sea, unable to extricate himself from his state of shock. Most are huddled in the groups they traveled with and are soaked, shivering, hungry and exhausted. Luke is treating as many of the injured as he can while Aristarchus is running from huddle to huddle making sure that everyone is alive. Julius motions with his hand to his men as his eyes dart around the grisly scene, mentally checking off the prisoners on his list. With everyone accounted for, he briefly displays a satisfied smirk. His command of the situation was remarkable, and his decisions were courageous. This will definitely look good on his résumé. As natives emerge from the thickets, our surreal moment of detachment quickly ends; controlled pandemonium ensues. With a fire built and everyone somewhat comfortable, we will exit this scene and peer one last time into the lessons this storm has taught us; those lessons that are critical to our existence.

Most often during my personal storms, I get to the point where I am so sick of listening to the wind, rain and pounding surf that I feel like poking holes in my eardrums—just to enjoy some silence. Although I know that I need to listen to God's voice, the clashing of the otherworldly forces that are battling all around me often drown it out. At times, I marvel at Paul's ability to tune it all out and listen to the voice of the angel. At other times, it becomes a completely natural process that I do not quite understand. Often we do not know how to hear from God during the storm and in the midst of all of this noise, but we must. It is both simple and difficult. It is something that affects each of us differently. For me it is a nagging knowing that I am doing something wrong or a sick feeling inside of me that will not go away or sleepless nights and tear-filled days. At other times, though, it is the sure confidence that I have somehow heard the voice of God speak to me about a particular situation, and of that I cannot let go. Whatever way He speaks to us, we need to focus on what He has spoken. We must hear His voice and heed the message.

To recap the lessons we have learned along the way. We know that Paul and the other prisoners were on this ship because they were in bondage to someone else, but there were others on the ship that were not in bondage to anyone. There were free men on board who consciously made the choice to board unassisted and unaided by any other human being. So what are the reasons we might be on board a ship similar to Paul's? There are three reasons why we might be on an "Alexandrian freighter," and with each of those reasons come lessons we should learn.

First, we may be like Paul and find ourselves captive on some boat. Our equivalence to Paul in this situation may be that we are an employee, church member or parishioner, spouse or sibling, convict, educator, patriot or club member. We have spotted foul weather ahead and keep raising the warning flags, but no one seems to be listening to us. Though we know that staying on board is the right thing to do in spite of the inevitable outcome, we must learn the following lessons.

• We can learn the discipline and perseverance it takes to make it through all that the storm unleashes against us, including an inevitable shipwreck.

• We can learn to gain control over our tongue without backbiting or complaining or otherwise speaking incorrectly. A key factor is also not attempting to gather support for an unlawful mutiny.

• We can learn to hear from God even in the midst of the tumultuous aggressions around us.

• We can learn to trust in the destination that God has ordained for us to arrive at despite any temporary losses or setbacks that we may encounter.

• We can learn to trust in God no matter what the weather is like. Once we realize that He is always there for us even when it looks like He isn't, we have gained a key victory over our own worst enemy, our carnal mind.

• We can learn to play a vital and important role in our own rescue rather than just expecting God to bail us out while we sit around and sing songs of deliverance. He requires that we do our part whenever it is possible.

• We can learn not to lose hope, because that is fundamentally worse than not having faith. Without hope, it is impossible to have faith. But when we have a clear word from God as to where we need to go (hope), then we can face down (faith) anything that tries to hinder or derail us (storm).

Second, we may be like the owner or captain of the ship and exercise final authority over all matters pertaining to our ship. Our equivalence to either of these men in this situation may be that we are a captain, boss, parent, eldest sibling, principal, CEO, pastor, elected official, chief, warden, or a leader in any type of organization either public or private. Our ship is full of precious cargo, and there are many obvious reasons why we cannot leave this ship. When faced with a dangerous situation and presented with a tempestuous storm, we must learn the following lessons.

• We must learn the trust and obedience involved in listening to God, or his mouthpiece, and to obey whatever is spoken (even if that direction comes from one of those under our guidance). We must learn that sometimes as leaders we have too much self-interest to make sound decisions by ourselves, and that we need other input in order to choose wisely.

• We must learn to listen the first time when a word of warning is announced from a reputable source. This will cause us less pain and may result in no net loss of cargo, livelihood or life.

• We must learn not to lean upon our excuses, experience or superior wisdom. When faced with potential danger, we must lay aside all of the excuses as to why we should not delay and all of the valid reasons why we should take the risk and go for

Rome now. Sometimes our superior attitude can take us places out of which our experience cannot bail us.

Third, we may be like one of the passengers and willingly boarded this ship of our own volition, or we may be like Julius and have had a pressing need or reason why we had to board this particular ship. Our equivalence to either the passenger or centurion in this situation may be that we are any of the people listed in the previous two examples. We now find ourselves sandwiched between the poor decision of boarding this ship and a raging inferno threatening to kill us and decimate our belongings. The lessons we need to learn in this scenario are the same as for both of the two previous scenarios. (Please refer to the lists above).

THE HORRORS OF THE STORM

I have outlined in the preceding chapters the situation that Paul and the passengers aboard the Alexandrian ship faced, but now I would like to backtrack a little in an attempt at bringing this closer to home. As I have stated before we, like Paul, may find ourselves aboard a ship whose fate is sealed. Having expressed our opinion and warned of the impending danger inherent in ignoring our advice, we return to our tent to find that the ship's captain and owner did not listen to us but decided to move on. With the wind picking up and the rain pelting down, we try to find some shelter from the precipitation as we stagger across the lurching deck. Winter is setting in with its glacial whiff surrounding us. We are far from home and long for our own bed and visibility, in any sense of the word, is non-existent. While everything around us is in an uproar and our location is a mystery, the only thing we are certain of is the inevitability of our shipwreck.

When we find ourselves plunged into this raging sea, we instantly recall a lifetime of choices that we somehow wish we could relive. Thrown from the deck of this ship only to land in a churning ocean forty plus feet below, and driven farther from the ship with each angry blast of old man winter's icy breathing, we find ourselves paddling with all available appendages while swallowing gallons of filthy sea brine. A stiff, assaulting wind howls all around us as the ship weakens and yearns for calmer weather and friendlier waters. Huge deep-sea undulations, which momentarily levitate our flailing torso that is barely distinguishable amidst the sea-corpses scattered atop the cresting swell, cruelly give way as they vacuum away beneath us. The troughs respond with equal glee as they reveal the hideous features of an ocean floor that we will shortly and violently encounter. With a firsthand knowledge of the hell we are experiencing, we struggle just to survive, trying to avoid being swept away from the others and attempting to get to a shore that we cannot see. No forethought went into our suicidal plunge, and we have no life-vest, no portable floatation device, no raft, no emergency radio beacon, no wetsuit, no goggles, no nose plugs and no idea where we are or what is around us.

We hear the crashing surf and surmise that there must be rocks close by. We know that a huge craft is breaking apart right behind us and that someone said they saw a beach. We were ordered to swim, but it has been so long since we have even been in the water that we are not sure we even remember how. We have been chained to a guard for weeks or have been locked in a prison cell for years. Our muscles have definitely atrophied to the point where they are nearly useless on the ground, let alone in an angry sea. We cannot even bear to face the next wave that picks us up and hurls us toward an unknown shore. Wicked undercurrents are tearing at our clothes and feet and trying to drag us away. The same crosscurrents that are pummeling the ship are also doing their best to make sure that we, too, do not survive. Flashes of loved ones scream through our minds, and photos of peaceful times hang upon the walls of our imagination. As the laughter of our children and loved ones momentarily drowns out the disaster around us, it all suddenly gets whisked away. We are left alone again with our painful reality; the reality that we are probably going to die. There are screams and cries all around us. Children are begging for help as they flail their tiny members in a vain attempt at staying afloat and not drowning. Women are unleashing blood curdling screams, vainly attempting to find their babies and begging God to lead them by motherly instinct. Grown men are crying, swimming, and vowing allegiance to God in exchange for His assistance. It is here that we find ourselves.

It is possible that we are like the captain, the one who first strutted onto this stage. Maybe we know that we alone are responsible for this state of affairs, that all of these lives aboard our ship were in our hands. Knowing that it is because of our poor judgment that these people have to endure this ordeal, we may well be lost in a deep depression. When we get back home, if we ever make it back, we will have to lay off the rest of our employees, maybe start bankruptcy proceedings, possibly lose our home and everything else that we own, and maybe even face criminal charges of manslaughter if any of these people drown. There will be hell to pay. We know now that we should have listened to Paul, but the fact is that we did not.

Another likely scenario is that we may find that we are like one of the prisoners finding ourselves suddenly free from the constricting shackles that moments ago bound us to our captor. Now thoughts of escape dominate our mind. Our mind races as we consider swimming to shore and escaping into the trees or into some swamp, free from our penal sentence–but free to do what? We don't even know where we are, and escape may pose more dangers than just sticking with this punishment.

On the other hand, maybe we find that we are like one of the crewmembers who tried to escape just hours ago. We are being beaten not only by the waves, but also by a couple of men from the ship who think we deserve a little more punishment for our cowardice than we got. Our ordeal will soon be one of the most intense, lonely, desperate moments of our lives. Thoughts of guilt plague us as our conscience condemns our earlier actions. We give up trying to fight off these men's blows and just let them come. We deserve this disaster, being beaten and the dangers of this sea. Choosing courage over cowardice could have been our reward; however, we tried to run and will now have to live forever with the disgrace and shame that our actions have brought upon us.

What God wants to know in all of this is (no matter which member of the boat we can identify with) can we still hear His voice and obey Him or will we let His voice get drowned out by all that is going on around us? Will we let His voice of reason lose its power and prominence in our life and waive its authority to that of the pleading voices around us? Like Pilate, will we refuse to listen to the right voice, chicken out in our decisive moment and disavow our responsibilities? Or will we allow our own words to take over or those of Job's friends or those of the mongrel horde that is trying to break through our Great Wall and take over our land? Whose voice will we listen to, God's or that of an imposter? At this critical juncture, will we finally listen to God and not to our better, rational judgment, business training or our superior intelligence and heed the still small voice of God? Life's moments are quickly ticking by. We must choose now.

Section Five

BALANCING THE SETTLEMENT SHEET

MANHANDLING A ROUGH CREW

OUR TRUE SELF

At their simplest explanation, the storms of life represent times of change that are difficult, at best, to handle. It is during these seasons of turmoil and heartache that we find out who our true self is. We can be, but we cannot always do. Who we are will always show up loud and clear when the blows come swinging in; we cannot fake it. The root question God wants to help us answer in the midst of each battle is the question of our heart. God wants each of us to know where our heart lies. Rapacious storms will leave their sickening stench upon us in the form of scars that we may bear the rest of our days, but what we must avoid is the intended wounding of all whom we come into contact with thereafter. Some of us will take the half-learned lessons of our storm and use them to destroy the faith of those around us, warning them of the inevitable loss and hopeless situations to come. In this case, we will have missed the point of our calamity—to grow, to adapt, to survive. When we give in and become aimless, no more a survivor but a victim, then we can never move beyond the wound of our demise. Instead, we will forever carry with us the pain of our loss, having never honestly dealt with our own selves. In effect we then become the walking dead while bearing a malignant sword. We will flail and cry out in desperate anguish to know the reason for the state of our lives, begging God to let us out of our atrocity. Many of us will even wish for death rather than bear the thought of enduring the tempest's wicked kicks. What we really do not want is to deal with these storms of life because they represent that which we would rather shy away from. Rather than having to deal with answering the difficult questions we must ask ourselves, we will do almost anything else. Driven by modern claims of the power we can wield, we would rather avoid the difficulties of life altogether. The questions we seek to avoid are painful. Are we the problem? Are the raging seas due to our own arrogance, ignorance or disobedience? Has someone close to us caused this storm to plow into us? Were we that naïve in our assessment of a prior warning? Have we become involved in the affairs of another man's ship that is destined to shipwreck? Does our faith need to be stretched? Do we really believe that our Heavenly Father cares for us? We long for an answer that will validate our superior spiritual accomplishments while pointing the fingers of blame at another. More often than not, though, the fingers of blame point directly back at us.

Why did this storm come and why would God allow this to happen to us? It is most often during the challenges of life that God wishes to reveal that which is truly within us. He wants to know how we will react, and He wants to show the footage to us. Will we shrink back and rely on those old, familiar habits that we have always counted on? Or will we step up to the home plate of life and hit a home run by allowing God to change us? When we are faced with the removal of that power we have grown accustomed to wielding, will we give up or will we choose another bat and swing away? If we are presented with an impossible storm while Christ is on board, will we cry out in desperation and rebuke God, or will we step up and speak the storm away? Will we vehemently wrap our cloaks of spirituality around us, or will we allow God to strip away our false self in order to show us who we really are and where we need to change? He wants us to have faith in Him and to remember that He cares. God wants to encourage us like the angel encouraged Paul to take heart. Our heavenly Father desires that we not continue to lose hope and courage. We must shake ourselves awake and confront the pain of what we are experiencing. Running below the deck to hide or accusing the master of sin will not do us any good. Admitting our sin may be the first step, but embracing it will make it our death sentence. All of the men we have studied had a window to their soul opened, allowing them to peer in and gaze upon their own nakedness. God will do the same for us. When we are given that opportunity, we must take it and change. Jonah made no changes that would again make his life worthwhile. He made no effort at all to change his attitudes and behaviors and to become known throughout the ages as a man who dared to change. Instead, he took the wound of his sin and made it his epitaph. I pray that we are wiser and more honest with ourselves than he was.

TOUGH CHOICES AND MOUNTING LOSSES

Surviving the storms of life is about making tough choices. It is about doing what has to be done in order to get through. When faced with adversity, we can speak the wind and seas into obedience, speak ourselves into obedience, or walk through the valley. Whichever solution we choose will require tough decisions that will not always come easily. Making it through the storms with all of our stuff is good, but making it through alive is the most important. We will not always make the correct choices and will sometimes falter and fall, but we can usually always do better than we did the last time. It is completely up to us.

In surviving the haughty aggressions, there are some losses that we may suffer. What is important is that we learn to expect these losses. Following is a list of some of the more common losses that will occur. Often when encountering treacherous squalls, we feel abandoned and begin to harbor bitter feelings toward those around us. We must fight this urge and understand that these losses are predictable and sometimes unavoidable. In fact, most of them are not emotional at all once we realize the mechanics of the situations in which we find ourselves. It is important that we accept these facts before the storms arrive so that we can deal with the difficulties better when they do affect our life. Pretty sunsets and silver-lined clouds are not the norm in life, and they are not the covenantal promise of God either. Sometimes we will be blessed by the incredible and abundant blessings of God. At other times, it will appear as if the wrath of Almighty God is directed solely upon us. As I said, not everyone will experience these losses; however, for some they may all become one long, unbroken chain of hellish events.

• Loss of communication. Gradually we will experience ever-increasing disruptions in our lines of communication causing successive small gaps to build to the point where we have lost all regular, necessary communication with those around us. What we must realize is that this is normal because the storm's intensity has the power to interrupt all forms of communication with the outside world. Falsely we may conclude that people are avoiding us and purposely not trying to stay in touch, but during a storm there is no way we will be able to maintain any regular contact with anyone except those on the ship with us (and even that will be stressed to its limits). We must rest assured that communication lines will eventually be reestablished after the storm has passed. In addition, when conditions do improve, many whom we had lost touch with will not even realize what happened, for it was of no intent of their own.

• Loss of respect. Because we are in a storm, many of the weak and immature around us will begin to question our Christian experience (and maybe rightly so). For those who are results oriented, a growing concern will fester that somehow we have faltered and can no longer be trusted. Though we may have had nothing to do with either the tempest's arrival or its refusal to leave, it will be concluded that we are in sin (and we may be); however, the cause does not matter, because the loss of respect in our ability to live right and make godly decisions will have already been established and the stamps of approval will have already been removed from us. What is important to remember here is that this will happen. Many of those around us (including members of our own faith or family) will not be able to handle what is taking place and will no longer feel that they can respect us, our decisions or our lifestyle (no matter how godly we may be). One final item here is that when a group of peers or family members all lose respect for us, it often leads to us losing our own self-respect.

• Loss of influence. When those around us lose their respect for us and our capacity to model a wise and prudent life, then they will no longer allow themselves to be influenced by us. Where we once had influence there will now be a void. No longer able to hold us in high regard, those around us may also no longer allow us to lead them. Many negative words and connotations will be spoken about us, and it will be advised that we no longer be heeded. This will be especially true when we are experiencing the hell of the onslaughts of life that cannot be spoken away. When we are not outwardly manifesting a certain aura of success, then our position of influence is in jeopardy. The loss of influence eventually leads to the next loss, that of association.

• Loss of employment or loss of association. This is a more permanent form of the first item (loss of communication) and is a real possibility when we are in a more horrific or prolonged storm. It is an inevitable, albeit usually unwise, outcome. Most of us are surrounded by or associated with a certain percentage of weak, immature people. It is one of these people who may be in the position of authority/leadership over us either in our place of employment or at our place of association (church, club, association, civic group, etc.). Excepting in situations where we are clearly in direct violation of a moral or ethical law, most will see our situation as that which warrants dismissal. As the basis for their decision, they will cite the onslaught we are experiencing and will draw (oftentimes false) conclusions about what is taking place and why. This will then cause that person to recommend or to carry out the worst form of arrogance, the execution of a complete and permanent separation where all ties with us are cut (typically against our will). Again, this is to be expected, though it will most usually be the worst decision that can be made. At a time when we need any anchor to hold, we will abruptly be cut off. [In defense of the axe swinger—there are times where letting someone who is in a gross, immoral or illegal situation go is the right solution; however, we are not discussing this type of a situation. In this instance, we are talking about the humiliating act of abandonment that so often follows the furiousness of our worst fight of faith.]

• Loss of appetite. In a prolonged fight, we often lose not only our ability but also our desire to eat. Hunger becomes just another distraction in the madness of our struggle. While too busy trying to survive, we often do not feel like we have time to eat. Sometimes we even believe that our loss of appetite will bring about our inevitable demise more quickly. This is something that we must fight because it is the one thing that will help us maintain our strength so that we may continue to fight. Surviving on our fat reserves will not carry us through. When we don't feed regularly, we get weak. It is that simple. Pulling away from God's word, that sustaining influence in our lives, and thinking that we can live on the meager scraps tucked away in our hearts is a deceit that will cost us our lives. We must remain in His Word in order to make it through our storms.

• Loss of control. The previous losses reveal that we no longer have control over anything, or so it seems. When we can no longer exercise any control over our communication systems, our sense of respect, and the influence we once enjoyed, then we feel doomed. We may struggle or bail or do all that we can only to have our futility harshly revealed by the will of the storm. We may no longer have control over external circumstances, but control over ourselves we can always maintain. One of the biggest problems in our world today is the loss of self-control. No one can take our self-control. Only we can willingly give it up. The most important thing we can do in the midst of life's maelstroms is not to allow ourselves to lose control over our tongue, our attitudes, our habits and our actions. We are not puppets in the storm. In truth we are living, breathing beings that have every right and all of the authority and power necessary to maintain ourselves. Though helpless to control anything around us we must, however, not lose control of ourselves.

• Loss of possessions. This may seem trite and obvious, but it inevitable in some of the more horrific eruptions that upend us. Whether our possessions are riches or habits, money or ideas, they represent anything that we own (good or bad). It is important to note here that God does not view our possessions in a negative way if they do not exercise control over us. What is of the utmost importance to Him is our obedience, not what we have accumulated along life's journey. In the case of earthly possessions, their loss may hurt us but will not destroy us (this could include houses, money, land, cars or boats, family members and other loved ones, businesses or partnerships). As it concerns unearthly possessions, our more critical loses are spiritual and internal (this could include hope, dignity, self-control, salvation or the interest in living). When the savageries seem unending, we may give up on everything that matters and defer to the storm or, worse yet, we may never allow those wounds to heal. Some of us, though, may find that through the storms of life, we will lose the very attitudes that have held us back. Recognizing the tumult and its purpose, we will ultimately gain the strength that it unwittingly offers us when we abandon our old philosophies, habits and methodologies. Realizing that these things keep us bound, we dare to dig beneath the surface, the deck of our ship, and root out the disobedience that is resident within. Losing some of our dearly held possessions, such as bad attitudes, unhealthy relationships and addictions, will enlighten us to the fact that, after our eventual reemergence from the storm, we are better off without them. With more of the weights that have hindered us laid aside, we will again be able to compete in the race of life, unhindered and reenergized.

• Loss of vision. In the middle of a vicious whirlwind, it is nearly impossible to see. The fog, cloud cover, darkness, blowing mist and rain, crashing waves, desolation and unfamiliar territory all combine to make visibility near zero. There is little we can do to reverse this. Unable to see, we start to lose sense of what is actually going on around us and subsequently misinterpret the sounds we hear. We give bumps in the night more credence than we should. Instead of realizing their true source, we give them wings that help them fly and fangs and talons with which they can tear us apart. It is at this time that we are most lost and vulnerable to losing our internal vision as well. Believing that dawn will never arrive and that down is our perpetual direction, we give away our vision of the future, those promises God has made to us personally, and we lose sight of the good that was around us and that can be again. Since it may appear that we will never make it out of this tempest alive, we also abandon all of our future hopes and dreams, thinking that they, too, must have been a trick or a joke intended to lure us onto this ship.

• Loss of hope. With the loss of our vision and bearings comes the suicidal wound of hopelessly abandoning our dreams. Unable to see the light of day leads us to believe that night will swallow us up into its unquenchable void and that we will never be again. Ultimately, we will come to the place where we do not believe that we will ever be able to escape the grasp of this storm. With that abandoned, we give up all of our good habits and positive progress and let our ship drift wherever the upheaval wills to drive us. Giving up on our knowledge and wisdom, and too tired from fighting, we throw up our hands and give in to the desires of the storm. Not only do we give up hope, but we also give up any interest in even being rescued. Nothing is important and nothing matters anymore.

• Loss of ourselves. This is the ultimate end when we deal foolishly with the explosive terrorisms that attack our lives. If we fail to learn the lessons that God puts before us, if we fail to recognize our desperate need of God and if we continue to live a life in perpetual oblivion to the realities around us, then we will lose our soul. We will lose all that we are, the essence of ourselves. As if it was not bad enough enduring the atrocities of life, we can make it worse by losing everything in the end. It would be better to come out bloody, bruised and stumbling than to come out in a cloud of disillusionment that will never lift. The Bible speaks of the man who gains the whole world and, yet, loses his soul. To that I would add this question: what does it gain a man to lose his soul for any reason? This is the final tragedy that we must avoid and the epitaph that we must not write.

IDENTIFYING THE VOICES

One of the greatest difficulties during a storm is in figuring out to which voice we should give credence. One of my favorite pastimes during the fall of each year is to hunt. During my first hunting season, I learned three valuable lessons in listening: The first was to become familiar with all of the different noises that the forest produces and to assign each noise to its perpetrator. The second was to learn what sounds a deer makes (since the deer was my intended prey). The third was to become proficient in localizing the source of any particular sound.

In the woods there are many sounds that are similar and some that are downright confusing and frightening, but when hunting there is only one set of sounds that I am interested in— those of my four footed and sometimes-antlered friend, the deer. That first year I hunted, however, I was like a whirly-gig. Every time I heard anything, I spun my head around and gave the sound and its perpetrator my intense scrutiny and attention. But as time wore on and I became more familiar with the sounds of the woods, beginning to distinguish subtle differences in leaves rustling or branches clacking together, I was gradually able to identify the sources without turning my head. What I didn't know that first year is that I needed to prepare in advance. I needed to know what to listen for before I got out there; I needed discernment. Now when I hunt I am more able to clearly determine which rustle of leaves is from a squirrel and which is from a deer, and that the shrieking sounds are birds and not a doe's cry. I am able to distinguish the difference between a crazy woodpecker's rat-a-tat-tat and two bucks engaged in battle. And no longer do I confuse the brushing sound of my whiskers rubbing against the collar of my vest with a buck rubbing the tree beneath my stand.

As silly as it may sound, these are the same lessons that we must learn during the cataclysms of life. There are many sounds and voices vying for our attention. Among them are the sounds of the shuddering ship, the atmosphere-direct sounds of the storm—like the wind and the rain—and the people around us on board the ship. In addition to those are the sounds of the waves and the sea, the flapping of the sails and the whipping of the ropes—all of which the storm causes to sing a different song. Finally, there is Satan's voice, the voice of life itself, our own voice, and, of course the voice of God. Amid the cacophony, there are dozens of distractions that are trying to monopolize our mind's attention, but there is only one supremely important pursuit—to listen intently for the voice of our Beloved. His voice, that still, small voice of God, is the only one with which we should be concerned. At times we turn this way and that whenever there is another whisper or cry; however, this will only turn our attention from where it should be.

What we must practice during life's assaults is to listen using intense concentration and scrutiny in order to filter through the voices that call out to us. This requires a familiarity with the voices prior to the storm; a familiarity that, unfortunately, only comes from experience. There are many who teach that when confronted with a desperate time in life, a storm if you will, that we must cry out annoyingly, that we must quote the word incessantly, that we must confess defiantly, and that we must pray unceasingly until the clouds are magically parted. What they really mean is that there should be little-to-no time where our lips are not quoting, shouting, praising or commanding. To these people, this is what it is all about: protecting our rights as blood-bought covenant holders by demanding courtesies from an omniscient God that we believe are rightfully ours because of our relationship with Christ. Prayer to these people is more of a monologue where we are the stars and Christ is our audience. What we fail to realize is that prayer is a conversation with our Heavenly Father that involves much more listening than the unceasing furor of our own demands allows. In prayer is where we must remain mostly still and silent, especially when attempting to ascertain the voice of God during the ferocities of life.

Sitting in my tree stand requires that I sit nearly motionless while I wait for the deer (or other game) to approach my location. I cannot talk and carry on, and I cannot move about freely and make lots of noise. Neither can I command the deer to pass my way nor pray the squirrels into silence. If I do participate in these types of behaviors, then my prize will never come near. The same is true during the storms of life. We must sit and be still, straining to hear the voice of God and analyzing all the sounds around us as we learn to filter out and ignore those that are not His. Realizing that the sounds of severe weather are always the same, we must concentrate intently upon the words coming from God's lips and then carry out those commands. All other sounds the storm may be making are irrelevant when compared with His voice. Listening for His voice is paramount, and recognizing His voice will be life changing. We must learn to filter out the sound of the wind, waves, thunder, boat creaking, wood breaking, ropes snapping, furniture crashing, people screaming, sails tearing and flapping, and anything else trying to establish its superiority and instead listen to God.

In speaking of the voices heard during a storm, William Nichols gives us a first-hand account after being rescued from the shipwreck of a civil war ship.

I supposed I had seen something like confusion in battle, but the scene at this time was sublime. The ship had 300 tons of coal, and as she lurched from side to side, the roar of the coal and water [in the hold of the ship] sounded like Niagara, and the water on the outside dashing against the ship was another distinct sound and horrid enough of itself. The wind was howling through the rigging like the demons of the sea, and to make it a perfect hell, the men, excited and yelling to each other, begrimed with black smut and engine grease. It was desperation intensified.[205]

There are many voices during a storm. Here are some of the more familiar ones that we may encounter in the midst of our darkest hours.

• the howling wind.

• the crashing waves.

• the pelting rain.

• the tearing and whipping sails.

• the structure of the ship as it gives in to the onslaught of the storm.

• the furnishings and gear of the boat as they shift and crash around.

• the murmuring and screaming of the other people on board.

• the crashing thunder.

• the navigational devices.

• the devil.

• our own voice.

• the voice of God.

• the voices inside of our heads from others not present (parents, relatives, friends, etc.).

TIED TO THE DOCK FOR THE FULL MOON

IN THE INTEREST OF CONTROL

As stated earlier when speaking of the loss of control, one of the most difficult situations that occurs during a storm of life is in dealing with ourselves. A common misconception perpetuated in some religious circles today is that we can always control that which is around us—even when in a calamitous situation. We are told that we can stop life and avoid trouble, magically making every unpleasantness go away with the whisk of our hand. With the mysterious intonations of our voice or the power of our beliefs, all we must do is speak God's name in two syllables (pronounced gawd-ah) and everything will go away. This is simply, flat-out and unconditionally not true. Being "slain-in-the-spirit" or having hands laid on us by Joe Somebody will not keep life's storms from knocking on our door. Having hands laid on our head or demons cast from us does not mean that our troubles are over either. Sometimes we are presented with situations where we can believe God to work the supernatural through us, and we can see those storm clouds part and go away. But often we cannot.

We display false humility as we act in the name of God when our root desire is our hidden interest in manipulative control. What we would like is to control everything because that makes us feel god-like and, most importantly, makes those around us notice how powerful our faith is. The truth is that He has not relinquished control of life to us—as hard as that pill may be for some of us to swallow. So, at times, we will be completely under some horrific event's authority. As stated before, the only person we can always control is ourselves, but this is hard work. This constant, repeated drudgery will not back down and is reluctant to let go of us. Dealing with our sinful tendencies and bad attitudes is well within our realm of control; however, even though we can exercise this control, we usually do not. God wants to help us conquer ourselves by letting Him be in complete control. This is eternity, and He is playing for keeps.

WHAT WAS GOD SAYING, IN SHORT?

In Paul's storm, he saw THROUGH the wind and waves.
In the disciples' storm, they ONLY
SAW the wind and the waves.
In Jonah's storm, HE WAS THE CAUSE
of the wind and the waves.

In Paul's storm, God was telling them DON'T GO.
In the disciples' storm, God was telling them DON'T FEAR.
In Jonah's storm, God was telling him DON'T RUN.

In Paul's storm, God was telling them LISTEN UP.
In the disciples' storm, God was telling them SPEAK UP.
In Jonah's storm, God was telling him to GROW UP.

In Paul's storm, God was teaching them PERSEVERANCE.
In the disciples' storm, God was teaching them ACTION.
In Jonah's storm, God was teaching him OBEDIENCE.

In Paul's storm, God was telling them LISTEN
TO THE VOICE OF THE MAN OF GOD.
In the disciples' storm, God was telling them
LISTEN TO THE VOICE OF JESUS.
In Jonah's storm, God was telling him LISTEN
TO THE VOICES OF THE CREW.

Paul practiced MEDITATION to overcome the
storm–Paul listened to the voice of God.
The disciples' practiced THINKING when taking
on their storm–the disciples were trying to figure
out what to do in order to get out of the storm.
Jonah was deep into IGNORING in the midst of his
storm–Jonah was unconcerned because he had given
up and was simply not interested in listening.

MOVING FORWARD WITH PROGRESS

The reader should note that in each storm story that we
have examined, the people involved traveled some distance
before, during, and after the storms hit. Jonah traveled three
days out on the boat, three days back to shore and 1200 kilometers over land in getting himself to Nineveh, but that did not
mean that God was pleased with his performance. Paul traveled
nearly 2000 kilometers from the time he set sail until he reached
Rome, but that did not preclude him from being shipwrecked a
fourth time. The disciples traveled only a few kilometers before
reaching their distant shore, but that did not excuse their rebuke
of the Master. The reason that this is significant is because we
often confuse movement with God's blessing. If we were Jonah,
we might consider three days journey toward Tarshish as a successful escape, but we would be wrong. Likewise, if we were
Paul, we might consider the first 1000 kilometers of the trip to
mean that we would not shipwreck, but we would be wrong.
Then finally, if we were the disciples, we might conclude that
the deliverance of the demoniac might justify our rebuke of
Christ, but the point would have been missed. The point is that
just because we are presently making some headway or have hit
an area of calm waters in the midst of our disaster does not mean
that we are on the right track. Movement alone is not an indicator of anything other than, well, movement.

It is interesting to note that all movement is relative.
When we say that we are traveling down the highway at fifty-

five miles per hour, we generally assume that we are not taking into consideration the speed of the earth's rotation, her orbital cycle, or the crustal plate's speed beneath us. We give our speed in relationship to those stationary objects around us. However, when traveling on the surface of the water (or in the air for that matter), the situation is a little more complicated. Since the surface of the water is constantly moving, we need some stationary reference point from which to judge our progress—something like the ocean floor. If the ship's engines are running wide open and our readings indicate that we are traveling at thirty knots, that may not actually be indicative of our forward progress. The reason is this: there are other factors that play into this equation which determine our actual forward speed—factors such as wind speed and direction and current. Our instruments may read thirty knots, but if the water beneath us is moving at thirty knots in the opposite direction, then our net speed is zero. In other words, we may be expending great amounts of energy and look like we are moving forward when in actuality we may not be moving at all relative to the ocean floor (this would be our point of reference). This would be a case of moving but not making any forward progress. What Christ envisions for us is that we make forward progress during the tempests that rage around us, and the only trustworthy point of reference by which to judge our progress is God's word. A flurry of activity is not necessary if we are no match for the wind and waves; in fact, it may be foolhardy.

For us to make acceptable forward progress during the storms of life, we must listen to God and to wise counsel in advance. Unfortunately, there is rarely time in the midst of an attack to stop everything and get a second opinion or take a course on storm survival tactics. Being prepared ahead of time is a key to our survival, and knowing how to react will help us to avert at least some tragedies. We see similar advanced techniques stressed in commercial pilot training courses and military personnel indoctrinations. They are dumped into helpless situations repeatedly during the safety of training exercises in order for the proper reactions to become second nature to them.

In this way, when the worst situations hit, they do not have to think but instinctively know what to do. Should we train any less thoroughly for Christ's army and the battles that we must fight? We, too, must know how to recognize the massacres of life and which direction to take in order to make it through. Preparing in advance will allow us to concentrate on doing what must be done in order to survive.

There are many times during life's conflicts that we confuse the two parts of wrongdoing. One part is doing what is wrong. The other part is not doing what is right. Our excuse that we did nothing wrong will not cut it, because the point is that we may not have done what was right in order to survive. We can never justify wrongdoing by evaluating the present or future circumstances. Coming out of a storm alive is good, but it is not good enough. If we simply survive it then we have learned nothing at all; however, if we learn from it, change through it and grow as a result, then we have done well.

Many times after a storm we vow to rebuild our lives as if nothing had ever happened. Pledging never to be driven away, we often recklessly rebuild in the very same place where disaster will once again find us waiting. Nevertheless, however noble this may at first appear following the cataclysms of life, we must honestly reevaluate our locale and reconsider the pros and cons of rebuilding our lives on that very same piece of ground. Naturally, this is no more apropos than in the recent disaster caused by Hurricane Katrina. What we have seen since this natural disaster is that many residents of those communities that were annihilated have vowed to rebuild upon the same foundations that were recently destroyed. The problem is that the homes of some Gulf Coast residents were built in ill-advised locations to begin with, either below sea level, near very old levees, or in areas prone to uncontrollable floodwaters. Now I do not mean to be condescending or mean, but it may not be wise to rebuild some of those homes. The reason? Because another storm will no doubt descend upon that locale and devastate whatever new structure it finds standing there. In light of this revelation, the questions that must be honestly asked and answered are: How many times will we rebuild in a place where our lives will constantly be put at risk and devastated? Should we not be more responsible in where we locate our new home, and build it in a location that affords more protection than we previously enjoyed?

To put this into a spiritual perspective, let me put things this way. When we have messed up in life and built our marriages or families or businesses upon questionable foundations or in places that are constantly under a barrage of attacks, might we not be better off in the long run if we rebuilt in a different place and in a different way next time? Why would Jonah, after he had missed God and run away, ever try to flee to Tarshish again? What would it have gained Peter, once he had denied Christ thrice, to stick around the crowds and deny Him once more? How do we convince ourselves to rebuild our lives beneath a dam that we know will burst again and again, destroying everything in its path every time? Wouldn't it sometimes be better if we did not rebuild our shattered lives upon the very foundations that failed us previously? Couldn't we realize more security in life if we avoided places prone to disaster and mayhem and destruction? I know that these are tough questions, but they have to be asked of every one of us because we seem to have a natural tendency to shy away from them. It may look tough and gritty to rebuild in the face of disaster, but the truth is that it may simply be foolhardy. This is not to say that we should be driven away with every wind, but it is to say that we must honestly reevaluate our locale after every storm that devastates the coastlines of our lives.

Following the storms of life, though, how can we know how well we have performed? By what measuring stick can we reliably and impartially judge ourselves? With a plethora of religions and a confusing array of self-proclaimed prophets, the answer may seem more impossible to grasp than it really is. As we have already discussed, the only infallible and unchanging measuring stick (or guidebook if you like) is the Word of God—the Bible. That is what we must measure our successes and failures by because it is what counts the most. Success in storm survival cannot be ascertained by man's rules, but can only accurately be measured by God. It is not up to me to give the answers to the storms of life here in this book. It is simply my purpose to lead us through the process. I do not have the solutions in my answer book for every storm that may arise, but I have defined the storms and the basic ways to behave properly. It is up to each individual to hear from God and to hone the gift of discernment in order to know what has to be done when another storm arises.

CUTTING OFF THE FORESKIN

The book of Joshua gives us a beautiful picture of what God wishes to accomplish through our difficulties in life. In chapter four, we find that God had dried up the waters of the Jordan River so that the Israelites could cross over and possess the land. This caused a great fear to melt the hearts of the Amorite and Canaanite kings because they knew what was in store for them. Nevertheless, just when God's people were getting ready to engage in battle at Jericho, God stopped them and told Joshua to do something odd. He told Joshua to circumcise the sons of Israel. Imagine what must have been going through the minds of these men who were about to be operated on. A procedure like that was supposed to have been performed on all male babies when they were eight days old (Genesis 17:12; Leviticus 12:3), not on men in the prime of their lives. Yet here, some of them were forty years old and about to go under the knife. Their surgery would not be performed by a member of the local medical association or in a clean room with sterilized equipment either. This rite of passage, this covenantal agreement, was going to be performed by a senior citizen on a dirty knoll with a sharp piece of rock! They were willing to let an elderly man cut into their most private place with a piece of flint!

There is not much personal dignity in a baby eight days old, but as a man grows older, he (hopefully) develops a clear sense of personal space and modesty that no other man may enter. It is even difficult sometimes to get a man to allow his own doctor to treat him if the problem area lies below the belt and above the knees. The area in question is a private realm and domain for most men that we are not comfortable letting other men see, let alone touch or hack away at with a rock. But this was what had to be done. Before Israel could enter the Promised Land, this procedure had to take place—on *every* adult male. No procedure meant not partaking of God's promise. And so as chapter five gets underway, the men are no doubt embarrassed at the thought of a grown man seeing their nakedness and fearful as to his ability to perform the task; however, each one of them stepped up the hill and allowed their foreskin to be cut off. Amazing! To have the courage that these men displayed in allowing God's man to cut something off in order for them to enter into His promises is truly remarkable. Some may question whether this was a necessary medical procedure, and the answer is no not in any natural sense. In fact, it was not a procedure that was practiced or performed by many. Circumcision was set up by God with Abraham as a sign or token of the covenant (promise or pledge) between himself and God. Medically it was unnecessary, but spiritually it was vital.

Often we lament when God desires to remove some of our flesh during the traumas of life due to the pain it causes us. We feel justified in having our possessions, validated by some of them in fact, but to God they do not even register on the chart because of their eternal insignificance. Many times we fight and kick trying to hold on to habits or attitudes that God is trying to remove. When we cry out that the storm is not our fault, He answers back that the cause of the storm is irrelevant because His purpose is always to cut away that which is unnecessary *spiritually.* He is most interested in how we handle the storm and not in our truckload of personal possessions. God's purpose is to loose us from our excess baggage more than to preserve our comfortable lifestyle. I'm not advocating that God doesn't want to bless us with material goods. What I am saying is that He is much more interested in clothing us spiritually and in allowing the difficult situations by which we can take another step toward spiritual maturity. Our eternal soul is what interests Him most.

Our minds are focused on our stuff, so it is inevitable that we are most concerned with how much our home cost to build, what color our Porsche is, and whether our socks and tie match for church. But to God these are minute details that just do not matter in the eternal realm. What we must guard against is the overwhelming desire we have for attempting to retain what God has deemed unnecessary. Jonah did not allow God to cut off that which was dragging the ship under, his disobedience. Oh, he gave in and let them throw him overboard, but he did not really give in to God and change. Paul was told to cut off discouragement when the angel of God visited him, and he did—forever becoming our shining example. The disciples took Christ's rebuke and changed their fear into faith (even though they continued to struggle with it later). In fact, it was not too long after their storm that Peter accepted Jesus' bidding and walked across the water (thus getting his next lesson in the faith of the storm). My point is that we all carry around weights that hinder our forward progress and encumbrances that drag us down and away from God. We must shed these burdens during the storms of life if we ever hope to make it through alive.

An important lesson to learn during all of this is that we can always get along with less than we thought we ever could. Though we have a way of liking our stuff (and I am not just talking about personal possessions and material wealth), what I am talking about is deeper and more fundamental to life itself. The items God typically wants to cut off are more a part of our psyche and include our attitudes, habits, behaviors, tendencies, shortcomings and skeletal remains. What we thought we needed in order to live, God can show us that we will be better off without. Often there is a higher purpose for our storm even beyond what we are experiencing. For Paul, the loss of his personal freedom, although frustrating, was something that he lived nearly five years without. His higher purpose was to witness of Christ in Rome to the highest authorities in the world at that time. God was intent upon getting the witness to Rome and not in whether or not Paul arrived there in chains or in a limousine. In our situations, it may not come to the point of physical imprisonment and chains, but it may come to the point where we have to deny ourselves some of the exclusivities that we so covet. We can get along without the trappings that we always thought we needed (or looked great carrying around). At times we will be requested to lay them down, and at other times the storm will make these life-changing decisions for us. Our critical point is in letting go no matter what. Usually God would rather that we chose to be circumcised before the storm arises, but oftentimes this is too painful a decision for us to make. When we become too attached to the way we have always been, then we are in the most danger of having these superfluities forcibly removed in a manner that will leave even the toughest of men crying like babies. The only thing worse for these men than being circumcised later in life on a hill would have been having that same procedure performed on the deck of a ship in the middle of a hurricane. Is the picture becoming clearer?

Not long ago I was interested in renewing my relationship with an old friend from my college days. After questioning a mutual friend as to its likelihood, he regrettably informed me that my old friend was no longer interested in getting together with me because I was not the same as I used to be. I was stunned. Because I was not the same as I was in college, I was no longer worthy of the friendship. What appalling behavior. My point in bringing this up is that if we do not change, and we remain the same as we were in high school or college or tech school, then we are doomed to continue to repeat all of our past failures. Our only hope is when we change, adapt, grow and ascend. I am glad that I am not the same as I used to be. God has had to cut some flesh out of my life, and unfortunately, some has been sheared off by the winds that have ripped through my life. Some has been beaten away by the pounding waves, while more has been thrown overboard by me once I saw the disobedience that was dragging my ship under. The people on board the ship with Paul realized after the storm that they could survive, even though their ordeal was horrific and seemingly a death march. They could do without it all and still make it, and so can we.

HEALING THE WOUND

Following their painful ordeal, the people of Israel all stayed in Gilgal until the men were healed. Our story does not end with the cutting off of the foreskin, but it continues on with the healing process that so many of us attempt to avoid. Once we have endured the barbarities of life and certain encumbrances have been removed, then we must allow a time of healing to take place before we again jump into battle. I know a dear friend of mine once shared with me that he never missed a day of work after his adult son died. He took the pain of that storm and poured it into his work and ministry. Am I saying that what he did was not right? Not necessarily. What I am saying is that the Biblical precedent is that we sit it out for a time and heal. No operation comes without some time for our natural body to repair itself, and no spiritual or emotional wound should be given any less consideration. Although it appears noble not to grieve and admirable not to miss work, when we take that chance we may be leaving a wound open that will never heal. Is it then worth it? I say that it is not. Joshua's words should stand tall in our minds following our spiritual circumcisions. Everything remained at a standstill until all the men were healed.

A CHANGE OF DIET

As our story continues and the men have fully healed, the children of Israel ate their last meal of manna. As Joshua put it, "And the manna ceased on the day after they ate of the produce of the land . . ." (Joshua 5:12 AMP). For forty years they had eaten manna, but now they were to eat of the fruit and bounty and produce of Canaan, the Promised Land—the land that flowed with milk and honey. Manna represented the way they used to live, the meal of their wilderness experience, but even their diet was about to change—another unneeded item cut off. Israel would no longer be in need of manna because the land they were entering was filled with bountiful produce. This meal represented a final departure from their old way of life. On the ship with Paul, a similar situation occurred in Acts 27:35–38 when they, too, ate the last meal of their storm experience. In order to proceed they had to cast off the old way, the grain, and embrace whatever came next. No longer able to continue with our burdens weighing us down, we, too, must release our old ways, habits and lifestyles and look forward to God's provision. For the Israelites, He was going to feed them with the bounty of their new homeland. Paul and his shipmates would be fed from the hands of the natives on Malta, and the disciples would be fed life-changing words of truth that defied their old ways of thinking and challenged them in every area. Jonah himself was fed to a fish that would help to get him back on track (unfortunately, he never seems to get back on track).[206]

3

Drowning in a Sea Full of Rumors

The Denial of Reality

There is a popular teaching traveling around religious circles today that basically instructs people to deny reality. If faced with a problem, say financial struggles or disease, we are instructed never to utter the words "I cannot afford" and we are not allowed to speak the name of the disease we are battling. Somehow we have been duped into thinking that saying those words is akin to agreeing with Satan's death sentence upon us. Speaking the truth of our current circumstances is not tantamount to cursing ourselves or denying the power of God. It is simply the current state of affairs. What we notice in the stories that we have studied is that God's people in the Bible did not deny the reality of what was happening, but they found a way (at least some of them) to rise above their circumstances or to plow through them. Only the vacillations of the unlearned amateur would cause him to deny the reality of what he was experiencing. When we are sick, then we had better know the name of the sickness so that treatment options or healing prayers may be focused correctly. Neither Paul nor the disciples stood and denied the storm and, though Jonah chose poorly in the end, he, too, faced the reality of his situation. God condemned none of them for doing so. In fact, there is no biblical precedent for denying the reality of any situation, be it good or bad. A faith built upon the shaky footings of a make-believe world cannot tear down the strongholds of any walled city, let alone the fortresses within our own hearts.

I propose that we grow up and call life as we see it, in a manner of speaking. Yes, we must have faith and believe God and are to stay away from negativity and doubt, but (as the old saying goes) if we see a duck, then we should call it a duck. If there are storms brewing on the horizon, no amount of positive confession is going to cause them all to blow the other way. We cannot deny the reality of our situations. Storms will come whether we recite positive or negative mantras, so let us not be ignorant of the realities in the world around us. In order to reach into the realm of what is not seen and bring it into the realm of the seen, we must have our feet firmly planted in the soils of reality and truth. A man's faith should not be established within the deceptive denial of the realities of life, but should be rooted in a hope that boldly reaches beyond our own realities to the ones that God has declared; this is what will bring about a miraculous change of circumstance. Faith in the midst of life's atrocities recognizes the turmoil that surrounds us and then reaches past those to the calm waters that lie beyond.

CHANGE AND UNDERSTANDING

In reference to the storms of life, the most tragic aftermath is epitomized by those emerging from the rubble as unchanged survivors. As I have stated before, the buzzword today is of being a survivor. Whether this means those who have endured domestic abuse, those who have been the victims of random acts of violence or those unfortunate enough to have lived through the horrors of molestation and rape, it is now in vogue to be labeled as a survivor. Nevertheless, what we are all missing when paying our dues to join the latest survivors club or rehabilitation association is this: who has changed during the storm and become a better person? Our focus is more on the horrors we have faced than in the people we have become. We have all survived something, but wearing that patch on our jacket is not very impressive. Have we become better people or are we still harboring bitterness and coddling open wounds inflicted upon us years ago? Do we care to forget the pain long enough to help someone else not become angry and vengeful toward their aggressors? Survival is not enough. Growing up in the process is the key. If we did not change through the storm into a more discerning, courageous person, then what was the point of going through it? Jonah's refusal to change doomed him. He remained the same, not able to practice what he knew to preach. Sometimes in the midst of a tempest, the most difficult thing is to put into practice what we know we should do. Hearing the right voice is not always the hardest thing. Sometimes obeying that voice is the most difficult part. Nevertheless, we must; we must become more than survivors.

Another overwhelming development in the midst of our adversities is when those around do not know how we feel or even how to help us. We must confront this difficult issue no matter how badly we wish to leave it alone. Our extended family or friends and counselors may not be equipped to give us any help or advice. They may feel so inadequate and overwhelmed that they cannot even speak. The storm that we are in may be so bewildering to them that they are lost as to any understanding of how to assist us. Often this is not due to lack of concern on their part, but is due to their ignorance of the realities of severe weather. It may indicate that they do not possess the skills necessary to help us. Understanding any of this, however, does not make it any easier to deal with. What we must acquire through our own storms are the skills necessary to overcome, as well as those needed in helping others through their tragedies. Without becoming angry over what our loved ones cannot provide us, we should graciously accept what support they do offer and expect no more. Though some of our closest friends may seem to be in a time warp, we should trust that they are doing the best they can. Again, we must seek to understand. Even when we are at the mercy of a hellish tempest and cannot help ourselves, we must be considerate of where others are emotionally and spiritually. So many people think that we can lash out at those who are not helping us (and believe me we all feel that way sometimes), but we must not give in to carnal thinking. Sometimes we have to experience the grief that comes from being tossed to and fro at the whim of the waves, because it is from our own helplessness that some of life's most important lessons are birthed. Understanding where we are and accepting only that help that others can give will help us avoid more losses during our agitations.

COMPLICATIONS WITH COMMUNICATIONS

As touched upon earlier in the section on mounting losses, another agonizing situation arises when our closest friends and allies seem to back away from our grievous situation and us. Disruptions in communications are often not due to lack of desire or effort but are likely due, in part, to the conditions in the atmosphere. (This is not to say that some will not abandon us during the storms of life, because some will—but most will not.) Reception in the middle of a turbulent atmospheric disturbance is generally not good and is typically non-existent. Poor weather disrupts the proper propagation of carrier waves, thus resulting in intermittent communication at best. A vital piece of information to remember during these times is that none of this is the fault of our friends, relatives or counselors who are not on board our ship. Our loved ones may be sitting tirelessly by the phone, trying their best to get a message through to us, but the weather may foil all of their attempts. Even though our radio may be tuned to the proper frequency, the atmospheric unrest will usually deny the message access to our radio's antenna. This is the same sort of phenomenon that occurs when our satellite television service is interrupted due to inclement weather or when we cannot receive the local network broadcast because our home is located deep in the next valley over from the antenna. Valleys are tough places to get a good, strong signal when the transmitter has no line of sight to our location. The atmospheric and geographic conditions sometimes combine to prevent us from receiving the proper signal. Does this mean that the television station does not wish us to see their programming? No, it simply means that sometimes the weather and our location mess with our ability to receive it. And so it is with us spiritually when we are surrounded by the storm clouds of life.

Another equally important reason why others often cannot contact us is because our position relative to theirs has changed dramatically. We are no longer in the close proximity we once were. The gap that separates us from those who are not directly within the scope of the storm has grown due to our movement away from them. As our tempest's winds have blown, we have been pushed off course and out to sea. Our family and friends still reside right where they always did; however, we are continually moving away as each day of our storm passes. It is important that we not worry or place blame during these times, though, because we will only drive a wedge between friends or family that may not easily be repaired. As a direct result of the tumult that has attacked us, we may experience this type of separation. Rest assured that it is only temporary. After the weather clears, we can return to familiar waters and again be back in contact just like before. A good point to remember in all of this is that this may be just as confusing for them as it is for us; we may seem to have dropped off the face of the earth in their eyes as well. Better days are ahead. Reuniting with our friends and family after the storm has run its course will be sweet and rewarding.

MULTIPLE PERSONALITIES, DISORDERED

Notice how different groups of people on the ship have different reactions to the storm. The owner, captain and sailors all have one thing on their minds. That is to get this ship through the storm while retaining as much of the cargo, crew, passengers and ship as possible. They are focused on navigating the tumultuous seas and finding a way to get through safely. Having no time for panic or worry, sometimes even their own fear has to take a back seat to more immediate tasks. The conditioning of a life at sea has hardened them to the flatlander's displays of emotion. There is no time for anything but decisive action and the discipline of focus. Intently consumed with survival and the responsibility they have to the ship's owner, the passengers and the captain, the mariners carry out their tasks in such a manner as to ensure everyone's safety on the ship (and to save the cargo and ship if possible). Severe weather tends to galvanize the crew toward a common goal and a group effort centered upon bringing the ship, crew, cargo and passengers through safely.

The passengers, however, have little to do during their harrowing ride other than to think about who is doing what wrong. With no duties to perform and no experience in these matters to speak of, they have nothing to distract them from becoming overwhelmed. In addition, once passengers become overwhelmed, they react with uncanny idiocy. Their interest in the storm is not scientific in nature but personal. No passenger is charting wind speeds and direction, calculating the wave-crest-to-trough-depth ratios, or estimating the quantity of water coming over the sides of the ship with each crashing wave. With intensity equal to that of the sailors' they are fiercely concerned with their own survival and could not care less about the technicalities of rough weather seamanship. Here is where we are often hung up. When we are passengers upon a ship in distress, our view gets out-of-focus and our eyes start resting upon what should not matter. Worrying about living through the night takes precedence over being obedient to what God has said. Wallowing in the pit of emotional distress, the passengers have little else to do except point the fingers of blame at the others on board. Like money-hungry, attack-dog style personal injury lawyers, they only seem to care about whom else is to blame for the mess that they are in. Distracted by their own finger pointing, they effortlessly divide themselves into groups of increasingly illegitimate causes. Discipline is lost and focus continues to deteriorate until they can only see the proverbial trees and not the forest that encompasses them. We must never allow our self-respect to degrade to such lowly proportions.

In a storm, we can feel both confident and overwhelmed at the same time. Our emotions can and will go haywire if we allow them to. Look at the disciples. Losing their discipline caused them to lose their focus. Instead, they jumped to ridiculous conclusions and acted as children. They had been in this type of weather before but failed to remember anything of their past encounters. Sometimes even being there before is not enough to help us or prepare us to make it through the next storm of life. Often, too much experience can be a negative because we feel like we have been there before and can handle it in our own strength. What we must remember is that each storm is a living, breathing entity that will require us to focus and not get off track. Hearing God's precious voice as to which way we should proceed is paramount to our survival.

REACTION IS EVERYTHING

It is interesting how people react to the news of a storm's impending arrival, especially if the storm is going to be a big one. There is a flurry of activity as the grocery stores and home improvement centers are jammed with people fighting each other for what's left in the dwindling stacks of supplies. Everyone is in a last minute frenzy preparing for the severe weather that they knew would be coming. With a winter storm approaching, people tend to buy extra shovels, snow scoops, candles and flashlights. If a hurricane is approaching, people buy plywood by the lift, rolls of tape by the dozens and sandbags by the gross. Each family hopes that one or all of these last minute purchases will keep them safe from the worst damage. What is tragic, however, is that no one seems even the least bit interested in preparing in advance for the brutal cataclysms that will eventually wreak havoc upon their lives. Why is that? How can we be so good about preparing for natural storms (albeit usually at the last minute) and so inexcusable when it comes to those of the spiritual realm? Do we think that spiritual storms are any less likely to cause catastrophic damage or do we simply ignore all of the warning signs, hoping that if we plead ignorance they will visit someone else instead? Human nature is fickle when it comes to preparing for the inevitable atrocities of life, but we must fight in order to change ourselves and to become more prepared.

During a natural storm, there are typically two groups of people: those who venture out into the fray and those who stay at home. Storms bring the crazy out of some people, and they go nuts driving around and exposing themselves to dangers that they should not just for the thrill of it. Still others venture out because they have obligations they must fulfill such as jobs or medical emergencies. The second group is comprised of people who remain paralyzed with fear because of the storm. Unable to risk even peering out their windows, they sit huddled together around the television watching the horrors replayed for them in Technicolor and Dolby Surround Sound. We must decide that we will be a part of neither group when pandemonium strikes our lives. Living in between them with a balance of common sense and courageous resolve is what will see us through.

To bring this home to where we live, let me expose some of our more common behaviors. When the storms hit, some are so blindsided by the obvious that they cannot operate in any normal capacity. Others take it all in stride and deal with it as best they can. Those hyped up on faith try their best simply to ignore the gale force winds that are attacking them and hope that maybe, just maybe, this storm is really only at the neighbor's house. The fearful turn into reclusive hermits who will never again venture out into life, while the vengeful become a boiling pot of activity that threatens to overpower even their own determination to forget. All of our reactions to conflicts are varied and come from different perspectives, but the one common thread is this: we all react. And this is the critical part. Our reactions are of the utmost importance to what lies beneath, for if there is nothing of substance there, then we are doomed. Severe weather situations bring out the best in some and the worst in others. Some succeed in facing down another of their giants, while others succumb to the numbing realization that we are grasshoppers in comparison to the wind and waves. An unexpected surprise, however, comes to the discerning ones after the destruction has passed. A bittersweet moment arrives after we have survived the storm and tallied the damages, a moment when we know that we made the right decisions and have grown because of the storm. Indifferent in a way to its passing, we mouth a simple thanks to the furious gale as it eases beyond our realm—nearly grateful for its rapacious violation because of what it revealed in us. When our decisive moment came, we lived up to it. We dealt with the beast and stayed our course. What we have done is finished the fight and managed to keep our faith. Congratulations are in order. "Good job. Well done."

MAKING FAST THE DECK LINES

WRAPPING UP SOME LOOSE ENDS

Briefly, I have compiled a list of some of the rules of storms. These may have been touched upon in other parts of this book, but because they are so critical, they bear repeating. Some others of these tidbits are matters of housekeeping that we must keep in mind as the atrocities of life repeatedly pillage our dwellings. In no descending order of importance, each one presents a nugget of truth that will free some part of the reader's soul and form the basic outline of a "Personal Plan-Of-Action" when it comes to preparing ourselves to face the storms of life.

• We will lose our bearings. In the midst of the storm, in the worst part of this personal nightmare, we will not be able to see where we are going or determine exactly where we are. Not knowing whether we are close to land or in the deepest part of the ocean will tend to panic us as our ship drifts helplessly along. When the darkness surrounds us and we cannot see or hear clearly, the urge to give up hope will attempt to overwhelm us. A key we must keep in mind is that the storm is against us, not the entire world, and that the chances of us making it back home are in our favor if we simply resist the urge to give up. We must gather ourselves and ascertain where we are as best we can, then leave the rest up to God as we make the wisest decisions we can based upon the limited data available.

• We cannot change the rules. With every type of storm comes an unbendable set of rules. These involve that which is beyond our control, cannot be manipulated and must not be misunderstood. "Faithing" away a storm of disobedience will never work. Requesting to disembark into the angry ocean and give up will not end the turmoil if the storm is one that we must walk through. Commanding away a storm God means for us to experience is a recipe for a more calamitous disaster. Rebuking our Lord for His inattentiveness to our plight may not bring about a generally happy situation. We must learn the rules of each storm presented in this book and abide by them. The prayer of faith will not magically deliver us every time—we have to realize this. A key that we must remember is that we cannot apply one storm's rules to another storm. It will never work. What we must do is discern which type of storm that we are in and then apply its rules without exception.

• We do not determine the storm's duration, course or intensity. In the midst of the storm, we must realize that every storm must run its course. Every storm system will continue to unleash its fury until the conditions that precipitated it have dissipated. Unless we have been thrust into a faith-building situation where God intends for us to speak the storm away, there is nothing we can do to alter anything about the storm (except our reaction to it). Therefore, we must endure its hellacious attack until it passes (or until we give up our disobedience and sin).

• We will find help. When our storms are finally over and we have reached the safety of the shore, help and relief will generally come from the most unusual and unexpected places. The Maltese natives, who were considered barbarians by some, cared for the passengers aboard the Alexandrian ship. Jonah found his assistants in the Phoenician crew. The disciples found a gift in the conversion of the demoniac. The most likely routes of help will be from those we least expect, and those we thought we could count on may very well have fallen away forever.

• We will struggle with our attitude. When the storm is at its worst and everything is crashing in around us, we should expect that our attitude, no matter how good it was prior to the storm, will tend to deteriorate. It may even get to the point where we get hurt, angry, confused, disillusioned and suicidal. We will want to jump or be thrown overboard, just as Jonah, and drown and end it all. Anything appears better than enduring another minute of the storm. But we must look up, for it has to get worse before it can get better. Mountains are not measured from arbitrary points of reference or from midway up their impressive summits, but are measured from the valleys that surround their foothills (except in the case of underwater mountains). Unless our attitudes decline to the depths of despair, then they can never soar into the stratosphere of God.

• We will find more of life beyond the safety of the shore. When the storm is finally over, we must realize that there is something beyond the shore. Yes, the shore represents the end of the storm, but we still have to make it to our ultimate destination. After the storm, Paul had to make it through the winter on the island and then go on to Rome to appear before Caesar. Christ had a demoniac to free after the storm, and Jonah had a devastating message to deliver. Joseph had nations to rescue. He may have believed that Potiphar's house was his ultimate destination and misinterpreted that to mean it was his place where his destiny (his Rome) would be realized, but it was not so. There was one final leg of his journey that was required. And, yes, sometimes being in a storm and on a boat does feel like being in prison or in chains, but we must hang on and remember that God has a work for us to do beyond our place of refuge (our Malta).

• We must stand up. In the midst of the storm, we must face the storm. Cowering below deck or tying ourselves to the mast will not cut it. We must stand up to its viciousness face-to-face and toe-to-toe and not allow ourselves to be bullied by the beast. Every time its wicked blows knock us down, we must stand back up.

• We will sustain wounds. It is foolish to think that we will pass through our storms unscathed and unaffected. Rest assured that the storm will beat up even the strongest soul. No matter how hard we try, our emotions will get the best of us sometimes—even when we have prepared well in advance. Feelings of sadness, loneliness, anger and depression are all normal and cannot be stopped. These represent some of the wounds the storms of life will inflict upon us. Helpless abandonment will continually attack the very underpinnings of our souls. Even some of the greatest men of faith in the Bible suffered deep depression and feelings of abandonment, so we should not think that we are any different form them. We will fall down, and we will get bloodied and bruised. That is the reality of being thrown around by the storms of life.

• We should not have to endure a storm alone. Nobody in life should have to endure a storm without at least one other person pulling for him or her. In reference to this, let us look at the following quote: "Human relationships are primary in all of living. When the gusty winds blow and shake our lives, if we know that people care about us, we may bend with the wind . . . but we won't break."[207] As the popular song says, "We all need somebody to lean on." Nothing is worse than knowing that no one else even cares if we make it through the storm alive. And, indeed, nothing is more comforting than knowing that someone else is in our corner and intimately interested in our survival and good name.

• We may not be delivered from our storm. In Acts 7:55 - 60, Stephen was stoned to death for the sake of the Gospel. Deliverance from the storm is not God's obligation to us, as some would have us believe. The suffering that we may endure during a storm is never wasted if we choose to allow it to work goodness inside of us. Some may never resurface after their most horrific malignity—a final curtain call it may be. It is not up to us to understand the whys of this, but we must simply accept that God knows best. Every person is appointed a time to die, and nowhere in holy writ does it say that every death will be a peaceful one.

• We must discern to learn. In Galatians 6:4a, Paul admonishes us with some powerful advice. "But let every person carefully scrutinize *and* examine *and* test his own conduct *and* his own work." If we would spend more time discerning and diagnosing our attitudes instead of griping about those of others around us, then we could move further along life's path. Practically we revere doctors and their abilities to cure us, but we dare not practice their rituals in our spiritual lives. Any doctor worth his weight observes the condition, documents the symptoms and then diagnoses the cause of the illness. Only then does he outline a course of action or prescribe a cure. So why don't we do the same with our own lives? What would cause our arrogance to blossom under the Son of God's penetrating gaze? Discernment is the key in learning how to handle the storms of life. Once we discern the situation and document its ferocity, then we can embark upon a course that will steer us out of the wind and waves.

• We may bear permanent reminders of our days of horror. There may be some indelible markings on us after the storm, permanent reminders of those terrible days. The Bible says that Job was disfigured beyond recognition in his storm, a grotesque physical specimen with scars that would make any man shudder. Oozing open wounds that were so irritating that he was finally forced to scrape his entire body with a shard of clay pottery (from the top of his head to the soles of his feet) left him as one large piece of scar tissue. What the Bible never indicates is that Job was ever healed from this disfigurement. Jonah's reputation bore an eternal blemish. David's son from his adulterous affair with Bathsheba did not come back to life. Therefore, we, too, may pass through the storms of life and come out better on the inside, but we may bear the scars forever on the outside.

PLEASE THROW ME A LIFE PRESERVER

While going through a storm, we often attack or blame each other for our circumstances. This is a bad idea that will not help. What we should do is help each other, throwing life preservers to anyone not already dead in the water. We should practice what the Bible preaches and do the good that we know to do. Following is a brief list of what we need during the storms of life and what we need to model to those around us. Taken together with the lists of items discussed in *Wrapping Up Some Loose Ends* and *A Bag Full of Tools,* this will complete our basic outline of a "Personal Plan-Of-Action" as it pertains to the storms of life.

• We should provide for one another. While docked in Sidon for the night, Julius allowed Paul to go to his friends so that they might provide for his needs. This was not confined to the physical act of treating his wounds or feeding him, but it also extended to the emotional comfort and assurance that they gave Paul. It is always helpful to have someone loving enough who is not personally involved in our storm to care for and comfort us and offer us a fresh perspective. Paul put it this way, "That is, that we may be mutually strengthened *and* encouraged *and* comforted by each other's faith, both yours and mine" (Romans 1:12 AMP).

• We need friendship and accountability. Without someone else there to help us get back up when we fall down, we may never make it through some of the rougher stretches in our lives. Paul had this in Luke and Aristarchus, who both voluntarily accompanied him upon this fateful journey. What relief it brings when we know that, though life may get more turbulent and venomous than we could have ever imagined, we have someone standing with us at its worst. Accountability is a natural outcropping of close friendships because we know that within the confines of our relationship we will find acceptance, encouragement and trust—three vital cords when we are drowning.

• We need a word from God. Although the entire company of the Alexandrian ship eventually gave up all hope of being saved, God did not. In the midst of life's infernos we must get a sure word from God, because we may not always have someone like Paul aboard our ship who will hear God's voice and let us know that it will be all right. We need someone with us who will continually encourage us to never give up our hope; we need someone who can help us fight our carnal urges. And when we are not experiencing an onslaught of life, then we should be that person to someone else.

• We need brutal honesty. When Paul reiterates that they should have taken his earlier advice he was being tactful and honest. In the midst of our horrors, we need someone to be brutally honest with us. Someone with nothing either to gain or lose who can point out the dark clouds that are hidden from our view by our blind spot—someone that we will listen to. It is critical that we have a trusted friend or confidant who will not be afraid to tell us the truth about our situation.

• We need sure anchors. When the Alexandrian ship got close to the rocks of an unknown shore, the crew dropped four anchors in an attempt to stop her forward movement toward the rocks. If we do not have our anchors securely sunk into the depths of Christ, then the storm may very well dash our ship against the rocks of despair. There is no hope if we are not anchored. Not only do we need to be anchored in God, but also we must have anchors in friends, family members, accountability relationships and a local church.

• We need to stick with our ship. In an attempt to escape from the ship, the crew tried to lie their way around an escape. Abandoning ship is never a good idea and is generally not the choice God wants us to make. Often when being mercilessly attacked, we seek the easiest way out. What we need is to have the strength and fortitude to cut off the carnal way of escape. We have to face the storm's fury in order to see God's way out. Too many of us seek escape when God wants us to walk it out.

A Bag Full of Tools

Many habits will assist us in living to tell about the pillaging onslaughts of life. Actually, the Bible is replete with examples for us to examine and from which we can learn. What I have compiled below is a brief list of some of the more common tools we can put in our bag and carry aboard our ship. This list is not all-inclusive and should only be considered as a starting point. We have the rest of our earthly lifetime to spend augmenting our arsenal with effective weapons of warfare.

• Philippians 1:9–11–We must have discernment—this is probably the most critical element in our lives.

• Psalm 1:1–We need to avoid ungodly counsel, the pathways of the sinner and not sit down and fellowship with scornful mockers.

• Psalm 1:3–We need to be firmly planted near the river of God.

• Luke 7:23; 2 Kings 5:10 - 12–We cannot become offended when God or His servants do not act as we expect.

• Psalm 1:2; 119:11–We need to hide God's word in our heart and habitually meditate upon it.

• Matthew 7:24, 25–Our lives (house) must be built upon the rock of God.

• Philippians 4:7; Colossians 3:15–We must have the peace of God which will rule our hearts.

• Ephesians 6: 10–17–We must put on the whole armor of God and then, when we have done all that the crisis demands, we must stand firmly.

• 1 Peter 5:5, 6–We must clothe ourselves with humility.

• 1 Peter 5:7–We must cast all of our cares, worries, anxieties and concerns upon God.

• 1 Peter 5:9–We must withstand the onslaught of the enemy of our soul by remaining firm in our faith, even when suffering for Christ's name.

• 2 Corinthians 10: 4, 5–We must cast down all thoughts and imaginations and refute the lofty theories and reasonings that would try to exalt themselves above the knowledge of God. When we do that, we are taking authority over these wicked arguments and purposes and leading them away captive–refusing to partake of their anarchy.

TESTING THE EMERGENCY BROADCAST SYSTEM

A SHIP FULL OF LIES

There are many times we blame God for the storms that we experience. We believe that He is toying with us, dangling us a carrot and then throwing it away. But God is not toying with us; the storm is. A fact that we should become intimate with is that storms will come and there is nothing we can do to stop them; however, we can often minimize their damage by our preparedness and by not causing more of our own doing. God does not lie to us, but the storm does so continually.

Powerful waves declare that they will lift us up to the heavens, and they do for an instant. But then the waves reveal what is hidden beneath them—the rocky, craggy, merciless ocean floor. They quickly release their lofty declaration and drop us from the crest to the depths of the trough. In fact, in some storms it is not uncommon for the waves to be so high and the troughs so deep that the actual ocean floor itself is uncovered (or close to it). Sometimes the very harbor water is sucked out to sea, and the harbor floor is left void of any water. The waves, which have promised us a cleansing flood, lie as they dash us against sand, stone and debris. In a perpetual yo-yo like motion we are helplessly launched to enormous heights only to experience the bottom once again.

The wind and sails lie in an intermingled dance. Howling through the rigging, the wind lies by telling us that it will fill our sails and blow us to safety. The sails lie by telling us that they will cup the wind and hold their form if only we will unfurl them and point them towards the wind's steady blast. However, as soon as we have complied with their wishes and as soon as we have given in to the strength of their promises, the wind laughs at our naiveté, and the sails whip and roll in an hysterical display as they tear apart in the face of the vengeful blast. Seams give way and threads pull loose as the integrity of the sails shreds before the knifelike wind. But before they finally give in, they allow the fury of the wind to push us deeper into the heart of the storm.

The furnishings and the gear on board lie by telling us that they will provide us with comfort and security. Beautifully crafted furnishings tell us that they will caress our bodies and store our riches while the oversized gear assures us of our safety even in the worst of conditions. A half-dozen anchors solemnly vow to hold us steady through the hurling winds and rolling waves, and the rudder swears to keep us heading in the right direction. Lanky masts boast of their flexibility in the wind, testifying as to their ability to remain stalwart and true while the railings pledge to keep all on-deck items aboard. Impressive bulwarks guarantee that they will manhandle the volume of the waves and keep our ship afloat. Corporately they spin us a yarn as they suddenly give way in a striking display of camaraderie, leaving us most vulnerable to the fury of the storm.

The rain lies as it vehemently defends its downward plummet, coaxing us into believing that it will pound down upon the waves until they subside. It also promises to wash the stench from the deck of our ship and erase the years of neglect and bloodshed. All we must do is go below and wait out its cleansing droplets. Then the rain rejoices as we accept its fabrication, falling harder and faster, mocking us where we stand while it hurls itself forth and fills our boat with unneeded weight. Half-frozen water that has plummeted from the heavens slices our face and reduces our visibility to zero, and yet all the while we believed its lies.

The boat creaks, groans, and vows that it will counteract the stresses of the storm that are attempting to separate its many members. Oaken joints cry out with shrieks of pain. Nails reverse their course with whining, biting singing. Tenons belie the depth of their mortises as they struggle to remain enclosed. But when they all see that the storm will not be denied, they give up in a lying chorus of shudders, cracking and splitting as they part company faster than they were joined together. Their integrity was a cruel joke, and it lasted just long enough to get us into the middle of the ocean.

The people on board the ship with us lie as well. Giving us their word that they will stick with us no matter what happens, they lie and let us down when our life begins to inconvenience or confuse them. They claim that they will stand beside us and bail the water back out of the boat and that nothing will make them turn away, but they all lie. There was never an honest intention of staying with us because they had already arranged a means of escape. Scheming while we were drowning, they knew that when the storm got bad they would be able to find some excuse to jump ship without us. Unable to handle the pain of the wind and the treachery of the waves, they knew their own weaknesses would be revealed if they stayed—and they would allow nothing to expose them, not even friendship or kinship.

The navigational devices deceive us and trick us into running the ship off course. The compass resolutely indicates north while it secretly conceals its malfunction. It lies as we swerve according to its untrue readings, desperately trying to escape the fury ahead—but the compass did not know where we were headed any more than we did. As the most trusted and respected piece of navigational equipment on board, it has dashed our hopes against the rocks of confusion while it conspired with the Loran in its deception. Even the depth gauge told us that the ocean floor lay far below us, but it could not react as fast as the swells gave way to the troughs. It lied about its ability to adapt to quickly changing conditions. As the hull rips open upon the ocean floor, we realize that our navigational equipment, too, was all part of the pack of lies.

The devil lies as he testifies that God has abandoned us here in the middle of this storm. He swears that he had nothing to do with it, that he has not the power to override our free will, and therefore could never be to blame. Suggesting that it must be God who is to blame for our unreasonable situation, he again convinces us that God is toying with us. With heady reminders of unanswered prayers and horrible sufferings, he sells us the lie that God is sadistic. Like lab mice in God's experimental labyrinth, he convinces us that we do not merit divine intervention. With the knowledge of good and evil, Satan convinces us of his superior wisdom and undying loyalty to our cause against the ruthless dictator that we serve. Crookedly he twists every sound until it matches his wicked convolutions.

Then our own voices lie to us. The words inside of our heads and hearts betray us as they demand a hearing. Telling us that we cannot make it through the storm, we lie to ourselves about the complete loss of hope. We also lie to ourselves that we have done nothing wrong, and that this storm must be God's fault because He has not kept His end of our covenantal agreement. Our own voices tell us that we are worthless, weak and inept. For all of the years that we have nurtured the voice within and for all of the hours we have spent reinforcing it with truth, it now swears allegiance with another. It abandons us and it lies all the way.

Finally, we have the voice of God. His voice is the only still, small voice in the midst of the storm—and it does not lie. Often we believe His voice to be so hard to hear because it is the only one not screaming at us; however, we can use that to our advantage. God's voice is the only voice not in our face with pounding fists and a red face. His voice is different and can easily be identified by peering through the fog and rain, over the waves and into the horizon. Listening to His voice alone will finally reveal the truth. With a steadiness in His voice and strength like no other, His words come across forcefully but not angrily. Assurances of our rescue come forth as He smoothly details His recommendations. We can choose to listen to His voice and live or we can choose to listen to one or all of the others and take our chances with them. The choice is ours alone. Free will has its dilemmas.

In the face of this ship full of lies, we would do well to heed the words of Solomon and choose wisdom and knowledge before the storms of life come upon us. After the storms have arrived, there may appear to be no answer from Heaven. As stated earlier, hearing His still, small voice in the middle of a screeching gale is difficult at best, but it is nearly impossible when we are not even familiar with its sound. Wisdom is based upon understanding the knowledge of God. Without knowledge, we are doomed. The best time to get that knowledge is before we even see the storm clouds approaching.

Wisdom cries aloud in the street, she raises her voice in the markets; She cries at the head of the noisy intersections [in the chief gathering places]; at the entrance of the city gates she speaks: How long, O simple ones [open to evil], will you love being simple? And the scoffers delight in scoffing and [self-confident] fools hate knowledge? If you will turn (repent) and give heed to my reproof, behold, I [Wisdom] will pour out my spirit upon you, I will make my words known to you. Because I have called and you have refused [to answer], have stretched out my hand and no man has heeded it, And you treated as nothing all my counsel and would accept none of my reproof, I also will laugh at your calamity; I will mock when the thing comes that shall cause you terror and panic—When your panic comes as a storm and desolation and your calamity comes on as a whirlwind, when distress and anguish come upon you. Then will they call upon me [Wisdom] but I will not answer; they will seek me early and diligently but they will not find me. Because they hated knowledge and did not choose the reverent and worshipful fear of the Lord, Would accept none of my counsel, and despised all my reproof, Therefore shall they eat of the fruit of their own way and be satiated with their own devices. For the backsliding of the simple shall slay them, and the careless ease of [self-confident] fools shall destroy them. But whoso hearkens to me [Wisdom] shall dwell securely and in confident trust and shall be quiet, without fear or dread of evil (Proverbs 1:20–33 AMP).

WHEN IT STILL DOESN'T WORK

Many people who are experiencing the terror of a storm cannot seem to make any of these approaches work. Some of these people may be like Jonah and may be so deep into the abyss that darkness is the only light they can see. To these I would say that maybe we need to take a deeper look into our ship; maybe we need to go back to the beginning, for surely there is a hope. The problem never lies with God, so in that absence, it must lie with us. There is always a way out of or a way through the storms of life. ALWAYS. Perhaps if we would be completely honest with ourselves there may be a way of escape that was overlooked or not attempted due to the uncertainty of its success (or the embarrassment of our admission). If only we could identify those areas in our own lives where we have rejected the wisdom and counsel of God, then we would know which course of action to take. Armed with that knowledge, we could return to God in a spirit of repentance, choosing wisdom instead of folly. This would cause us to dwell securely. But, alas, there are many times when we choose our own folly and reject wisdom and knowledge, instead choosing our own understanding.

Many times we look at knowledge and ignore or reject it, choosing instead to go our own way based upon our emotional imbalances. I cannot stress enough the importance of self-examination before, during and after the storms of life have rolled through. If a man does not examine himself, then he knows not what filth he may be transporting to the next turbulent disaster in life. When some people go off on tangents and contradict even the most fundamental teachings of the scriptures, we wonder how they could be so blind. The simple answer is that they have rejected wisdom and knowledge and are now consumed in their folly and self-importance. Repeated storms of life will come upon them and overtake them and Wisdom will laugh at their calamity. Continually embracing knowledge, wisdom and understanding will be what keeps us from perishing. It is not enough to hear the minister deliver his message and then go home and eat lunch. We must learn to feed for ourselves upon the knowledge of God, because wisdoms footings are poured on top of that knowledge. The reason why none of this may be working could be that we have rejected that knowledge, thinking instead that emotional outbursts would better support our house.

If it is not working, then we must make a repair in order to get our ship moving towards life. Some of the questions we should be constantly asking ourselves are as follows: What am I supposed to learn through this storm? Why have I accused God foolishly? What is there in my life that needs to change? Why do I doubt that God cares for me? What attitudes do I harbor that are dragging me down to Hell? Why do I assign the blame for every storm upon Satan? What do I need to let go of and cast off my ship? Why do I not admit my own fears, shortcomings and sin and then lay that disobedience aside? What can I do for someone else the next time I see them going through a storm? These are only some of the more common questions that we must answer honestly. The storms of life are about making it through, bearing the scars of our battles well and using the wisdom gained to help others avoid painful mistakes. It is about Him, not us. Life is about our wild, wide-open adventure and daily communion with God in order to learn how to navigate through the storms of life. So if it is still not working, then we must go back to square one—our salvation—and start all over again.

6

AT HER USUAL BERTH

THE CRUX OF THE MATTER

What I have been saying in this whole book, the real point that I want to get across to the reader is this: There is no one way to deal with the storms of life. That is why discernment is the critical key with which we can unlock the direction of God. We must know God and continually converse with Him. Without Him, we will give up during the storms of life or we will run and hide in the wrong places and lose all that we have gained. Disobedience will cause us to walk away from what God has graciously granted in order to follow after the base and evil desires that reside deep within. Faithfully listening for the sound of the wind as it begins it descent, and correctly interpreting the signs the storm is broadcasting, will help us to avoid many calamities in life. Honesty in admitting the carnal desires and cowardice buried within us will never steer us wrong. Now it is up to us to take this manual on the storms of life and to embrace discernment and let her lead our ship through to safe harbors.

As I said in the introduction to this book, this is why we must spend so much time putting our anchors deep into God. This is why we must examine the realities of life around us and become clever and cunning, spending more time thinking about how and where to anchor our ship than on what to wear or watch. For example, if we know of certain predilections that our family members have dealt with (uncles, aunts, fathers, mothers, cousins, grandparents or other close relatives), then we must doggedly prepare to travel another path, willfully determining that our ship will not rest in the graveyard where their ships are rotting. In order to avoid their disasters we will have to put forth a herculean effort, but it is possible to blaze our own new trail. When we know that, for instance, certain immoral situations have been a pattern with past family members, then we can be more than certain that these proclivities will also try to darken our door—naturally endeavoring to drag us down as well. So in those areas we must make sure that we have set our anchors deep into the good ground of morality and godliness and have run out enough cable (catenary) so that the anchor will hold. We must put some spiritual distance between that anchor and us so that it can effectively keep our ship from falling into the rocks of destruction.

AN ANCHOR TO HOLD

The more I study the art of anchoring, the more I am convinced that these techniques must be adapted spiritually for the church to survive the horrors of life. Without a solid understanding of these principles, what anchors we do lay out will not hold. In speaking of a catenary (the deep curve of the rope between the ship and the anchor), most will question my sanity, but the spiritual application of this principle is staggering. When laying out an anchor for a ship, one of the main principles in how effectively the anchor will hold is found in how horizontal the catenary is (that is how much distance there is between the ship and the anchor). With little line put out between a ship and its anchor, the more vertical the catenary will be and the greater the chances of the anchor not holding; however, the more cable put out between our ship and the anchor, the more horizontal this line will be and the greater the chances that the anchor will hold. The reasoning is simple:

The catenary is essential for two reasons, the first being that the deeper the curve the more horizontal the eventual pull on the anchor, which tends to bury the anchor flukes deeper into the ground. The second is that with the elasticity provided by a deep curve in the cable a vessel is preventing from snubbing to her anchor as she rides to a sea (snubbing may be defined as bringing the vessel to a sudden stop, as when letting go an anchor with too much way on).[208]

So what does that mean to us in life during our terrifying debacles at sea? It means that how we anchor is critical. Every area of our lives must be securely anchored—preferably into ground that will hold—like God and His word. With many voices promising us commitment and security, it is God alone who speaks truthfully and who provides an unchanging bed into which we can sink our anchors. Everything else will eventually falter and fall away (even our best friends will at times abandon us), but God and His word alone never change.

Why have I made such a big deal of the catenary? The first part of my answer concerns the thought of the deeper the catenary curve, the more horizontal the pull on the anchor we have set out. We can parlay this into spiritual terminology by saying that the more effort we put into and time we spend putting out, say, an anchor against pornography or lying or financial misrepresentations, the better our chances are that this anchor will not break loose or become dislodged. How can we accomplish this? By putting time and distance between our sins and us and by repeatedly spending time "in God" (i.e. at church, praying, reading the Bible, fellowshipping with other Christians, worshipping God) while successfully denying temptation a foothold in our life. In a word, sanctification. This is the lengthy process whereby we are purified and set apart from sin. It is a journey that it can never be summed up by one event. Freedom from the sins of our past starts with a prayer, a deliverance if you will or an understanding acknowledgement of our plight without Christ, but there is infinitely more to it than that. The only sure remedy and defense is to put a lot of time and distance between those weaknesses to which we are prone and our indulging in them as is possible. AA members use a simple counting of days such as "Hi, my name is Bob and I have been alcohol free for two hundred and twenty-six days." This organization has realized that the greater the distance between the temptation and the person the less chance there is of a repeat saturation. As Christians, we would do well to adopt this truth rather than believing that one supernatural instance will fix all of our spiritually broken down places. Finding lasting freedom comes from continually denying ourselves access to our weaknesses, thereby setting that anchor and putting a great distance between us and those struggles that we are susceptible to. Even Christ, when He forgave sins, told those he healed, delivered and set free to go *and sin no more.* Christ recognized that the process went far beyond the initial act of deliverance and extended into the future of not doing it again, so why can't we?

The second part of my answer concerns the thought of the elasticity provided by a deep, curved catenary. When distance is put between the ship and the anchor, it provides a deep level of protection in that the anchor line insulates or isolates the effects of tremendous blows or huge ocean swells from the ship. The elasticity of a long length of rope (or chain or cable) acts like a shock absorber as it lessens what might be a fatal blow to the ship's structure. Instead of a huge swell suddenly jarring every part of the ship's core, the anchor line absorbs the brunt of the strain and transfers the intensity of the blow to the ship in smaller amounts spread out over a greater length of time. In spiritual terminology, this would equate to several steps in the long line of distancing ourselves from any particular sins. It would start with Paul's admonition to Timothy to "Study *and* be eager *and* do your utmost to present yourself to God approved (tested by trial), a workman who has no cause to be ashamed, correctly analyzing *and* accurately dividing [rightly handling and skillfully teaching] the Word of Truth" (2 Timothy 2:15 AMP). The process would continue with making ourselves accountable in all areas of our lives to our spouse, pastor, best friend and God Himself. What we need between those anchors against sin and ourselves are stalwart members who will not be moved by our fetishes and propensities. We need people in our lives that will absorb some of the shock and strain of our storms and release it to us in chunks that are more manageable. When we find someone like that, we must do everything within our power to hold on to that person—for these are rare people indeed.

THE RULES OF ANCHORING

As I stated before, there are a variety of religions and sciences that promise their members sure footing, but there is only one true God who is Himself supreme and unchanging. All others are imposters who sell their lies built upon the shifting sands of human intellect and emotions. Therefore, in life, we must be sure of what we are anchoring ourselves to in order to survive. Anchoring to lies or untested ground will result in shipwreck and disillusionment. An anchor set into something firm, secure and unchanging will hold through any severe weather that may come against us. Obviously, God is the one we should continually be anchored to, but there are other fine soils into which we must also set our anchors—thereby creating an atmosphere of commitment that will not be easily broken free and a web of anchor lines that reach out in many directions. Following is a list of anchoring priorities that will help us to establish what is important to be firmly fixed to.

• God.

• Spouse.

• Family (first immediate, then extended).

• Friends.

• Theology.

• Church.

What do I mean when I say "anchoring to God" or "anchoring to friends and family"? The answer is simple. When we commit, then we are anchored. Whether this means that we get married, make a public profession of our born again experience, become a member of a church, become a partner in a business, parent a child, give our word or commit in some other way to another individual or organization, it all adds up to being anchored to that person or thing. Anchoring in life is where a certain level of commitment comes to rest upon another, complete with the trust and confidence necessary to maintain that relationship. It is further a firm belief in the honesty and good intentions of that other party as it pertains to our relationship. [A brief list of synonyms for being anchored in life is as follows: friendship, marriage, member, partner, sibling, parent, president or CEO.]

When we anchor in life, there are a few nautical rules that apply to the anchorages we choose. In order for our anchors to hold when the storms are trying to unsettle our ship and dash it into the rocks, we also have to follow the proper techniques established for anchoring. Not to do so is to admit our own ignorance and to believe that we can ignore the lessons of the past in favor of our higher enlightenment; however, failure to follow these simple rules will result in losses we cannot imagine.

• Every vessel under way upon the seas is to be fitted with an anchor of appropriate size, weight and design that can perform under the worst conditions that that vessel can expect to experience. In doing this, the vessel can be assured with a large degree of certainty that when the worst conditions arise, that the ship's ground tackle system will not fail. [Ground tackle is a term used when referring to the anchor and all of the parts related and attached to it, including rope, chain, shackles, and any winches or capstans used with it.] Before setting sail we must realize what the worst case scenario of our journey may be and then prepare ourselves to meet that challenge–whether that be any or all of the losses we discussed earlier. Doing this will also help take the bite out of disillusionment.

• Before anchoring, every captain must determine what type of ground he is anchoring into in order to establish the likelihood that the anchor, once set, will hold. If the ground is found to be unsuitable, then the captain should be compelled to find a better berth for the ship. In ascertaining the trustworthiness of the ground (friends, family, deity, etc.) we wish to anchor into, we can avoid abandoning established relationships when we later find them lacking.

• Before anchoring, every captain should choose his resting spot only after careful observation of the anchorage, sea conditions, prevailing wind directions and other boats already present in the anchorage. After making these considerations, the captain can place the boat in the best possible location whereby it can avoid any unnecessary negative interactions with the obstacles present—such as banging into other boats in the night or facing side-to the prevailing wind direction, both of which could spell disaster if the worst was to be encountered. In other words, we must take care not to rest our ship amidst too many dangerous obstacles. [Note: An anchorage is any harbor, cove, inlet, mooring or other location where a ship may be secured for a period of time.]

• Successful anchoring comes only from careful preparation, well-practiced routines and common sense. It may sound silly to practice anchoring, but it is the only way by which we can become proficient. Without knowing the techniques like the back of our hand, in times of crisis we will falter for that split second that may irreversibly send us into eternity. Unfortunately, as we grow up, we are constantly learning from our stinging mistakes how not to anchor.

• Every captain and crew should know what the weak links are in the ground tackle equipment and should inspect them frequently. When areas of weakness are known, such as familial tendencies, then these items should be the focus of intense and unwavering scrutiny at regular intervals in order to make certain that no parts are wearing thin or giving way. What we need most is for the weakest links in our ground tackle system to be more than strong enough to handle the worst life has to throw at us.

One of our biggest mistakes in life, though, is not in being unanchored, but rather in being anchored in the wrong location or to substandard holding ground. We anchor ourselves to people who constantly drag us under, to old ideas and habits that never were in the plan of God and to vocations that have no intent on letting us live out our destiny. The real problem with anchoring to the wrong thing lies in the great effort it takes to break that anchor free from its resting place, especially the longer it has remained set. Anchoring is not difficult, but it is absolutely necessary. Placing our anchors into suitable ground should only be attempted after careful consideration and prayer, and with godly counsel and advice from trusted peers. Removing our anchors from unsuitable ground is equally necessary, but may require additional help in order to be accomplished.

Before launching our boat out into the sea of life there are two critical areas in which we, as Christians, should be competent. The first critical area is good seamanship. There have been countless sailors who have been lost at sea during severe weather, many of whom were challenged by the storms and found wanting. Generally, they lacked the proper skills required in sailing and navigation in order to survive (many also lost their will to survive). Instead of gaining the real experience and expertise they needed in order to survive severe weather, they spent the bulk of their energy in pursuing other interests. They indulged their lifestyle more than honing the skills necessary to survive on the high seas. The second critical area is in having the proper ground tackle aboard the ship. Being a free spirit with no roots, commitments or obligations is not a healthy long-term lifestyle. Having anchors set in some place is the norm in life and should not be avoided or discouraged. There have been many documented cases in the past twenty-five years where people's ships and lives have been lost at sea during severe weather based solely upon one simple fact: They had failed to put any anchors aboard their vessels. Choosing to risk it all based upon their perceived superiority over the weather, or in the interest of shaving unwanted weight while in the heat of competition, they shunned common sense and paid the ultimate price. Though this situation is tragic, it is all too common in life. We tend to think that we really do not need connections or commitments of any kind. How many basic laws of life are we willing to breach in order to risk it all on the unknown?

UNRESOLVED EXPECTATIONS

In closing this book, I have one final lesson that I feel is important. This one deals with the period immediately following the storm, a period often forgotten by most due to the blindness of complete exhaustion. Once our storm has passed and we are finally able to stand up and look around, we may not like what we see. Lost, alone, abandoned and forgotten, we may find ourselves in a strange place or in a land far from our choosing. There may be downed trees and power lines, overturned houses and wrecked vehicles, and missing beaches and properties. Buoyed atop immeasurable velocities, entire chunks of our lives have been carried away and the wreckage is strewn for miles. Just when we have made it through a tough test of faith, we find ourselves having arrived at a destination that may not be what we had in mind. Like Paul, we may find ourselves not even able to recognize the area around us, or in a similar fashion to Jonah, we may find that we have been spit up onto a shore not far from our home but equally unappealing. The last problems arise when the storms of life dump us into unfamiliar territory and leave us in places where we did not expect to be. This is when we arrive at our final, pivotal point of the storm. Presented with this one last hurdle, it is critical that we react properly, reexamine each lesson that we have previously studied here in this book and make some tough determinations.

During life, we find it comforting to preplan our destinations. Even if we do not know exactly where we may end up, we at least have a picture of it in our mind. So what happens when the coups de main of life leave us bloodied and bruised but still alive on a deserted stretch of ground that defies every one of our previous expectations? How should we react? An unexpected layoff or firing at work, the death of a loved one, a disease that is quickly destroying who we are and used to be, or a financial burden that has broken our life in half. What should we do if we find that we have been dumped into one of these unexpected places? In short, we need to find out where God intends for us to be, then we can move on. Again, it all comes back to discernment.

Christ's disciples found themselves in the region of the Gerasenes with a crazy, demon-possessed man who was known to attack anyone that tried to pass his way. Did they like it there and want to stick around? In the natural, probably not. They had fished in Kursi's waters before and had done all within their power to avoid an encounter with this lunatic. Surely, because of this, the region of the Gerasenes was not on the top-ten list for sightseers and tourists. But the fact is that the disciples ended up in a place that was, at best, uncomfortable for them. Jonah ended up in Nineveh, the place he hated almost as much as he hated himself. Miserable to be where he ended up, he hated the fact that he was there as much as the reason why. When he ran in the night to Joppa and boarded that ship, he never expected that he would ever see or hear of Nineveh again, but he found himself there nevertheless. Paul landed on an island in chains (and later in Rome), right where God had told him that he would end up. Noah landed on the top of a mountain in a very large ship without friends, houses or anything other than what he carried with him in the ark. Job lost his great influence in the city, his children, and all of his wealth and worldly possessions (at least during the storm), stranded in a place no father or husband ever wants to be found in. Each one of these had to deal with and confront the pain of their storm, the disillusionment that arrived upon the heels of their disaster and the loss of respect from friends and associates. In a way, they were all outcasts in a world that would judge them harshly.

My point is that we, too, may find ourselves in equally unexpected places. How we handle this last major hurdle is what will justify or condemn us. How we react to the unexpected or unwanted places is what will lead us on or ruin all that we have accomplished. It is not enough to make it through the storms of life, but we must finish it out, as they say, in style by finishing our course and keeping our faith. We must learn the freedom that comes from completely abandoning our will to His greater purposes no matter what our preconceived expectations were. Let us refuse to be like Jonah, who grudgingly accepted his Nineveh in lieu of a death at the bottom of the sea. May we not be like the disciples who may have preferred to be elsewhere. Instead, let us be like Paul and make the most of where we land with the right attitude. Notice that I did not say the best attitude that we can muster. No, we must have the right attitude, and if we do not have it, then we must pray and ask God to help us obtain it. Life could be worse; we may not have survived at all. It is vital that we find the contentment Paul spoke about in whatever place the storm has dumped us. So what did Paul mean when he spoke about contentment? Though this is a lengthy definition, I feel that it will enlighten us as to the true meaning of the spirit of contentment. With that in mind, let us take a look:

Contentment is having the ability to be strong enough for a situation and, hence, being capable, able and willing to raise a barrier to ward off any feelings of dissatisfaction, greed, envy or the desire for more than we have the capacity to carry, hold or handle. It is to be willing and pleased within our current circumstance to the point where we express agreement with our place and a restrained compliance and happiness with what we possess. Further, contentment displays itself in not desiring more than what we currently have and not being disturbed by a desire for something different. It also means to have Christ's power poured into us in sufficient supply so that we are pleased with whatever is available to us and thus we feel adequately sup-

plied and fulfilled with what we expected and received. Part of the manifestation of contentment is to continue to hold ourselves together while remaining bright in our countenance, knowing that we have the necessary resources in Christ in order to get along without further help or assistance. True contentment is to comply with our present situation without protest, struggle, dispute or the need to strive and fight for something that we do not possess. The picture contentment paints is of a person satisfied with that which is contained within, knowing that what we have is enough and that we have need of no more. Finally, it means to be willing in our attitude to be at peace and at rest with the meaning or significance of our situation as opposed to its form.

Let us deal with some realities here concerning places of unexpected arrival. The following practical examples will help us tune in to exactly what I am saying and will show us where, exactly, we need to feel this contentment. Maybe our storm is marital strife and, instead of the divorce that we secretly hoped for, we still find ourselves stuck in this failing marriage relationship. Or maybe our storm is financial devastation and, instead of the bankruptcy we had prayed would wipe our slate clean, we are stuck paying back our creditors for the next twenty years. A final example may be that our storm is a physical challenge resulting from years of gluttony and binging on junk food to the point where, instead of the liposuction or gastro-intestinal bypass surgery that we were sure would fix us, we are left with the agonizing realities of diabetes, obesity and heart disease. What are we to do when we had our hopes set high upon a mountain that we could never climb? How should we proceed when we have been dumped into a situation that we would rather not be in? The first thing we must know is that God is still on the throne and in control, but that He may not wave His magic wand and put us back into a place of comfort and ease.

If we find ourselves standing in a place similar to any that I have described or are faced with an unexpected reality that we are having difficulty dealing with, then we must carefully proceed with a clear word from our heavenly Father. It may be that our location after the storm is merely a temporary displacement, but it could also signal a permanent relocation that we have to deal with. There are not many ways we can react. In the following list, I will give only the essentials. Though there may be more and different ways to react, those listed here are the only primary ways by which we should proceed.

• If we find that we are in an uncomfortable place where we are temporarily detained, then we must do whatever good it is that our hands find to do in that place. For the disciples and Jesus, it was to heal this demoniac. They had ministry to do after the storm. How vital it was to that man that they not jump back in their boats and head back to Capernaum (a place of comfort) before they had accomplished their mission. Although an example of a temporary relocation, they had to be obedient to the wishes of the master before they could return home.

• If we find ourselves in a situation where we have run from the call and command of God, then once we are spit back up on shore, we must get ourselves moving immediately back towards the destination God commanded. It may take days, months or years to get back to that place, but without being in the right geographic location, that place that God said to go, then we can have no peace, no relief, and no hopeful future.

• If we find ourselves shipwrecked and stranded like Paul, then we must take comfort in the fact that the Father, indeed, will see to it that we make it to our "Rome". We must deal with where we are because it is where we are supposed to be, and even though this may tilt some or our thinking, being stranded on this island was part of Paul's destiny. We must make the most of the time that we have while stranded and use it for the glory of God, realizing that it is part of our destiny.

• If we find ourselves in a place of comfort and honor and responsibility after the storm, like the three Hebrew children and Joseph and Daniel, then we must act humbly and responsibly. We must take our new position with meekness and carry out our newfound responsibilities with the mind and character of Christ. In these times, we will have been strategically placed there by God and will have a specific mandate to carry out for Him. The most critical element is in finding out what that mission is and then carrying it out to the glory of God.

I have to be honest; many of the storms that have struck my life have left me in the worst possible places imaginable to me. Severe weather has dumped me into rough situations, uncomfortable places and detestable locations. I naively thought that once the storm was over that I was done, but there is always the aftermath to deal with. No one ever told me that the storm might dump me off in a place that I despised. No one told me that I might have to bulldoze down the remnants of my home and start all over again. Often the storms have hit me with such speed, intensity, and fury that I have not had time during the battle to get a bad attitude. In fact, there have been times when I barely had time to fight at all. When the pandemonium is finally over with and I am exhausted from the struggle, the last thing I want to do is have to deal with my attitude. Unfortunately, for me at least, this is usually the time when I let down my guard and my greatest challenge arrives—keeping my attitudes in check.

Ending up where we do not want or did not expect to be can be a more difficult pill to swallow than the storm itself. The simple answer as to how to deal with this is not simple at all, because the answers are complex at best. If we are in an uncomfortable, unexpected or unwanted place but are exactly where God wants us to be, then we must deal with it.

BIBLIOGRAPHY

Archaeological Institute of America, Monographs New Series, Number 5, Sacred and Secular: Ancient Egyptian Ships and Boats, by Cheryl A. Ward, Kendall/Hunt Publishing Co., Dubuque, Iowa, 2000.

Ship and Boat Models in Ancient Greece, by Paul Forsythe Johnston, Naval Institute Press, Annapolis, Maryland, 1985.

Crossroads in Ancient Shipbuilding, Edited by Christer Westerdahl, Oxbow Books, Park End Place, Oxford, OX1 1HN, 1994.

The Archaeology of Boats and Ships, by Dr. Basil Greenhill with Professor John Morrison, Naval Institute Press, Annapolis, Maryland, 1995.

"Golden Age Treasures" by George F. Bass, National Geographic Magazine, March 2002.

The New Bible Dictionary, Inter-Varsity Press, Tyndale House Publishers, Inc., Second Edition, Wheaton, Illinois, Reprinted 1986.

The Sea of Galilee Boat: An Extraordinary 2000 Year Old Discovery by Shelley Wachsmann, Plenum Press, New York 1995.

The Sea of Galilee and Its Fishermen in the New Testament by Mendel Nun, 1989, Published by Kibbutz Ein Gev: Tourist Department and Kinnereth Sailing Co.

Ancient Stone Anchors and Net Sinkers From the Sea of Galilee by Mendel Nun, 1993, Published by Kibbutz Ein Gev: Tourist Department and Kinnereth Sailing Co.

Gergesa (Kursi): Site of a Miracle Church and Fishing Village by Mendel Nun, 1989, Published by Kibbutz Ein Gev: Tourist Department and Kinnereth Sailing Co.

Twenty-Six Translations of the Bible, Volume III, New Testament, Matthew–Revelation, Curtis Vaughan, General Editor, Published for AMG Publishers, Chattanooga, Tennessee, (copyright 1985, The Zondervan Corporation, Grand Rapids, Michigan).

http://worldfacts.us/Israel-geography.htm

http://www.us-israel.org/jsource/Society_&_Culture/geo/rift.html

http://www.infoplease.com/ce6/world/A0821681.html

http://community.gospelcom.net/Brix?pageID=4937

http://community.gospelcom.net/Brix?pageID=1853

http://www.infoplease.com/ce6/world/A0821681.html

http://www.us-israel.org/jsource/Society_&_Culture/geo/rift.html

http://www.ukdiving.co.uk/ukdiving/world/redsea/erez/

http://www.ourfatherlutheran.net/biblehomelands/galilee/jordanriver.htm

http://www.connect.ab.ca/~dmoore/page5.htm

http://www.bartleby.com/65/gr/GreatRif.html

http://www.ubfellowship.org/

http://www.keyway.ca/htm2002/seagal.htm

Egyptian Boats and Ships by Steve Vinson, Shire Egyptology Series, Shire Publications Ltd., Buckinghamshire, UK 1994.

Webster's New World Dictionary of American English, Third College Edition, Victoria Neufeldt, Editor in Chief, Simon and Schuster, Inc., New York, 1988.

The American Heritage Dictionary of the English Language, William Morris, Editor, American Heritage Publishing Co., Inc., Houghton Mifflin Company, New York, 1973.

Expository Dictionary of Bible Words, Lawrence O. Richards, Zondervan Publishing House, Grand Rapids, Michigan, 1985.

Vine's Expository Dictionary of New Testament Words, W.E. Vine, M.A., MacDonald Publishing Company, McLean, Virginia, date unknown.

Dictionary of Word Origins, John Ayto, Arcade Publishing, New York, 1990.

The Ship: An Illustrated History by Bjorn Landstrom, Doubleday and Company, Inc., Garden City, NY 1961.

Ships and Seafaring in Ancient Times by Lionel Casson, University of Texas Press, 1994.

Piracy in the Ancient World by Henry A. Ormerod, The Johns Hopkins University Press, 1997.

The Influence of Sea Power on Ancient History by Chester G. Starr, Oxford University Press, New York 1989.

Herodotus

Ships and Sea Power Before the Great Persian War by H.T. Wallinga, E.J. Brill, Leiden, The Netherlands, 1993.

The Ancient Mariners, Seafarers and Sea Fighters of the Mediterranean in Ancient Times by Lionel Casson, Princeton University Press, Princeton, NJ 1991.

http://ina.tamu.edu/ub_main.htm

Ancient Shipwrecks by K.C. Smith, Pub. By Franklin Watts, a division of Grolier Publishing, 2000.

http://www.cyprus-holidays-hotels.com/Kyrenia/ship_wreck_museum.html

http://www.anomalist.com/features/tartessus.html

Seagoing Ships and Seamanship in the Bronze Age Levant by Shelley Wachsmann, Chatham Publishing, 1998.

Egypt, Canaan, and Israel in Ancient Times, by Donald B. Redford, Prince University, 1992.

http://ancientneareast.tripod.com/Levant.html

Ships and Seamanship in the Ancient World, by Lionel Casson, The Johns Hopkins University Press, 1995.

http://www.biblesearch.com/files/ot3.pdf

http://www.geocities.com/centrevillechurchofchrist/smelser_j/exile.htm

Eerdmans Atlas of the Bible with A–Z Guide to Places, reprinted, August 1987, William B. Eerdmans Publishing Company, Grand Rapids, Michigan.

The Ancient Assyrians by Mark Healy, Osprey Publishing Ltd., 1991, Reprinted 2003.

The Assyrian Empire by Don Nardo, 1998, Lucent Books, San Diego, CA.

Ancient Records of Assyria and Babylonia, Volume 1, Daniel D. Luckenbill, ed., Chicago: University of Chicago Press, 1926. Reprint: New York: Greenwood Press, 1968.

The Might That Was Assyria by H.W.F. Saggs, Sidgwick and Jackson Limited, London, Great Britain, 1984.

The Assyrians by Elaine Landau, The Millbrook Press, Inc., Brookfield, CT, 1997.

Manners and Customs of Bible Lands by Fred H. Wight, Moody Press, Chicago, Illinois, 1953.

Bible Manners and Customs by George M. Mackie, Fleming H. Revell Co., New York.

http://mediatheek.thinkquest.nl/~11118/en/development/types.list.gregale.html

http://www.uscg.mil/hq/g-m/mse4/boatlb-rb.htm

http://laws.justice.gc.ca/en/S-9/C.R.C.-c.1436/48511.html#rid-48565

Word Pictures in the New Testament, Volumes I-VI by Archibald Thomas Robertson, 1930, Baker Book House, Grand Rapids, Michigan.

http://dictionary.reference.com/search?q=home%20port

The Interpreter's Dictionary of the Bible, An Illustrated Encyclopedia, Eleventh Printing, Abingdon Press, Nashville, Tennessee, 1980. [Original copyright 1962].

http://www.boatsafe.com/nauticalknowhow/terms0101.htm

http://www.sailorschoice.com/Terms/scphrases.htm

Staying Put! The Art of Anchoring by Brian M. Fagan, Caractacus Corporation, Santa Barbara, CA, 1993.

The Complete Book of Anchoring and Mooring, Revised Second Edition by Earl R. Hinz, Cornell Maritime Press, Centreville, Maryland, 2001.

Anchors, An Illustrated History by Betty Nelson Curryer, Naval Institute Press, Annapolis, Maryland, 1999.

Heavy Weather Tactics Using Sea Anchors & Drogues by Earl R. Hinz, Paradise Cay Publications, Arcata, California, 2000.

The Acts of the Apostles, An Historical Commentary, [Volume 5 of the Tyndale New Testament Commentaries Series] by E. M. Blaiklock, Litt.D., William B. Eerdmans Publishing Company, Grand Rapids, Michigan, Reprinted 1979.

The New Unger's Bible Dictionary, Revised and Updated Edition by Merrill F. Unger, Edited by R. K. Harrison, Moody Press, Chicago, Illinois, 1988.

Lectures on the Book of Acts by H.A. Ironside, Litt.D., Loizeaux Brothers, New Jersey, Twentieth Printing, 1988.

The New Testament, An Expanded Translation by Kenneth S. Wuest, William B. Eerdmans Publishing Company, Grand Rapids, Michigan, Reprinted 1984.

The Holy Bible, New International Version, UltraThin Reference Edition, Holman Bible Publishers, Nashville, Tennessee, 1986.

"Scripture taken from the HOLY BIBLE, NEW INTERNATIONAL VERSION. Copyright © 1973, 1978, 1984 International Bible Society. Used by permission of Zondervan Bible Publishers."

The (AMP)lified Bible, The Zondervan Corporation and the Lockman Foundation, Zondervan Publishing House, Grand Rapids, Michigan, 1987.

"Scripture taken from THE (AMP)LIFIED BIBLE , Old Testament copyright © 1965, 1987 by the Zondervan Corporation. The (AMP)lified New Testament copyright © 1958, 1987 by the Lockman Foundation. Used by Permission."

The Works of Josephus: New Updated Edition, Complete and Unabridged in One Volume, Translated by William Whiston, a.m., Hendrickson Publishers, Peabody, Massachusetts, 1987, Seventeenth printing, 2003.

Wilson's Old Testament Word Studies by William Wilson, MacDonald Publishing Company, McLean, Virginia, (no copyright date given).

Theological Wordbook of the Old Testament, Volumes I & II by the Moody Bible Institute of Chicago, Edited by R. Laird Harris, Moody Press, Chicago, Illinois, 1980.

The Prophets of Israel by Leon J. Wood, Baker Book House, Grand Rapids, Michigan, 1979, Eighth Printing, June 1989.

Exploring the Old Testament by Beacon Hill Press, Edited by W.T. Purkiser, Ph.D., Beacon Hill Press of Kansas City, Missouri, 1955.

A Popular Survey of the Old Testament by Norman L. Geisler, Baker Book House, Grand Rapids, Michigan, 1977, Fifteenth Printing, September, 1989.

A History of Babylonia and Assyria by Robert William Rogers, Volumes I & II, Second Edition, Eaton & Mains, New York, 1900.

Nineveh and its Remains, A Narrative of an Expedition to Assyria by Sir Austen Henry Layard, The Lyons Press, Guilford, Connecticut, 2001, Revised abridgement originally published in 1882.

The Book of Acts by Stanley M. Horton, Gospel Publishing House, Springfield, Missouri, 1981.

Wild at Heart, Discovering the Secret of a Man's Soul, John Eldredge, Thomas Nelson Publishers, Nashville, Tennessee, 2001.

U.S. Army Survival Handbook, Department of the Army, The Lyons Press, Guilford, Connecticut, 2002.

(Footnotes)

Preface

[1] U.S. Army Survival Handbook, Department of the Army, The Lyons Press, Guilford, Connecticut, 2002, Pg. 7.

[2] The Tragedy of King Richard the Second by William Shakespeare; Act 2, Scene 1.

[3] See http://k12.0cs.ou.edu/teachers/glossary/p.html

[4] U.S. Army Survival Handbook, Department of the Army, The Lyons Press, Guilford, Connecticut, 2002, Pg. 5.

[5] It is estimated that there are between 12,000 and 14,000 radio stations in the United States. See <http://www.nab.org/radio/radfacts.asp>; <http://www.fcc.gov/mb/audio/totals/bt031231.html>

[6] It is estimated that there are over 1700 television stations in the United States. See <http://www.fcc.gov/mb/audio/totals/bt031231.html>

[7] It is estimated that there are over 21,500 television stations and 44,000 radio stations worldwide. See <http://www.nab.org/irc/virtual/faqs.asp#US-Totals>

[8] See <http://www.srh.noaa.gov;ohx/vision.html>

[9] See <http://www.fema.gov/about/history.shtm>

[10] Gordon MacDonald, The Effective Father, (Wheaton, Illinois: Living Books, Tyndale House Publishers, 1989).

[11] "Destructive Storms Drive Insurance Losses Up, Will Taxpayers Have to Bail Out Insurance Industry?"
by Seth Dunn & Christopher Flavin, March 26, 1999. See < http://www.worldwatch.org/alerts/990325.html>

[12] Ibid

[13] "The Cost Of Storms" Editor: Cheryl Dybas, November 19, 1999. See <http://www.nsf.gov/od/lpa/news/tips/99/tip91119.htm>

[14] See < http://www.factmonster.com/ipka/A0001441.html>

[15] See <http://www.turkishpress.com turkishpress/news.asp?ID=29379>

[16] See <http://story.news.yahoo.com/news?tmpl=story&u=afp/2 0050222/wl_sthasia_afp/ asiaquakesrilankamaldives&cid=1535&ncid=2337>

[17] See < http://www.msnbc.msn.com/id/9329293/>, <http://www. msnbc.msn.com/id/9329293/page/2/> and <http://aolsvc.news. aol.com/business/article.adp?id=20050910151109990001>

[18] See < http://www.msnbc.msn.com/id/9454308/>

[19] See <http://www.msnbc.msn.com/id/9118428/> and <http:// www.msnbc.msn.com/id/9454308/>

[20] See VHS documentary: The History Channel, Modern Marvels, Weather Predictions, Catalogue #: AAE-42296, ©1998, A&E Television Networks.

[21] See http://en.wikipedia.org/wiki/Low_pressure_system

[22] See http://en.wikipedia.org/wiki/High_%28atmospheric%29

[23] See http://en.wikipedia.org/wiki/Pressure_system

[24] Bringing up Boys, Dr. James Dobson, Tyndale House Publishers, Inc., Wheaton, Illinois, 2001, Pg. 235.

[25] This adaptation is loosely based upon and contains many revisions of continuity and thought for clarification and better language flow based upon information from the following sources: Matthew 8:24–27; Luke 8:1–26; Word Pictures of the New Testament by A.T. Robertson, Volumes I & II; Vine's Expository Dictionary of New Testament Words by W.E. Vine; The Acts of the Apostles by E.M. Blaiklock; The New Testament, An Expanded Translation by Kenneth S. Wuest; Nelson's Illustrated Bible Dictionary, Editor Herbert Lockyer, Sr.; Expository Dictionary of Bible Words by Lawrence O. Richards; Abingdon's Strong's Exhaustive Concordance of the Bible by James Strong; Twenty-Six Translations of the Bible, Volume III, General Editor Curtis Vaughan; Webster's New World Dictionary, Third College Edition; The American Heritage Dictionary of the English Language, Roget's International Thesaurus, Fourth Edition, Revised by Robert L. Chapman; The New Bible Dictionary, Second Edition; The New Unger's Bible Dictionary, Revised and Updated Edition, and my own personal flair.

[26] See http://dictionary.reference.com/search?q=home%20port

[27] The New Bible Dictionary, Inter-Varsity Press, Tyndale House Publishers, Inc., Second Edition, Wheaton, Illinois, Reprinted 1986, Pg. 177.

[28] The Interpreter's Dictionary of the Bible, An Illustrated Encyclopedia, Eleventh Printing, Abingdon Press, Nashville, Tennessee, 1980, Pg. 533. [Original Copyright 1962].

[29] Nelson's Illustrated Bible Dictionary, Herbert Lockyer, Sr.-Editor, Thomas Nelson Publishers, Nashville, Tennessee, 1986, Pg. 206–207.

[30] The New Unger's Bible Dictionary, Revised and Updated Edition, Merrill F. Unger, Moody Press, Chicago, Illinois, 1988, Pg. 209.

[31] Word Pictures in the New Testament, Volume II, The Gospel According to Luke, Archibald Thomas Robertson, Baker Book House, Grand Rapids, Michigan, 1930, Pg. 97.

[32] See http://www.keyway.ca/htm2002/seagal.htm

[33] The New Bible Dictionary, Inter-Varsity Press, Tyndale House Publishers, Inc., Second Edition, Wheaton, Illinois, Reprinted 1986, Pg. 403, 404.

[34] The Works of Josephus, Translated by William Whiston, Hendrickson Publishers, Peabody, Massachusetts, 1987, New Updated Edition, Seventeenth printing—March 2003, Pg. 637. [From the Wars of the Jews, Book II, Chapter 21, Section 8].

[35] The Sea of Galilee Boat: An Extraordinary 2000 Year Old Discovery by Shelley Wachsmann, Plenum Press, New York, 1995), Pg. 112, 113.

[36] The Sea of Galilee and Its Fishermen in the New Testament by Mendel Nun, 1989, Published by Kibbutz Ein Gev: Tourist Department and Kinnereth Sailing Co., Pg. 6.

[37] The New Bible Dictionary, Inter-Varsity Press, Tyndale House Publishers, Inc., Second Edition, Wheaton, Illinois, Reprinted 1986, Pg. 404.

[38] Nelson's Illustrated Bible Dictionary, Herbert Lockyer, Sr.-Editor, Thomas Nelson Publishers, Nashville, Tennessee, 1986, Pg. 402.

[39] See http://www.boatsafe.com/nauticalknowhow/terms0101.htm

[40] Gergesa (Kursi): Site of a Miracle Church and Fishing Village by Mendel Nun, 1989, Published by Kibbutz Ein Gev: Tourist Department and Kinnereth Sailing Co., Pg. 15.

[41] Gergesa (Kursi): Site of a Miracle Church and Fishing Village by Mendel Nun, 1989, Published by Kibbutz Ein Gev: Tourist Department and Kinnereth Sailing Co., Pg. 6.

[42] Gergesa (Kursi): Site of a Miracle Church and Fishing Village by Mendel Nun, 1989, Published by Kibbutz Ein Gev: Tourist Department and Kinnereth Sailing Co., Pg. 3.

[43] Gergesa (Kursi): Site of a Miracle Church and Fishing Village by Mendel Nun, 1989, Published by Kibbutz Ein Gev: Tourist Department and Kinnereth Sailing Co., Pg. 6.

[44] The New Bible Dictionary, Inter-Varsity Press, Tyndale House Publishers, Inc., Second Edition, Wheaton, Illinois, Reprinted 1986, Pg. 1107.

[45] The New Bible Dictionary, Inter-Varsity Press, Tyndale House Publishers, Inc., Second Edition, Wheaton, Illinois, Reprinted 1986, Pg. 1107.

[46] Ancient Stone Anchors and Net Sinkers From the Sea of Galilee by Mendel Nun, 1993, Published by Kibbutz Ein Gev: Tourist Department and Kinnereth Sailing Co., Pg. 11, 12.

[47] Ancient Stone Anchors and Net Sinkers From the Sea of Galilee by Mendel Nun, 1993, Published by Kibbutz Ein Gev: Tourist Department and Kinnereth Sailing Co., Pg. 9.

[48] Ancient Stone Anchors and Net Sinkers From the Sea of Galilee by Mendel Nun, 1993, Published by Kibbutz Ein Gev: Tourist Department and Kinnereth Sailing Co., Pg. 11.

[49] Ancient Stone Anchors and Net Sinkers From the Sea of Galilee by Mendel Nun, 1993, Published by Kibbutz Ein Gev: Tourist Department and Kinnereth Sailing Co., Pg. 16.

[50] Ancient Stone Anchors and Net Sinkers From the Sea of Galilee by Mendel Nun, 1993, Published by Kibbutz Ein Gev: Tourist Department and Kinnereth Sailing Co., Pg. 17.

[51] Ancient Stone Anchors and Net Sinkers From the Sea of Galilee by Mendel Nun, 1993, Published by Kibbutz Ein Gev: Tourist Department and Kinnereth Sailing Co., Pg. 20.

[52] The Sea of Galilee and Its Fishermen in the New Testament by Mendel Nun, 1989, Published by Kibbutz Ein Gev: Tourist Department and Kinnereth Sailing Co., Pg. 16.

[53] The Sea of Galilee and Its Fishermen in the New Testament by Mendel Nun, 1989, Published by Kibbutz Ein Gev: Tourist Department and Kinnereth Sailing Co., Pg. 18.

[54] The Sea of Galilee and Its Fishermen in the New Testament by Mendel Nun, 1989, Published by Kibbutz Ein Gev: Tourist Department and Kinnereth Sailing Co., Pg. 19.

[55] The Sea of Galilee and Its Fishermen in the New Testament by Mendel Nun, 1989, Published by Kibbutz Ein Gev: Tourist Department and Kinnereth Sailing Co., Pg. 23.

[56] The Sea of Galilee and Its Fishermen in the New Testament by Mendel Nun, 1989, Published by Kibbutz Ein Gev: Tourist Department and Kinnereth Sailing Co., Pg. 29.

[57] The Sea of Galilee and Its Fishermen in the New Testament by Mendel Nun, 1989, Published by Kibbutz Ein Gev: Tourist Department and Kinnereth Sailing Co., Pg. 31.

[58] The Sea of Galilee and Its Fishermen in the New Testament by Mendel Nun, 1989, Published by Kibbutz Ein Gev: Tourist Department and Kinnereth Sailing Co., Pg. 32.

[59] The Sea of Galilee and Its Fishermen in the New Testament by Mendel Nun, 1989, Published by Kibbutz Ein Gev: Tourist Department and Kinnereth Sailing Co., Pg. 32.

[60] Ancient Stone Anchors and Net Sinkers From the Sea of Galilee by Mendel Nun, 1993, Published by Kibbutz Ein Gev: Tourist Department and Kinnereth Sailing Co., Pg. 35.

[61] Ancient Stone Anchors and Net Sinkers From the Sea of Galilee by Mendel Nun, 1993, Published by Kibbutz Ein Gev: Tourist Department and Kinnereth Sailing Co., Pg. 44.

[62] Ancient Stone Anchors and Net Sinkers From the Sea of Galilee by Mendel Nun, 1993, Published by Kibbutz Ein Gev: Tourist Department and Kinnereth Sailing Co., Pg. 47.

[63] See http://www.sailorschoice.com/Terms/scphrases.htm

[64] Gergesa (Kursi): Site of a Miracle Church and Fishing Village by Mendel Nun, 1989, Published by Kibbutz Ein Gev: Tourist Department and Kinnereth Sailing Co., Pg. 8.

[65] See http://worldfacts.us/Israel-geography.htm

[66] Nelson's Illustrated Bible Dictionary, Herbert Lockyer, Sr.-Editor, Thomas Nelson Publishers, Nashville, Tennessee, 1986, Pg. 402.

[67] The Sea of Galilee and Its Fishermen in the New Testament by Mendel Nun, 1989, Published by Kibbutz Ein Gev: Tourist Department and Kinnereth Sailing Co., Pg. 54.

[68] The Sea of Galilee Boat: An Extraordinary 2000 Year Old Discovery by Shelley Wachsmann, Plenum Press, New York 1995, Pg. 121.

[69] See http://www.ourfatherlutheran.net/biblehomelands/galilee/jordanriver.htm

[70] See http://www.us-israel.org/jsource/Society_&_Culture/geo/rift.html

[71] See http://worldfacts.us/Israel-geography.htm

[72] See http://www.ukdiving.co.uk/ukdiving/world/redsea/erez/

[73] See http://www.boatsafe.com/nauticalknowhow/terms0101.htm

[74] See http://www.sailorschoice.com/Terms/scphrases.htm

[75] This adaptation is loosely based upon and contains many revisions of continuity and thought for clarification and better language flow based upon information from the following sources: Theological Wordbook of the Old Testament Volumes I & II; The Prophets of Israel by Leon J. Wood; Exploring the Old Testament, Edited by W.T. Purkiser; Old Testament Word Studies by William Wilson; A Popular Survey of the Old Testament by Norman L. Geisler; A History of Babylonia and Assyria by Robert William Rogers, Volumes I & II; Nineveh and its Remains by Austen Henry Layard; Nelson's Illustrated Bible Dictionary, Editor Herbert Lockyer, Sr.; Expository Dictionary of Bible Words by Lawrence O. Richards; Abingdon's Strong's Exhaustive Concordance of the Bible by James Strong; Twenty-Six Translations of the Bible, Volume II, General Editor Curtis Vaughan; Webster's New World Dictionary, Third College Edition; The American Heritage Dictionary of the English Language, Roget's International Thesaurus, Fourth Edition, Revised by Robert L. Chapman; The New Bible Dictionary,

Second Edition; The New Unger's Bible Dictionary, Revised and Updated Edition, The Thompson Chain-Reference Bible compiled and edited by Frank Charles Thompson and my own personal flair.

[76] See http://www.ussrankin.org/id430.htm

[77] The Prophets of Israel, Leon J. Wood, Baker Book House, Grand Rapids, Michigan, 1979, Pg. 123.

[78] The Prophets of Israel, Leon J. Wood, Baker Book House, Grand Rapids, Michigan, 1979, Pg. 292.

[79] Exploring the Old Testament, W.T. Purkiser, Editor, Beacon Hill Press, Kansas City, Missouri, 1955, Pg. 293.

[80] The New Unger's Bible Dictionary, Revised and Updated Edition, Merrill F. Unger, Moody Press, Chicago, Illinois, 1988, Pg. 705.

[81] The Prophets of Israel, Leon J. Wood, Baker Book House, Grand Rapids, Michigan, 1979, Pg. 289.

[82] The Ancient Assyrians, Mark Healy, Osprey Publishing Ltd., 1991, Reprinted 2003, Pg. 6.

[83] See http://www.biblelights.com/chart3.htm

[84] A Popular Survey of the Old Testament, Norman L. Geisler, Baker Book House, Grand Rapids, Michigan, 1977, Pgs. 130–135.

[85] The Prophets of Israel, Leon J. Wood, Baker Book House, Grand Rapids, Michigan, 1979, Pgs. 122–129.

[86] A History of Babylonia and Assyria, Volume Two, Robert William Rogers, 1900, Eaton & Mains, New York, Reprinted

2003, Lost Arts Media, Long Beach, California, Pg. 103.

[87] The Assyrians, Elaine Landau, The Millbrook Press, Brookfield, Connecticut, 1997, Pgs. 29–31.

[88] The Prophets of Israel, Leon J. Wood, Baker Book House, Grand Rapids, Michigan, 1979, Pg. 290.

[89] See http://www.mrdowling.com/603mesopotamia.html

[90] See http://news.nationalgeographic.com/news/2001/05/0518_crescent.html

[91] Nineveh and its Remains, A Narrative of an Expedition to Assyria, Sir Austen Henry Layard, The Lyons Press, Guilford, Connecticut, 2001, Pg. 340.

[92] The Assyrians, Elaine Landau, The Millbrook Press, Inc., Brookfield, CT, 1997, Pg. 29.

[93] The Assyrians, Elaine Landau, The Millbrook Press, Inc., Brookfield, CT, 1997, Pg. 31.

[94] The Prophets of Israel, Leon J. Wood, Baker Book House, Grand Rapids, Michigan, 1979, Pg. 290.

[95] The Might That Was Assyria, H.W.F. Saggs, Sidgwick and Jackson Limited, London, Great Britain, 1984, Pg. 131.

[96] The Assyrians, Elaine Landau, The Millbrook Press, Inc., Brookfield, CT, 1997, Pg. 12.

[97] The Ancient Assyrians, Mark Healy, Osprey Publishing Ltd., 1991, Reprinted 2003, Pg. 3.

[98] The Assyrian Empire, Don Nardo, Lucent Books, San Diego,

CA, 1998, Pgs. 11,12.

[99] The Ancient Assyrians, Mark Healy, Osprey Publishing Ltd., 1991, Reprinted 2003, Pgs. 7,8.

[100] The Assyrian Empire, Don Nardo, Lucent Books, San Diego, CA, 1998, Pg. 39.

[101] This quote is originally from the 'Annals of Assurnasirpal' and is quoted in Daniel D. Luckenbill, ed., Ancient Records of Assyria and Babylonia. 2 volumes. Chicago: University of Chicago Press, 1926. Reprint: New York: Greenwood Press, 1968, Volume 1, pg. 146. The Assyrian Empire by Don Nardo, Lucent Books, San Diego, CA, 1998, Pg. 41.

[102] The Assyrian Empire, Don Nardo, Lucent Books, San Diego, CA, 1998, Pg. 45.

[103] The Thompson Chain-Reference Bible, compiled and edited by Frank Charles Thompson, B. B. Kirkbride Bible Company, Inc., Indianapolis, Indiana, original copyright 1908, 71st printing, 1982, Pg. 351.

[104] See http://www.battlebelow.com/glossary.htm

[105] The New Unger's Bible Dictionary, Revised and Updated Edition, Merrill F. Unger, Moody Press, Chicago, Illinois, 1988, Pg. 459.

[106] The New Bible Dictionary, Inter-Varsity Press, Tyndale House Publishers, Inc., Second Edition, Wheaton, Illinois, Reprinted 1986, Pg. 406.

[107] The New Unger's Bible Dictionary, Revised and Updated Edition, Merrill F. Unger, Moody Press, Chicago, Illinois, 1988, Pg. 103.

[108] See http://www.searchgodsword.org/enc/isb/view.cgi?number=T3684 (from the International Standard Bible Encyclopedia as found on this site)

[109] See http://community.gospelcom.net/Brix?pageID=1853

[110] The New Bible Dictionary, Inter-Varsity Press, Tyndale House Publishers, Inc., Second Edition, Wheaton, Illinois, Reprinted 1986, Pg. 614.

[111] The New Bible Dictionary, Inter-Varsity Press, Tyndale House Publishers, Inc., Second Edition, Wheaton, Illinois, Reprinted 1986, Pg. 936.

[112] The New Bible Dictionary, Inter-Varsity Press, Tyndale House Publishers, Inc., Second Edition, Wheaton, Illinois, Reprinted 1986, Pg. 614.

[113] See http://www.anomalist.com/features/tartessus.html

[114] Manners and Customs of Bible Lands, Fred H. Wight, Moody Press, Chicago, Illinois, 1953, Pg. 274.

[115] Manners and Customs of Bible Lands, Fred H. Wight, Moody Press, Chicago, Illinois, 1953, Pg. 276.

[116] Bible Manners and Customs, George M. Mackie, Fleming H. Revell Co., New York, (no date), Pg. 146.

[117] See http://www.netours.com/2003/Dic/D36ViaMaris.htm

[118] See http://community.gospelcom.net/Brix?pageID=1546

[119] Webster's New World Dictionary of American English, Third College Edition, Victoria Neufeldt, Editor in Chief, Simon and Schuster, Inc., New York, 1988, Pg. 1119.

[120] The Ship: An Illustrated History, Bjorn Landstrom, Doubleday and Company, Inc., Garden City, NY 1961, Pg. 34.

[121] Manners and Customs of Bible Lands, Fred H. Wight, Moody Press, Chicago, Illinois, 1953, Pg. 276.

[122] The Ship: An Illustrated History, Bjorn Landstrom, Doubleday and Company, Inc., Garden City, NY 1961, Pg. 34.

[123] The Ship: An Illustrated History, Bjorn Landstrom, Doubleday and Company, Inc., Garden City, NY 1961, Pgs. 22, 23.

[124] See http://www.cyprus-holidays-hotels.com/Kyrenia/ship_wreck_museum.html

[125] Piracy in the Ancient World, Henry A. Ormerod, The Johns Hopkins University Press, 1997, Pgs. 15, 16.

[126] The Ancient Mariners: Seafarers and Sea Fighters of the Mediterranean in Ancient Times, Lionel Casson, Second Edition, Princeton University Press, Princeton, NJ, 1991, Pg. 20.

[127] The New Bible Dictionary, Inter-Varsity Press, Tyndale House Publishers, Inc., Second Edition, Wheaton, Illinois, Reprinted 1986, Pg. 935.

[128] The New Unger's Bible Dictionary, Revised and Updated Edition, Merrill F. Unger, Moody Press, Chicago, Illinois, 1988, Pg. 1006.

[129] The New Unger's Bible Dictionary, Revised and Updated Edition, Merrill F. Unger, Moody Press, Chicago, Illinois, 1988, Pg. 485.

[130] The New Unger's Bible Dictionary, Revised and Updated Edition, Merrill F. Unger, Moody Press, Chicago, Illinois, 1988, Pg. 485.

[131] See http://www.battlebelow.com/glossary.htm

[132] See http://www.geocities.com/cjstein_2000/dictionary.html

[133] Seagoing Ships and Seamanship in the Bronze Age Levant, Shelley Wachsmann, Chatham Publishing, 1998, Pgs. 39.40.

[134] Ships and Seafaring in Ancient Times, Lionel Casson, University of Texas Press, 1994, Pg. 101.

[135] Ships and Seafaring in Ancient Times, Lionel Casson, University of Texas Press, 1994, Pg. 102.

[136] See http://ina.tamu.edu/ub_main.htm

[137] Ancient Shipwrecks, K.C. Smith, Published by Franklin Watts, a division of Grolier Publishing, 2000, pg. 22.

[138] See http://www.ussrankin.org/id430.htm

[139] See http://www.biblestudy.org/question/castlots.html

[140] See http://www.bartleby.com/65/lo/lots.html

[141] See http://www.ussrankin.org/id430.htm

[142] See http://www.battlebelow.com/glossary.htm

[143] Theological Wordbook of the Old Testament, Volume II, R. Laird Harris editor, Moody Press, Chicago, Illinois, 1980, Pgs. 557, 558.

[144] See http://www.sailorschoice.com/Terms/scterms.htm

[145] See http://www.battlebelow.com/glossary.htm

[146] Manners and Customs of Bible Lands, Fred H. Wight, Moody Press, Chicago, Illinois, 1953, Pg. 270.

[147] Manners and Customs of Bible Lands, Fred H. Wight, Moody Press, Chicago, Illinois, 1953, Pg. 271.

[148] Manners and Customs of Bible Lands, Fred H. Wight, Moody Press, Chicago, Illinois, 1953, Pg. 271.

[149] The New Bible Dictionary, Inter-Varsity Press, Tyndale House Publishers, Inc., Second Edition, Wheaton, Illinois, Reprinted 1986, Pg. 269.

[150] See http://www.sailorschoice.com/Terms/scterms.htm

[151] Theological Wordbook of the Old Testament, Volume I, R. Laird Harris editor, Moody Press, Chicago, Illinois, 1980, Pg. 322.

[152] This phrase originally came from a sermon preached by Pastor Barry Bowman at Church of the Holy Spirit in Rhode Island.

[153] The math of this time frame is as follows: Jonah's first call (1:1) and subsequent preparations to travel until the time when he is spit up on shore by the great fish (2:10) is estimated to be seven days. Jonah's second call (3:1) and subsequent preparations to travel until the time that he reaches Nineveh (3:4a) is estimated to be fifty days. Jonah's prophetic preaching (3:4b) until Jonah's sulking East of the city (4:5) is estimated to be the original forty days of Jonah's message. The rest of the book (4:6–4:11 presumably all takes place on the same day following the original forty days Jonah spoke about in his message. Thus 7+50+40+1=98. 98/30=3 months and 8 days or approximately 13 weeks.

[154] The math of this population estimate is as follows: God's statement that there are more than 120,000 persons in Nineveh

not yet old enough to know their right hand from their left. We assume that this means children under the age of about four, and this would total 120,000. We assume that most of these children would have had two parents, and this would total 240,000. We assume that each of these children would have had, on average, at least two siblings (not uncommon in those days), and this would total 240,000. Thus 120,000+240,000+240,000=600,000 people plus their livestock.

[155] See http://www.sailorschoice.com/Terms/scterms.htm

[156] The Prophets of Israel, Leon J. Wood, Baker Book House, Grand Rapids, Michigan, 1979, Pg. 276.

[157] The Prophets of Israel, Leon J. Wood, Baker Book House, Grand Rapids, Michigan, 1979, Pg. 276.

[158] The Ancient Assyrians, Mark Healy, Osprey Publishing Ltd., 1991, Reprinted 2003, Pg. 5.

[159] The Might That Was Assyria, H.W.F. Saggs, Sidgwick and Jackson Limited, London, Great Britain, 1984, Pgs. 124, 125.

[160] The Might That Was Assyria, H.W.F. Saggs, Sidgwick and Jackson Limited, London, Great Britain, 1984, Pg. 126.

[161] The Might That Was Assyria, H.W.F. Saggs, Sidgwick and Jackson Limited, London, Great Britain, 1984, Pg. 127.

[162] The Prophets of Israel, Leon J. Wood, Baker Book House, Grand Rapids, Michigan, 1979, Pg. 289.

[163] The Might That Was Assyria, H.W.F. Saggs, Sidgwick and Jackson Limited, London, Great Britain, 1984, Pg. 125.

[164] The Assyrians, Elaine Landau, The Millbrook Press, Brookfield,

Connecticut, 1997, Pgs. 34–37.

[165] The Might That Was Assyria, H.W.F. Saggs, Sidgwick and Jackson Limited, London, Great Britain, 1984, Pg. 126.

[166] This adaptation is loosely based upon and contains many revisions of continuity and thought for clarification and better language flow based upon information from the following sources: Word Pictures of the New Testament by A.T. Robertson, Volume III; Vine's Expository Dictionary of New Testament Words by W.E. Vine; The Acts of the Apostles by E.M. Blaiklock; The New Testament, An Expanded Translation by Kenneth S. Wuest; Lectures on the Book of Acts by H.A. Ironside; Nelson's Illustrated Bible Dictionary, Editor Herbert Lockyer, Sr.; Expository Dictionary of Bible Words by Lawrence O. Richards; Abingdon's Strong's Exhaustive Concordance of the Bible by James Strong; Twenty-Six Translations of the Bible, Volume III, General Editor Curtis Vaughan; Webster's New World Dictionary, Third College Edition; The American Heritage Dictionary of the English Language, The Book of Acts by Stanley M. Horton; Roget's International Thesaurus, Fourth Edition, Revised by Robert L. Chapman; The New Bible Dictionary, Second Edition; The New Unger's Bible Dictionary, Revised and Updated Edition, and my own personal flair.

[167] The New Bible Dictionary, Inter-Varsity Press, Tyndale House Publishers, Inc., Second Edition, Wheaton, Illinois, Reprinted 1986, Pg. 404.

[168] The New Bible Dictionary, Inter-Varsity Press, Tyndale House Publishers, Inc., Second Edition, Wheaton, Illinois, Reprinted 1986, Pg. 890.

[169] The New Unger's Bible Dictionary, Revised and Updated Edition, Merrill F. Unger, Moody Press, Chicago, Illinois, 1988, Pg. 978.

[170] The New Encyclopaedia Britannica, Volume 20, Macropaedia, Knowledge in Depth, Fifteenth Edition, 1993, Encyclopaedia Britannica, Inc., Pg. 325.

[171] The New Unger's Bible Dictionary, Revised and Updated Edition, Merrill F. Unger, Moody Press, Chicago, Illinois, 1988, Pg. 108.

[172] The Interpreter's Dictionary of the Bible, An Illustrated Encyclopedia, Volume A-D, 1962, Abingdon Press, Nashville, Tennessee, Eleventh Printing, 1980, Pg. 548.

[173] Word Pictures in the New Testament, Volume III, The Acts of the Apostles, Archibald Thomas Robertson, Baker Book House, Grand Rapids, Michigan, 1930, Pg. 461.

[174] The New Unger's Bible Dictionary, Revised and Updated Edition, Merrill F. Unger, Moody Press, Chicago, Illinois, 1988, Pg. 191.

[175] The New Bible Dictionary, Inter-Varsity Press, Tyndale House Publishers, Inc., Second Edition, Wheaton, Illinois, Reprinted 1986, Pg. 155.

[176] See http://www.sailorschoice.com/Terms/scterms.htm

[177] See http://www.sailorschoice.com/Terms/scterms.htm

[178] The Ancient Mariners: Seafarers and Sea Fighters of the Mediterranean in Ancient Times, Lionel Casson, Second Edition, Princeton University Press, Princeton, NJ, 1991, Pg. 212.

[179] Ships and Seafaring in Ancient Times, Lionel Casson, University of Texas Press, 1994, Pg. 126.

[180] Ships and Seafaring in Ancient Times, Lionel Casson,

University of Texas Press, 1994, Pgs. 123, 124.

[181] Ships and Seafaring in Ancient Times, Lionel Casson, University of Texas Press, 1994, Pg. 127.

[182] Ships and Seafaring in Ancient Times, Lionel Casson, University of Texas Press, 1994, Pg. 106.

[183] The Ancient Mariners: Seafarers and Sea Fighters of the Mediterranean in Ancient Times, Lionel Casson, Second Edition, Princeton University Press, Princeton, NJ, 1991, Pg. 209.

[184] Ships and Seafaring in Ancient Times, Lionel Casson, University of Texas Press, 1994, Pg. 124.

[185] Ships and Seafaring in Ancient Times, Lionel Casson, University of Texas Press, 1994, Pg. 125.

[186] The Ancient Mariners: Seafarers and Sea Fighters of the Mediterranean in Ancient Times, Lionel Casson, Second Edition, Princeton University Press, Princeton, NJ, 1991, Pgs. 198,199.

[187] The New Unger's Bible Dictionary, Revised and Updated Edition, Merrill F. Unger, Moody Press, Chicago, Illinois, 1988, Pg. 1090.

[188] The Ancient Mariners: Seafarers and Sea Fighters of the Mediterranean in Ancient Times, Lionel Casson, Second Edition, Princeton University Press, Princeton, NJ, 1991, Pg. 206.

[189] The New Unger's Bible Dictionary, Revised and Updated Edition, Merrill F. Unger, Moody Press, Chicago, Illinois, 1988, Pg. 1090.

[190] Ships and Seafaring in Ancient Times, Lionel Casson, University of Texas Press, 1994, Pg. 101.

[191] Ships and Seafaring in Ancient Times, Lionel Casson, University of Texas Press, 1994, Pg. 104.

[192] The Ancient Mariners: Seafarers and Sea Fighters of the Mediterranean in Ancient Times, Lionel Casson, Second Edition, Princeton University Press, Princeton, NJ, 1991, Pgs. 207, 208.

[193] The Ancient Mariners: Seafarers and Sea Fighters of the Mediterranean in Ancient Times, Lionel Casson, Second Edition, Princeton University Press, Princeton, NJ, 1991, Pg. 208.

[194] See http://www.boatsafe.com/nauticalknowhow/terms0101.htm

[195] See http://www.sailorschoice.com/Terms/scterms.htm

[196] See http://www.sailorschoice.com/Terms/scterms.htm

[197] See the PDF (portable document file) titled, Annex K–Mediterranean Sea, QINETIQ/S&E/SPS/CR020850/1.0, Section K.2.6.4, Main regional and local winds, by Trudi Webster, Pages K-11, 12 found at the United Kingdom's Ministry of Defence website. See mod.uk/linked_files/dpa/S2087EIA/Annex K - Mediterranean Sea.pdf

[198] See http://mediatheek.thinkquest.nl/~11118/en/development/types.list.gregale.html

[199] Heavy Weather Tactics Using Sea Anchors and Drogues, Earl R. Hinz, Paradise Cay Publications, Arcata, California, 2000, Pgs. 31, 32.

[200] Heavy Weather Tactics Using Sea Anchors and Drogues, Earl R. Hinz, Paradise Cay Publications, Arcata, California, 2000, Pgs. 32, 33.

[201] Heavy Weather Tactics Using Sea Anchors and Drogues, Earl

R. Hinz, Paradise Cay Publications, Arcata, California, 2000, Pg. 33.

[202] The New Bible Dictionary, Inter-Varsity Press, Tyndale House Publishers, Inc., Second Edition, Wheaton, Illinois, Reprinted 1986, Pg. 1107.

[203] See http://www.boatsafe.com/nauticalknowhow/terms0101.htm

[204] See http://laws.justice.gc.ca/en/S-9/C.R.C.-c.1436/48511.html#rid-48565

[205] "Lost Gold, Bounty From a Civil War Ship", Priit F. Vesilind, National Geographic, September, 2004, Pg. 116.

[206] This entire section concerning Joshua and the circumcision of his men was inspired by a sermon from my pastor, Rev. Steve Edlin, senior pastor of Faith Temple in Rochester, NY.

[207] The World According to Mister Rogers, Important Things to Remember, Fred Rogers, 2003, Hyperion Books, New York, Pg. 94.

[208] Anchors, An Illustrated History, Betty Nelson Curryer, Naval Institute Press, Annapolis, Maryland, 1999, Pg. 9.

Contact author Stanley P. Jordan
or order more copies of this book at

TATE PUBLISHING, LLC

127 East Trade Center Terrace
Mustang, Oklahoma 73064

(888) 361 - 9473

Tate Publishing, LLC

www.tatepublishing.com